Emblems for a Queen

Francis Clouet, *Mary, Queen of Scots*, c.1559. London, Victoria and Albert Museum.

Emblems for a Queen

The Needlework of Mary Queen of Scots

Michael Bath

First published 2008 by Archetype Publications Ltd.

Archetype Publications Ltd.
6 Fitzroy Square
London W1T 5HJ
www.archetype.co.uk

Tel: 44(207) 380 0800
Fax: 44(207) 380 0500

© 2008 Text Michael Bath

Note: The right of Michael Bath to be identified as the author of this work has been asserted by him in accordance with the Copyright, Designs and Patents Acts 1988.

ISBN 978-1-904982-36-4

British Library Cataloguing in Publication Data
A catalogue record for this book is available from the British Library.

All rights reserved. No part of this publication may be reproduced, stored in a retrieval system, or transmitted, in any form or by any means, electronic, mechanical, photocopying, recording or otherwise, without the prior permission of the publisher.

Printed on acid-free paper

Typeset by Kate Williams, Swansea
Printed and bound in Italy by Printer Trento srl

Contents

Mary Queen of Scots: Timeline of Key Events   vii
List of Illustrations   ix
Illustration Credits   xv
Acknowledgements   xvii

Chapter 1   The Embroideries   1
Chapter 2   Emblems   23
Chapter 3   Incriminating Emblems   49
Chapter 4   Birds and Beasts   69
Chapter 5   The Language of Flowers   113

Catalogue of the Embroideries:

Appendix 1   The Oxburgh Hangings   127
Appendix 2   The Oxburgh Valance   133
Appendix 3   Two Hardwick Cushion Covers   135
Appendix 4   The Hardwick Octagons   137
Appendix 5   Detached Panels   141
Appendix 6   Mary's Bed of State: Collated Entries from Four Early Descriptions of Bed Hangings no Longer Extant   147

Notes   159
Bibliography   165
Index   169

Mary Queen of Scots: Timeline of Key Events

1503 Marriage of James IV of Scotland to Margaret Tudor, daughter of Henry VII of England

1538 Marriage of James V to Mary of Guise/Lorraine

1542 Birth of Mary Stewart (8 December), later spelled 'Stuart' following her upbringing in France, since French does not use the letter 'w'. Death of James V (14 December) makes infant Mary Queen of Scots

1543 Mary's coronation (9 September), following the signing of the Treaties of Greenwich which agree the eventual marriage of Mary to Edward VI, son and heir apparent of Henry VIII

1544 Birth of François, son and heir to Henri II of France and Catherine de Medici, leads to Scottish repudiation of the Treaties of Greenwich, and the betrothal of Mary to Dauphin François, provoking an English invasion of Scotland ('the rough wooing')

1547 Death of Henry VIII, who is succeeded by Edward VI, followed by Battle of Pinkie Cleugh near Edinburgh (10 September) in which the Scots are routed by the English

1548 Mary's arrival in France to be brought up as future dauphine and eventual Queen of France

1550 Mary's mother, Mary of Guise, visits her seven-year-old daughter in France

1558 Mary's betrothal and marriage, aged 15, to 14-year-old François (24 April). Death of Mary Tudor of England, who is succeeded by her half-sister Elizabeth I. Her descent from Margaret Tudor makes Mary heir presumptive to the throne of England and in France she is proclaimed Queen of England, Ireland and Scotland, assuming the royal arms of England as well as those of Scotland and France

1559 Death of Henri II in a tilting accident (10 July), when a splintered lance pierces his eye, makes Dauphin François king (François II), and Mary Queen of France

1560 Death of Mary's mother, Mary of Guise, Regent of Scotland, makes Mary responsible for Scottish affairs. Treaty of Edinburgh provides for withdrawal of English and French troops from Scotland, conditional on Mary's disuse of the English royal coat of arms; Mary, however, refuses to ratify the treaty which would mean renouncing her claim to the English throne. Lords of the Congregation in Scotland introduce legislation securing a Protestant confession of faith. Death of François II (5 December) makes Mary a young widow, dowager Queen of France

1561 Mary leaves France (14 August) to return and rule Scotland, the native country which she has not seen since she was six years old

1565 Marriage (29 July) to Henry Stewart, Lord Darnley, Catholic son of the exiled Earl of Lennox, who also has some claim, through his mother, to the English throne. Protestant resentment of the marriage leads to rebellion led by Mary's half-brother, Lord James, Earl of Moray, which is suppressed by Mary in the military expedition known as the 'Chaseabout Raid'

1566 Murder of Mary's servant David Rizzio followed by the birth of Prince James (19 June), future James VI of Scotland and I of England

1567 Murder of Darnley (10 February). In April, the Earl of Bothwell takes Mary to Dunbar Castle where he seduces, or perhaps rapes, her; in May she marries him thereby increasing public disquiet and suspicions that they both had been complicit in, and had an ulterior motive for, the murder of Darnley. They have to raise an army to combat the lords who want to remove the queen from Bothwell's influence, but surrender at

1567 Carberry Hill in June, when Bothwell is outlawed and Mary taken prisoner. In July she is forced to abdicate, and James VI becomes King of Scotland under Regent Moray

1568 Mary escapes from Lochleven, where she was imprisoned, but her supporters are defeated (13 May) at Langside near Glasgow. A few days later she sails across the Solway Firth into exile in England. She receives protective custody in Carlisle Castle until July, when she is moved to Bolton Castle, Yorkshire. In October the York Conference is called to enquire into Scottish allegations of her complicity in Darnley's murder, reconvened at Westminster in November, though Mary is not allowed to appear in person. The proposal that she should marry the Duke of Norfolk appeals to her, and she begins correspondence with him, though they never meet

1569 Mary is transferred to the custody of the Earl of Shrewsbury at Tutbury Castle, Staffordshire, and, later this year, to Wingfield Manor, to Chatsworth, to Sheffield Castle, and finally back to Tutbury. In November the rebellion of the northern earls, who seek to place Mary on the throne of England and restore the Catholic faith, is quashed, and Norfolk is temporarily imprisoned, although there no evidence of his or Mary's involvement in the rebellion. Most of the extant embroideries are executed about this time, in the company of the Countess of Shrewsbury ('Bess of Hardwick')

1571 The Ridolfi plot to depose Elizabeth and put Mary on the English throne, leads to Norfolk's rearrest and his execution the following year

1574 Charles IX of France dies and is succeeded by his brother Henri III

1583 Throckmorton plot uncovered, a plot to invade England led by the Guises in France with Scottish Catholic support

1584 Mary's defence that she played no part in plots to unseat her cousin Elizabeth leads to the Act of Association, providing the death penalty for anyone implicated, even unknowingly, in such plots. Mary is transferred to custody of Sir Ralph Sadler

1585 Mary is transferred at Tutbury into the stricter custody of Sir Amyas Paulet, and in December moved to Chartley Hall

1586 Mary is implicated in the Babington plot (July) to murder Elizabeth, and tried at Fotheringhay Castle, Northamptonshire (14–16 October)

1587 Elizabeth signs the death warrant, and Mary is executed, aged 44 years, at Fotheringhay (8 February)

1603 Death of Elizabeth of England without offspring and hence leaving no direct heir to the throne leads to the union of the crowns and accession of James VI by virtue of his mother Mary's descent from Margaret Tudor, thus initiating the so-called 'Stuart' dynasty in England which takes its name from the French spelling of the name of Mary Stewart, Queen of Scots

1612 Mary's mortal remains are removed from Peterborough Cathedral to Westminster Abbey, where her son James I/VI erects a monument to her memory; he also builds a similar monument to her cousin Elizabeth

1617 King James returns for the only time following the Union of Crowns on a state visit to Scotland, a visit for which the elaborate embroideries executed by his mother for her Bed of State are sent to London for repair and reuse.

List of Illustrations

Frontispiece Francis Clouet, *Mary, Queen of Scots*, c.1559. London, Victoria and Albert Museum.

Figure 1.1 Artist unknown, *Mary, Queen of Scots*, 1578, oil on canvas. Edinburgh, Scottish National Portrait Gallery.

Figure 1.2 Artist unknown, *Henry Stewart, Lord Darnley*, c.1566. Edinburgh, Scottish National Portrait Gallery.

Figure 1.3 Artist unknown, *Elizabeth, Countess of Shrewsbury*. The Devonshire Collection, Hardwick Hall, Derbyshire.

Figure 1.4 Marian Hanging, panel E, showing the *impresa* of Marguerite de Navarre, sunflowers following the sun with the motto 'Not having followed lower things'. Oxburgh Hall, Norfolk.

Figure 1.5 Marian Hanging, panel A, with anagrams on Mary's name; although no sunflower is depicted the border inscription implies it: SA VERTV MATIRE [Its strength draws me]. Latin *virtus* can also mean moral perfection, virtue, strength of character and is a keyword in Mary's emblematic vocabulary. Oxburgh Hall, Norfolk.

Figure 1.6 'Elephant', detached panel showing corners filled with other details; when mounted on the surviving hangings such corner details were apparently cut off to leave just the cruciform centre panel. The elephant is copied from Conrad Gessner's *Historia animalium*. London, Victoria and Albert Museum.

Figure 1.7 Rowland Lockey, *Lady Arbella Stuart aged 13*, 1589. Daughter of the Earl of Lennox and Elizabeth Cavendish, she was brought up by her grandmother Bess of Hardwick. In 1611 she sold a number of pieces of needlework made by the late Queen of Scots (her aunt) to Mary Talbot (who was also her aunt). The Devonshire Collection, Hardwick Hall, Derbyshire.

Figure 1.8 The Marian Hanging. Oxburgh Hall, Norfolk.

Figure 1.9 The Shrewsbury Hanging. Oxburgh Hall, Norfolk.

Figure 1.10 The Cavendish Hanging. Oxburgh Hall, Norfolk.

Figure 1.11 Pinkie House, Musselburgh, long gallery painted ceiling c.1613 by an unknown artist. These were almost certainly the 'inscriptions' which Ben Jonson asked William Drummond to send him in 1619 when, instead, Drummond sent Jonson the emblems and mottoes on Queen Mary's embroidered Bed of State.

Figure 1.12 Unsigned French inventory, compiled sometime between September 1586 and October 1587, of devices embroidered on Mary's Bed of State. National Archives, SP 53/21, fol. 108r.

Figure 2.1 *Nutrisco et extinguo* [I nurture and destroy], the salamander device of François I (Claude Paradin, *Devises heroïques*, 1557, p. 16).

Figure 2.2 *Securitas altera* [Another safeguard], device of Henry VIII (Claude Paradin, *Devises heroïques*, 1557, p. 36).

Figure 2.3 *Te stante virebo* [Whilst you stand I shall flourish], the *impresa* of the Cardinal of Lorraine (Claude Paradin, *Devises heroïques*, 1557, p. 72).

Figure 2.4 Armorial manuscript showing knights jousting, each surmounted by a shield showing his *impresa*, including the *Te stante virebo* obelisk entwined with ivy. The Earl of Leicester's association with the *Te stante virebo* shield is suggested by the Dudley device of the ragged staff on his horse bard. London, College of Arms.

Figure 2.5 *Te stante, virebo* emblem (Geffrey Whitney, *A Choice of Emblemes*, 1586, p. 1).

Figure 2.6 *Malo oppressus, deterius formidat* [Oppressed with one evil, it dreads a worse one], the captive dove fears a greater evil if it escapes into the talons of the predatory eagle (Hadrianus Junius, *Emblemata*, 1565, no. 39).

Figure 2.7 Andrea Alciato, *Cum larvis non luctandum* [There is no contest with the dead] (*Emblemata*, 1551, p. 166, with engravings by Pierre Vase).

Figure 2.8 *Los plenos de dolor y Los vazios de speranza* [Those that are full are full of sorrow, those that are empty, of hope] (Paolo Giovio, *Dialogo dell'imprese*, 1560, p. 28).

Figure 2.9 The *Las pennas passan* panel, with the motto *Las pennas passan y queda la speranza* [Sorrows pass but hope survives]. London, Victoria and Albert Museum.

Figure 2.10 *Monstrant Regibus astra viam* [The stars show the way to kings], device of the Order of the Star founded by Jean de France in 1351 (Claude Paradin, *Devises heroïques*, 1557, p. 18).

Figure 2.11 *Ardua deturbans, vis animosa quatit* [The strength of courage shatters higher things], device not ascribed to any bearer (Claude Paradin, *Devises heroïques*, 1557, p. 87).

Figure 2.12 *Nodos virtute resolvo*, impresa of Jacques d'Albon, Mareschal de St André (Claude Paradin, *Devises heroïques*, 1557, p. 214).

Figure 2.13 *Non inferiora sequutus* [Not having followed lower things], impresa of Marguerite de Navarre (Claude Paradin, *Devises heroïques*, 1557, p. 41).

Figure 2.14 *Quis contra nos?* [Who is against us?], biblical device not ascribed to any bearer (Claude Paradin, *Devises heroïques*, 1557, p. 187).

Figure 2.15 *Ditat servata fides* [Loyalty makes one rich], device not ascribed to any bearer (Gabriele Simeoni, *Le imprese heroiche et morali*, 1560, p. 31).

Figure 2.16 *Vias tuas domine demonstra mihi* [Show me your ways, O Lord], imperial device displayed on the ship of Admiral Andrea Doria (Claude Paradin, *Devises heroïques*, 1557, p. 88).

Figure 2.17 Jetton of Mary Queen of Scots dated 1579, a ship with a broken mast in a storm and the motto *Nunquam nisi rectam* [Never if not upright]. Mary sewed this device with the same motto on her Bed of State embroideries. Edinburgh, National Museum of Scotland.

Figure 2.18 Shrewsbury Hanging centrepiece, modelled on Claude Paradin's Aesopic fable of the thirsting crow; the grotesque-work border uses motifs copied from ornament prints by Hans Vredeman de Vries. Oxburgh Hall, Norfolk.

Figure 2.19 *Ingenii largitor* [Bestower of talent], device not ascribed to any bearer (Claude Paradin, *Devises heroïques*, 1557, p. 141).

Figure 2.20 Lucas or Johannes Duetecum after Hans Vredeman de Vries, engraving from the *Caryatidum* series (Antwerp, c.1565). The Shrewsbury Hanging centrepiece copies the second and the sixth of these architectural ornament figures from Vredeman's print.

Figure 2.21 Lucas or Johannes Duetecum after Hans Vredeman de Vries, *Hercules and the Centaur*, engraving from the *Grottesco* series (Antwerp, 1565). The frame details, bottom right and left. are copied on the Shrewsbury Hanging centrepiece and also at Prestongrange. Stedelijk Prentenkabinet, Antwerp.

Figure 2.22 Painted ceiling, Prestongrange, Lothian, using a detail from Vredeman's *Hercules and the Centaur* print that is also copied on the Shrewsbury Hanging.

Figure 2.23 Cavendish Hanging centrepiece showing tears falling on quicklime with the motto *Extinctam lachrimae testantur vivere flammam* [Tears witness that the quenched flame lives]. Oxburgh Hall, Norfolk.

Figure 2.24 François Clouet, *Catherine de Medici*, engraving combining her portrait with her *impresa*. Paris, Bibliothèque nationale.

Figure 2.25 Medal of 1589, reverse with Catherine de Medici's quicklime device showing tears falling on quicklime with the motto *Ardorem extincta testantur vivere flamma* [Though extinguished, the flame shows that love endures]. Edinburgh, National Museum of Scotland.

Figure 2.26 *Latet anguis in herba* [A snake lurks in the grass] (Claude Paradin, *Devises heroïques*, 1557, p .70).

Figure 2.27 Marian Hanging, panel C, crowned monogram spelling the names MARIA/ELIZABETH with flowers symbolising the three kingdoms of France, England and Scotland. The motto means 'The bonds of virtue are lighter than those of blood'. Oxburgh Hall, Norfolk.

Figure 2.28 Marian Hanging, panel F, tortoise climbs a crowned palm tree with the motto *Dat gloria vires* [Glory gives strength]. Oxburgh Hall, Norfolk.

Figure 2.29 Mary *ryal*, coin first minted in 1565, the year of her marriage to Darnley, showing a tortoise climbing a crowned palm tree marked with a scroll: *Dat gloria vires* [Glory gives strength]. Edinburgh, National Museum of Scotland.

Figure 2.30 *Invidia integritatis assecla* [Envy pursues the upright] (Hadrianus Junius, *Emblemata*, 1565, no. 9).

Figure 2.31 Printer's mark of Christoph Froschauer, Zürich, showing frogs climbing a tree. Based on a design by Hans Holbein in 1526, this version is the one used on the title page to volumes II, III and IV of Gessner's *Historia animalium* (1554–1560).

Figure 2.32 Medal of Mary Queen of Scots, 1560, showing two earthly crowns beneath a star-filled sky with the motto *Aliamque moratur* [And awaits another]. This is certainly the original of the device which Henri III inherited or adapted from his sister-in-law Mary in 1574. Edinburgh, National Museum of Scotland.

Figure 2.33 *Manet ultima caelo* [The last awaits in heaven], device of Henri III (Adrien d'Amboise, *Devises royales*, 1621, p. 42). Henri inherited the two crowns of France and Poland, but would earn the heavenly crown only through his wise policies in the cause of religious reconciliation.

According to Amboise, Henri borrowed the device from a very similar one borne by Mary Queen of Scots.

Figure 2.34 Medals of François II (Jacques de Bie, *La France métallique*, 1636, fol. 61). The device showing two globes with a crown on the point of a sword and the motto *Unus non sufficit orbis* [One world is not enough] can be seen top right.

Figure 2.35 Book of hours printed in Paris in 1549 with luxurious binding showing the initial 'F' for François II with his dolphin motif as Dauphin of France, and an *impresa* panel showing the *Unus non sufficit orbis* emblem. Probably given to Mary by her husband, this book was left as a parting gift in 1561 with her aunt, who was abbess at Pierre-les-Dames where Mary stayed on her journey back to Scotland. Bibliothèque de Reims.

Figure 3.1 Sketches of devices on a watch owned by Mary in 1575. These four were engraved 'About the sides of the Diall'. National Archives (England) SP 53/10.

Figure 3.2 Devices on Mary's watch, with a header for this page recording 'A Diall wth a watche wherin upon the cover of the boxe opening over the houers was this figure'. National Archives (England) SP 53/10.

Figure 3.3 Sketch of the dial of Mary's watch showing 'The hande wth the howers'. National Archives (England) SP 53/10.

Figure 3.4 John Dunstall's copy of the device alluding to the myth of Mercury charming Argos with his hundred eyes and the motto 'Eloquence has closed many eyes'. British Library, MS Cotton Calig. CV, fol. 73r.

Figure 3.5 John Dunstall's copy of the device showing an eclipse and the motto 'She takes from herself the light that she envies'. British Library, MS Cotton Calig. CV, fol. 75r.

Figure 3.6 Sketch of the device on Mary's watch showing 'The botome of the Diall'. National Archives (England), SP 53/10.

Figure 3.7 Dunstall's copy of the device alluding to the myth of Cadmus's foundation of Thebes, showing weapons growing out of the ground and the motto 'God will put an end to these also'. British Library, MS Cotton Calig. CV, fol. 73r.

Figure 3.8 *Quis contra nos?* [Who is against us?], St Paul shakes off the viper that bit his finger as he fuelled the fire: God will protect the faithful (Claude Paradin, *Devises heroïques*, 1557, p. 187).

Figure 3.9 Reverse of medal of Queen Elizabeth of England by Jacobo Primavera, *c.*1572. British Museum.

Figure 3.10 Hieroglyphic signifying a woman who has only given birth once (Horapollo Nilus, *De sacris notis* [= *Hieroglyphica*], 1551, p. 179).

Figure 3.11 Marian Hanging, centrepiece; a vine is being pruned with the motto *Virescit vulnere virtus* [Virtue flourishes from its wounds], with Mary's monogram and the royal arms of Scotland. Oxburgh Hall, Norfolk.

Figure 3.12 Silver hand bell engraved with emblematic devices of Mary Queen of Scots, possibly the *clochette d'argent de sus la table de Sa Majesté* recorded in the Chartley inventory in 1586, here showing the *Virescit vulnere virtus* emblem. Private collection.

Figure 3.13 The same silver hand bell, showing ChiRho monogram with the inscription IN HOC VINCE [Triumph in this].

Figure 3.14 Silver hand bell: engraving inside the bell with numbers and lettering that can be read as CLAMAT SVAS [She calls her own].

Figure 3.15 Jetton of Mary Queen of Scots: reverse showing the *Virescit vulnere virtus* device. Edinburgh, National Museum of Scotland.

Figure 3.16 Sketch of Mary's *Virescit vulnere virtus* device (J. Dorat, *Recueil de devises*, MS Bibliothèque de l'Arsenal Ms. 3184), owned by royal herald Hector le Breton who died in 1652. Paris, Bibliothèque nationale.

Figure 3.17 Arms of the earls of Galloway with their crest showing the 'Pelican in her Piety' who feeds her young with her own lifeblood and the *Virescit vulnere virtus* motto (Lyon Court, Edinburgh, MS 21, 'Kings and Nobilitys Arms', *c.*1638).

Figure 3.18 The vine-pruning emblem with the *Virescit vulnere virtus* motto also featured as the crest to the heraldic arms of Alexander Burnett of Leys, here shown on the sculptured panel *c.*1596, Crathes Castle, Aberdeenshire.

Figure 3.19 *Virescit vulnere virtus*, emblem of the herb that gives out greater fragrance when trodden on (Gabriele Simeoni, *Imprese heroiche et morali*, 1560, p. 33).

Figure 3.20 Medal or jetton of Mary Queen of Scots, dated 1579: a vine being sprinkled from a watering can, one branch flourishing while the other is dead, and the motto *Mea sic mihi prosunt* [Thus are mine unto me]; we are expected to infer that the vine is being watered with wine, which will kill it. Edinburgh, National Museum of Scotland.

Figure 3.21 Marcus Gheeraerts the Younger, *The Persian Lady*, *c.*1600. The motto *Mea sic mihi* [Thus mine to me] can be seen on the tree trunk. Hampton Court, The Royal Collection, by gracious permission of H.M. Queen Elizabeth II.

Figure 3.22 Illustrations of medals of François II and Mary (Jacques de Bie, *La France metallique*, 1636, fol. 62).

Figure 4.1 'An Ape of Turky', unmounted panel from Oxburgh Hall, T33DD. Note how the corner segments of the centre roundel have not been cut off in these unmounted panels but are filled with further embroidered details, whereas on all the mounted panels they are invariably cut off to create a cruciform panel showing only the animal. London, Victoria and Albert Museum.

Figure 4.2 Tobias Stimmer, *Portrait of Conrad Gessner*, 1564. Schaffhausen, Switzerland, Museum zu Allerheiligen.

Figure 4.3 'A Gene Skyn', unmounted panel from Oxburgh Hall, T33FF. London, Victoria and Albert Museum.

Figure 4.4 Skin of the jenet, woodcut (Conrad Gessner, *Historia animalium*, I, 1551, p. 1102).

Figure 4.5 'Sea Moonke' on the Marian Hanging, panel 20, Oxburgh Hall, Norfolk.

Figure 4.6 Monkfish, or genus of sea monster having a human face and monk's cowl sometimes seen in the Forth estuary, according to Conrad Gessner (*Historia animalium*, IV, 1560, p. 174).

Figure 4.7 Monkfish, woodcut (Pierre Belon, *La nature et diversite des poissons*, 1555, p. 33).

Figure 4.8 'A Lion of the Sea' on the Oxburgh Valance, panel 13. Oxburgh Hall, Norfolk.

Figure 4.9 Sea lion, woodcut, first of the sequence of 'sea monsters having some sort of human appearance' (Conrad Gessner, *Icones animalium*, 1560, p. 173).

Figure 4.10 'Sea Hors', part of a detached, damaged panel from Oxburgh Hall. London, Victoria and Albert Museum.

Figure 4.11 Sea horse, woodcut (Pietro Andrea Mattioli, *Commentarii in Dioscoridis*, 1558, p. 176).

Figure 4.12 'Solen Goose' or gannet, Marian Hanging, panel 1. Oxburgh Hall, Norfolk.

Figure 4.13 'Bass-rock or Scottish Goose', Gessner's name for the gannet (*Historia animalium*, III, 1555, p. 158).

Figure 4.14 'Byrd of America' or toucan, Marian Hanging, panel 6. Oxburgh Hall, Norfolk.

Figure 4.15 Toucan, woodcut (André Thevet, *Les singularitez de la France antarctique*, 1558, p. 91).

Figure 4.16 Toucan, or *Pica Bressillica*, woodcut (Conrad Gessner, *Icones animalium*, 1560, p. 130).

Figure 4.17 'A Byrde of America', Cavendish Hanging, panel 15. Oxburgh Hall, Norfolk.

Figure 4.18 Unnamed fruit-eating and large-crested bird from Brazil, woodcut (André Thevet, *Les singularitez de la France antarctique*, 1558, p. 116).

Figure 4.19 'A Pye of Persia', Shrewsbury Hanging, panel 3. Oxburgh Hall, Norfolk.

Figure 4.20 Strange Brazilian bird called 'Pa, en Persien', woodcut (André Thevet, *Les singularitez de la France antarctique*, 1558, p. 45).

Figure 4.21 This illegible label would undoubtedly have identified this animal on the Oxburgh Valance as the fabulous creature allegedly discovered in Brazil and known as a su. Oxburgh Hall, Norfolk.

Figure 4.22 A Brazilian beast known as a su that carries its young away on its back when hunted by natives for its skin, woodcut (André Thevet, *Les singularitez de la France antarctique*, 1558, p. 109).

Figure 4.23 'A Tatou' or armadillo, Cavendish Hanging, panel 12. Oxburgh Hall, Norfolk.

Figure 4.24 'Tatus', woodcut (Conrad Gessner, *Icones animalium*, 1560, p. 103).

Figure 4.25 'A Stork of the Montaynes', Shrewsbury Hanging, panel 1. Oxburgh Hall, Norfolk.

Figure 4.26 Oripelargus or mountain stork, woodcut (Conrad Gessner, *Icones animalium*, 1560, p. 5).

Figure 4.27 Sea monsters that haunt the northern oceans (as illustrated in Sebastian Munster's *Cosmographiae universalis*, 1575).

Figure 4.28 Studio of Nicholas Hilliard (attrib.), *Queen Elizabeth I*, c.1599. The dress is decorated with what are probably painted animals and flowers, including sea monsters similar to those copied from contemporary prints in Mary's needlework. The Devonshire Collection, Hardwick Hall, Derbyshire.

Figure 4.29 Cushion cover embroidered with the myth of Europa and the bull, copying a woodcut by Virgil Solis after Bernard Salomon from a sixteenth-century edition of Ovid's *Metamorphoses*. The Devonshire Collection, Hardwick Hall, Derbyshire.

Figure 4.30 'A Scolopender', Marian Hanging, panel 21. Oxburgh Hall, Norfolk.

Figure 4.31 Scolopender, woodcut (Conrad Gessner, *Historia animalium*, IV, 1560, p. 1009).

Figure 4.32 'Zyphwhale', Marian Hanging, panel 14. Oxburgh Hall, Norfolk.

Figure 4.33 Zyphwhale, a formidable sea monster unlike any other (according to Conrad Gessner, *Icones animalium*, 1560, p. 249).

Figure 4.34 Xiphia, woodcut (Olaus Magnus, *Historia de gentibus septentrionalibus*, 1555, p. 743).

Figure 4.35 'Thorne Back', Marian Hanging, panel 25. Oxburgh Hall, Norfolk.

Figure 4.36 Fish which 'Spaniards and Latinists write and call a ray … Germans and Flemish roach and English knows as a thornback', woodcut (Conrad Gessner, *Historia animalium*, IV, 1560, p. 941).

Figure 4.37 Man-eating ray, a Danish species that attacks swimmers with the help of a pack of 'dog' fish who do its hunting for it (Olaus Magnus, *Historia de gentibus septentrionalibus*, 1555, p. 764).

Figure 4.38 'A Rhinocerote of the Sea', Marian Hanging, panel 23. Oxburgh Hall, Norfolk.

Figure 4.39 Monster resembling a rhinoceros that eats giant lobsters, woodcut (Conrad Gessner, *Historia animalium*, IV, 1560, p. 348).

Figure 4.40 'Reindeer', Shrewsbury Hanging, panel 12. Oxburgh Hall, Norfolk.

Figure 4.41 Reindeer being milked, woodcut (Conrad Gessner, *Historia animalium*, I, 1551, p. 950).

Figure 4.42 Reindeer milking, woodcut (Olaus Magnus, *Historia de gentibus septentrionalibus*, 1555, p. 596).

Figure 4.43 'A Pellican', Marian Hanging, panel 9. Oxburgh Hall, Norfolk.

Figure 4.44 Conrad Gessner's illustration of 'The Pelican as it is commonly represented by painters', i.e. the Christian 'Pelican in her Piety', shown pecking her breast to feed her young with her own lifeblood (*Historia animalium*, III, 1555, p. 639).

Figure 4.45 'A Shofler', or spoonbill, detached panel T33.X. London, Victoria and Albert Museum.

Figure 4.46 Pelecanus, German *Löffler* (as named and illustrated in Conrad Gessner, *Icones avium*, 1560, p. 92).

Figure 4.47 Damaged embroidery panel with an unidentified bird, but copying what Gessner describes as an Onocratalus, known in German as *Kropffvogel*. London, Victoria and Albert Museum, T33.R.

Figure 4.48 Onocratalus, or bird resembling the pelican with its large pouch, woodcut (Conrad Gessner, *Historia animalium*, III, 1555, p. 605).

Figure 4.49 'A Porphyry', Shrewsbury Hanging, panel 15. Oxburgh Hall, Norfolk.

Figure 4.50 Porphyrion, woodcut (Conrad Gessner, *Icones avium*, 1560, p. 126).

Figure 4.51 'A Robin', Shrewsbury Hanging, panel 13. Oxburgh Hall, Norfolk.

Figure 4.52 Rubecula, robin redbreast, woodcut (Conrad Gessner, *Icones avium*, 1560, p. 48).

Figure 4.53 Trochilus, i.e. robin, woodcut (Pierre Belon, *L'histoire de la nature des oyseaux*, 1555, p. 343).

Figure 4.54 'Delphin', Marian Hanging, panel 9. Mary's inclusion of her crowned initials undoubtedly signals the close identification she felt, as sometime Dauphinesse of France, with this creature. Oxburgh Hall, Norfolk.

Figure 4.55 'A She Dolphin', Marian Hanging, half of composite panel 27 with an unidentified fish sewn onto it. Oxburgh Hall, Norfolk.

Figure 4.56 The female dolphin shown with attached foetus, woodcut (Conrad Gessner, *Historia animalium*, IV, 1560, p. 381).

Figure 4.57 'A Bon Brek', Shrewsbury Hanging, panel 4. Oxburgh Hall, Norfolk.

Figure 4.58 'Ossifragus' or bone-breaker, i.e. Lämmergeier falcon, woodcut (Pietro Andrea Mattioli, *Commentarii in Dioscoridis*, 1558, p. 213).

Figure 4.59 'Knotted Serpentes', Cavendish Hanging, panel 22. Oxburgh Hall, Norfolk.

Figure 4.60 'Senecta Anguium', woodcut (Pietro Andrea Mattioli, *Commentarii in Dioscoridis*, 1558, p. 193).

Figure 4.61 'Sand Cockles', Oxburgh Valance, panel 5, Oxburgh Hall, Norfolk.

Figure 4.62 'Chamae' woodcut (Pietro Andrea Mattioli, *Commentarii in Dioscoridis*, 1558, p. 180).

Figure 4.63 'A Dotrel', Oxburgh Valance, panel 6, Oxburgh Hall, Norfolk.

Figure 4.64 'Ovum' woodcut (Pietro Andrea Mattioli, *Commentarii in Dioscoridis*, 1558, p. 210).

Figure 4.65 'A Spider', Oxburgh Valance, panel 3, Oxburgh Hall, Norfolk.

Figure 4.66 'Araneus', woodcut (Pietro Andrea Mattioli, *Commentarii in Dioscoridis*, 1558, p. 222).

Figure 4.67 'Scorpions', Cavendish Hanging, panel 10. Oxburgh Hall, Norfolk.

Figure 4.68 'Scorpio terrestris' woodcut (Pietro Andrea Mattioli, *Commentarii in Dioscoridis*, 1558, p. 165).

Figure 4.69 Cushion cover with illustrated fables, The Devonshire Collection, Hardwick Hall, Derbyshire.

Figure 4.70 Cushion cover with illustrated fables, The Devonshire Collection, Hardwick Hall, Derbyshire.

Figure 4.71 The fable of the crow and the snake, copperplate (Gabriele Faerno, *Fabulae centum*, 1563, no. 24).

Figure 4.72 The fable of the two thirsting frogs at a well, copperplate (Gabriele Faerno, *Fabulae centum*, 1563, no. 37).

Figure 4.73 *Impunitas ferociae parens* [Licence is the parent of ferocity], the mice mock the cats caught in their trap, woodcut (Hadrianus Junius, *Emblemata*, 1565, no. 4).

Figure 4.74 The fable of the fox and the eaglet, copperplate (Gabriele Faerno, *Fabulae centum*, 1563, no. 60).

Figure 4.75 'A Catte', detached panel with Mary's monogram, copying Gessner's woodcut, to which the detail of the mouse is added. Margaret Swain suggests that Mary made this cat ginger so as to reflect Elizabeth I's famous red hair, though her claim that the embroidery shows the cat 'wearing a small gold crown' (1973, p. 78) is not accurate. Ginger cats are, in any case, invariably male. Royal Collection, by gracious permission of H.M. Queen Elizabeth II, Edinburgh, Palace of Holyroodhouse.

Figure 4.76 The fable of the cat and the cock, copperplate (Gabriele Faerno, *Fabulae centum*, 1563, no. 42).

Figure 5.1 Cherry branch, Shrewsbury Hanging, octagon C, with the motto 'As fleeting as it is beautiful'. Oxburgh Hall, Norfolk.

Figure 5.2 'Cerasia', woodcut (Pietro Andrea Mattioli, *Commentarii in Dioscoridis*, 1558, p. 147).

Figure 5.3 Turnip, Shrewsbury Hanging, octagon B, with the motto 'The outcome stands in God's own hands'. Oxburgh Hall, Norfolk.

Figure 5.4 'Rapum', woodcut (Pietro Andrea Mattioli, *Commentarii in Dioscoridis*, 1558, p. 266).

Figure 5.5 Apple tree, Marian Hanging, octagon B, with the motto that means 'Let it be given to the fairer', alluding to the classical Judgement of Paris. Oxburgh Hall, Norfolk.

Figure 5.6 Monogrammatist HE (?Hans Eworth), *Elizabeth I and the Three Goddesses*, 1569. Holding an orb, not an apple, Elizabeth overwhelms the three classical goddesses with her beauty in a replay of the Judgement of Paris. Royal Collection, by gracious permission of H.M. Queen Elizabeth II.

Figure 5.7 Cedar tree, Cavendish Hanging, octagon D, with the motto 'True happiness is always unscathed'. Oxburgh Hall, Norfolk.

Figure 5.8 'Cedrus Phoenicea', woodcut (Pietro Andrea Mattioli, *Commentarii in Dioscoridis*, 1558, p. 94).

Figure 5.9 Laurel branch, Hardwick Hall, octagon 9, mounted on a modern screen with the motto 'The reward of virtue'. Oxburgh Hall, Norfolk.

Figure 5.10 'Laurus', woodcut (Pietro Andrea Mattioli, *Commentarii in Dioscoridis*, 1558, p. 97).

Figure 5.11 Rye grass with two cocks eating seeds, Hardwick Hall, octagon 11, mounted on a modern screen with the motto 'Do not walk in the highway'.

Figure 5.12 'Lolium', woodcut (Pietro Andrea Mattioli, *Commentarii in Dioscoridis*, 1558, p. 253).

Figure 5.13 Plantain, Hardwick Hall, octagon 10, mounted on a modern screen with the motto 'Do not turn off the highway'.

Figure 5.14 'Plantago Maior', woodcut (Pietro Andrea Mattioli, *Commentarii in Dioscoridis*, 1558, p. 281).

Figure 5.15 Gladdon, or stinking iris, Hardwick Hall, octagon 3, mounted on a modern screen with the motto 'Pluck not the crown'.

Figure 5.16 'Xyris', woodcut (Pietro Andrea Mattioli, *Commentarii in Dioscoridis*, 1558, p. 446).

Figure 5.17 Lily of the Valley, Hardwick Hall, octagon 21, mounted on a modern screen with the motto 'Do not walk in the highway'.

Figure 5.18 'Lilium Convallium', woodcut (Pietro Andrea Mattioli, *Commentarii in Dioscoridis*, not included in early editions – this illustration is taken from the 1598 edition, p. 631).

Figure 5.19 Teazle, Hardwick Hall, octagon 14, mounted on a modern screen with the motto 'Endure what cannot be avoided, rather than complaining at it'.

Figure 5.20 'Dipsacus', woodcut (Pietro Andrea Mattioli, *Commentarii in Dioscoridis*, 1558, p. 356).

Figure 5.21 Hawthorn, Hardwick Hall, octagon 29, mounted on a modern screen with the motto 'I wound from all sides alike'.

Figure 5.22 'Acuta Spina', woodcut (Pietro Andrea Mattioli, *Commentarii in Dioscoridis*, 1558, p. 100).

Figure 5.23 Orpine, Hardwick Hall, octagon 16, mounted on a modern screen with the motto 'Set about thy task with Minerva's aid'.

Figure 5.24 'Telephium', woodcut (Pietro Andrea Mattioli, *Commentarii in Dioscoridis*, 1558, p. 340).

Figure 5.25 Mandrake, Hardwick Hall, octagon 12, mounted on a modern screen with the motto 'Vices hidden give less offence'.

Figure 5.26 'Mandragora', woodcut (Pietro Andrea Mattioli, *Commentarii in Dioscoridis*, 1558, p. 535).

Illustration Credits

Copyright in the figures is held as follows:
Author: Figures 3.13, 3.14, 3.17, 4.14, 4.18, 4.20 and 4.22
Bibliothèque nationale de France: Figures 2.24 and 3.16
Bibliothèque de Reims: Figure 2.35
British Library: Figures 3.4, 3.5 and 3.7
Court of the Lord Lyon King of Arms, Edinburgh: Figure 3.17
The College of Arms, London: Figure 2.4
Lord Balfour of Burleigh: Figure 3.12
Museum zu Allerheiligen, Schaffhausen, Switzerland: Figure 4.2
National Archives, England: Figure 1.12, 3.1, 3.2, 3.3 and 3.6
National Library of Scotland: Figures 4.34, 4.37, 4.42, 4.71, 4.72, 4.74 and 4.76
National Museums of Scotland: Figures 2.17, 2.25, 2.29, 2.32 and 3.19
National Trust Photo Library: Figure 1.3 (Graham Challiflower), Figures 1.7, 1.10, 4.28, 4.29 and 4.69 (John Hammond), Figures 4.70, 5.9, 5.11, 5.13, 5.15, 5.17, 5.19, 5.21, 5.23 and 5.25 (R. Thrift)
The Royal Collection 2007, Her Majesty Queen Elizabeth II: Figures 3.20, 4.75 and 5.6
Royal Commission on the Ancient and Historical Monuments of Scotland, Crown Copyright: Figures 1.11 and 2.22
Scottish National Portrait Gallery, Edinburgh: Figures 1.1 and 1.2
Stedelijk Prentenkabinet, Antwerpen: Figure 2.21
Trustees of the British Museum: Figure 3.9
University of Glasgow Library, Department of Special Collections: Figures 2.1, 2.2, 2.3, 2.5, 2.6, 2.7, 2.8, 2.10, 2.11, 2.12, 2.13, 2.14, 2.15, 2.16, 2.19, 2.26, 2.30, 2.31, 2.33, 2.34, 3.8, 3.10, 3.18, 3.21, 4.4, 4.6, 4.7, 4.9, 4.11, 4.13, 4.14, 4.15, 4.26, 4.31, 4.33, 4.36, 4.39, 4.41, 4.44, 4.46, 4.48, 4.50, 4.50, 4.52, 4.53, 4.56, 4.58, 4.60, 4.62, 4.64, 4.66, 4.68, 4.73, 5.2, 5.4, 5.8, 5.10, 5.12, 5.14, 5.16, 4.18, 5.20, 5.22, 5.24 and 5.26
University of St Andrews Library: Figure 4.27
Victoria and Albert Museum, London: Frontispiece and Figures 1.4, 1.5, 1.6, 1.8, 1.9, 2.9, 2.18, 2.20, 2.23, 2.27, 2.28, 3.11, 4.1, 4.3, 4.5, 4.8, 4.10, 4.12, 4.14, 4.17, 4.19, 4.21, 4.23, 4.25, 4.30, 4.32, 4.35, 4.38, 4.40, 4.43, 4.45, 4.46, 4.49, 4.51, 4.54, 4.57, 4.59, 4.61, 4.63, 4.65, 4.67, 5.1, 5.3, 5.5 and 5.7

Acknowledgements

I am indebted to numerous friends and colleagues for help with this book over the past six or seven years. Linda Woolley and Susan North gave me access to the Marian embroideries in the care of the Victoria and Albert Museum, and Deborah Clarke to those at the Palace of Holyroodhouse. They also provided help in identifying and supplying photographs, Susan North offering crucial assistance in arranging for comprehensive new photography of the Oxburgh embroideries, which has supplied the high quality images reproduced in this book for the first time. John Guy, Sir Roy Strong, Gervase Hood at National Archives, and Michael Pearce of Historic Scotland, all identified key documents. Robert, Lord Balfour of Burleigh, gave me the opportunity to examine and discuss the various historical artefacts of interest in his possession while Ian, Lord Stewartby, shared his thoughts on the Mary *ryal* and Scottish coinage. Anne Sweeney and Peter Davidson alerted me to the writings of Robert Southwell that use the same iconography as the embroideries, and supplied vital texts of the relevant poems some time before these became more widely available in their superb new edition of Southwell's *Collected Poems*. Naomi Tarrant very kindly provided access to the papers of the late Margaret Swain. David Bostwick supplied information on the sixteenth-century household at Sheffield Manor, K.J. Höltgen helped me with emblems of the two pillars, and Donato Mansueto provided invaluable feedback on the *Manet ultima caelo* device. Betty Knott-Sharpe identified the biblical allusion in Mary's famous *Virescit vulnere virtus* emblem and improved or corrected some of my transcriptions and translations of Latin mottoes. Theo van Heijnsbergen of Glasgow University responded to a somewhat desperate cry for help with palaeography by co-opting an ever widening circle of Scottish renaissance colleagues who, eventually, ensured that my transcripts of the Hawthornden manuscripts contained fewer errors than would otherwise have been the case: Jamie Reid Baxter, Priscilla Bawcutt, Peter Davidson, Alison Adams and John G. Harrison all gave much needed help with this. Responsibility for any remaining transcription errors is, of course, entirely my own.

Parts of this book are based on articles which have appeared in various journals: *Emblematica*, *Review of Scottish Culture*, *History Scotland* and *Architectural Heritage*, all of which are listed in the Bibliography.

I am grateful to the Arts and Humanities Research Board for funding my initial work under their Research Leave Scheme in various libraries, including the British Library, the National Library of Scotland, Edinburgh University Library, Glasgow University Library, the University of Aberdeen, and in the Victoria and Albert Museum and at Oxburgh Hall. The Carnegie Trust for the Universities of Scotland provided vital funding towards illustration costs incurred by Archetype Publications in producing this book. The Strathmartine Trust and the Pasold Research Fund awarded grants to cover my own expenses in obtaining the necessary images and permissions for the large number of illustrations which are the heart of this book and upon which its argument rests.

I

The Embroideries

The many pieces of embroidery made by Mary Queen of Scots and Elizabeth Countess of Shrewsbury ('Bess of Hardwick') are among the best-known and most fascinating examples of historical embroidery to have come down to us. Particular examples have frequently been reproduced in book illustrations or studies of the decorative arts, and the fact that they were executed by two very famous women – whose lives have attracted a great deal of interest for other reasons – has undoubtedly contributed to their familiarity and fascination. But although there have been several previous studies of the embroideries as a group it is not easy for the non-specialist to discover just how many pieces of needlework exist, where they are all located, what they were used for, or what exactly they represent. Surprisingly, a full and accurate *catalogue raisonné* has never been produced despite the interest and importance of these embroideries, and the many questions surrounding their meaning and purpose. More importantly, questions regarding the sources and patterns used for their imagery remain unanswered. The purpose of this book is to address at least some of those questions, in particular the extent to which the embroideries executed by the two women constitute a single, distinctive body of creative work.

One practical, if rather shallow, reason for treating the various pieces as a distinct corpus stems from our uncertainty as to who actually sewed what. Although quite a few of the pieces are signed with the embroiderer's initials, the majority are not identified, which means that any study of the needlework of Mary alone would need to pay attention to a large number of pieces that may not actually be hers. However it will quickly become apparent that the work of Mary and Bess has so much in common that any attempt to study the work of either in isolation would be to make a wholly artificial distinction. The reason for this is that nearly all the surviving embroideries were executed while Mary was living in exile in England in the custody of Bess's fourth husband, the Earl of Shrewsbury, and much of the work of the two embroiderers was evidently sewn in each other's company, often using the same pattern books and print sources. A good case can be made for regarding all these embroideries as the product of a rather remarkable, if not unique, development of shared interests and common creative urges by two people whose personalities and ages (Mary was 28 years old when she arrived in England in 1568 whereas Bess was 50) were otherwise rather different. Admittedly before they completed the last of these embroideries, some time in the 1580s, the two women had fallen out following a famous quarrel. All the more remarkable, then, that before this date they appear to have achieved so much in common.

Mary is known to have practised embroidery long before she met her fellow worker, and Bess continued her hobby for some years after Mary's death in 1587, when she began rebuilding Hardwick Old Hall as well as the new Hardwick Hall (in Derbyshire) where so many of the other textiles which she either executed or commissioned can still be seen in what remains the richest repository for the decorative arts to have survived from late Elizabethan England. The Hardwick Hall textiles, for which Bess was chiefly responsible, have been well documented in an excellent study by Santina Levey (1998), but although they remain a most important resource for our understanding of the decorative arts at this period in Britain and although they include at least one group of embroideries (the octagonal plant slips) which belongs with the distinctive 'Marian' embroideries examined in this book (below), their diversity and their likely dates set them apart from the distinctive body of work the two women practised together. That corpus of collaborative work has sufficient features that distinguish it from the needlework later executed by or for Bess alone, or that practised by noblewomen more generally at this period, to justify treating it as a single and separable oeuvre.

Biographical background: Mary Queen of Scots

As the characteristics of this work thus seem to have developed at a particular stage in the lives of each of the two women concerned, a reminder of the biographical context might be helpful. Mary's biography must be one of the most frequently retold stories in history, and I shall not retell it here except to record events which are especially salient to her embroideries. Born to Mary of Guise in December 1542 at the palace of Linlithgow, Mary became Queen of Scots only days later on the death of her father, James V, and was crowned the following year in Stirling, by which time she was already betrothed to Edward, son and heir to England's Henry VIII, in the type of matrimonial trafficking required by hereditary monarchies. Scottish indifference to the English engagement, faced with overtures from France, led to what Scottish history describes as 'the rough wooing' in 1544 when Henry sent troops to invade Scotland and lay waste to the country. In 1548 the Earl of Arran, as Governor of Scotland, arranged a new betrothal of the five-year-old queen to the four-year-old Dauphin François II of France, and Mary left her native Scotland to begin her French upbringing as the future Queen of France. It was here that she learned the art of decorative needlework, an increasingly fashionable amateur pastime among members of the European nobility, particularly in France where Catherine de Medici had brought professional embroiderers from her native Italy; indeed it seems likely that it was Catherine, wife of Henri II and thus her future mother-in-law,

Figure 1.1 Artist unknown, *Mary, Queen of Scots*, 1578, oil on canvas. Edinburgh, Scottish National Portrait Gallery.

who taught Mary how to embroider, though there is no contemporary confirmation of this. In 1558, at the age of 15, Mary married her dauphin and a year later became Queen of France when Henry II died following the tiltyard accident in which his (Scottish) opponent's splintered lance pierced his eye. The accession of Elizabeth I, also in 1558, made Mary heir presumptive to the throne of England; she thenceforth held some title to the thrones of no fewer than three different countries – Scotland, France and England – which she was keen to see reflected, as will become obvious later, in the way their various coats of arms and emblems were marshalled in her embroidery and furnishings. The sickly young François II died after less than two years on the throne, leaving Mary as dowager Queen of France. The death of her mother, Mary of Guise – regent of Scotland since the year of Mary's birth – led to Mary's return to her native Scotland in 1561.

In 1565 Mary married Henry, Lord Darnley, and in 1566 her servant Rizzio was murdered in front of her only months before the birth of her son, the future James VI of Scotland. The murder of Darnley and Mary's imprudent marriage to the Earl of Bothwell in 1567 began the sequence of events that led to her abdication, her imprisonment in Lochleven Castle, and the defeat of her supporters at the battle of Langside, after which she sought the help of her cousin Elizabeth and sanctuary in England.

The belief that the embroideries that concern us all derive from the period of her final 19 years of exile rests on the date 1570 embroidered on one of the panels signed by Bess of Shrewsbury, the large centrepiece to the so-called 'Shrewsbury Hanging' at Oxburgh Hall (Norfolk). There are a number of earlier records, however, of Mary's activity as a needleworker during her seven years as queen in Scotland. In 1561 the English ambassador, Thomas Randolf, reported that Mary sat sewing while conducting her business as queen: 'I was sent for into the Council Chamber,' he writes 'where she herself sitteth the most part of her time, sowing some work or other.'[1] During the ten and a half months of her captivity in Lochleven Castle, Mary wrote asking the Lords and Council for 'an imbroiderer to draw forth such worke as she would be occupied with'. The request was refused, although in July 1567 she was sent canvas with 18 flowers painted on it and outlined in black silk. We know that Pierre Oudry, who painted the well-known Sheffield portrait of Mary had already been her professional embroiderer in France. Mary also employed other named embroiderers, and in the 1580s, if not earlier, Bess also employed embroiderers on her staff. The job of such a professional assistant was, as Mary's request from Lochleven suggests, to 'draw forth' the pattern on canvas which she would then fill with needlework in appropriate stitches and colours from her stock of silken or gold and silver threads. In December 1575 Mary asked Elizabeth to be allowed to go to the baths in Buxton, and to take an embroiderer to occupy her in doing something to pass the time; she also asks specifically for her maidservant Mlle. de Rallay to be with her. We shall hear more of this maidservant, for it was to Renée de Rallay that Mary bequeathed most of the pieces of embroidery that she possessed at the end of her life. Mary comments around this time on the skill of her embroiderer, Bastien Pagez, who 'in this dreary time cheers me by the work he invents, after my books, the only exercise that is left me'.[2]

The designs traced on pieces of canvas by her embroiderer would then be worked on a small embroidery frame that could be held in the lap. The job of the embroiderer also involved joining these pieces together or mounting them into larger hangings, sometimes cutting up rich cloths or ecclesiastical vestments, which the reformed church no longer required, for use as backing. Indeed, the Scottish Wardrobe inventory for 1562 records that Mary 'took for hir self ain cape a chasuble four tunicles to mak a bed for the King. All brokin and cuttit in her awin presence.'[3] Whether or not the tasks of the professional *brodisseur* also included finishing off the actual piece of embroidery when his mistress grew tired of it, or had other things to do, cannot be known, though

Figure 1.2 Artist unknown, *Henry Stewart, Lord Darnley*, c.1566. Edinburgh, Scottish National Portrait Gallery.

Figure 1.3 Artist unknown, *Elizabeth, Countess of Shrewsbury*. The Devonshire Collection, Hardwick Hall, Derbyshire.

She sayd that all the day she wrought with her needil, and that the diversitie of the colors made the worke seme lesse tedious, and continued so long at it till the very payn did make her to give it over; and with that layd her hand upon her left syde and complayned of an old grief newly increased there. Upon this occasion she entered upon a prety disputable comparison betwene karving, painting and working with the needil, affirming painting in her own opinion for the most commendable qualitie. I answered her grace, I could skill of neither of them, but that I have read *Pictura* to be *veritas falsa*. With this she closed up her talke, and bidding me farewell, retyred into her privy chamber.[4]

This account of Mary at work suggests not just the prolonged labour involved but at least something of the learned spirit in which she was prepared to discuss her art, though the exact spirit in which she launched into her *paragone* debate with her English visitor on the rival arts of design is not easy to judge. Before he left Tutbury, White also noted a motto on her 'Clothe of Estate': *En ma fin est mon commencement* [In my end is my beginning], which he did not understand ('which is a ryddil I understande not'). The same motto is recorded on one of the embroideries she executed for the Bed of State that William Drummond described in a letter to Ben Jonson, and its meaning is not particularly obscure, as we shall see. There is another, often noted, description of Mary's activity as a needlewoman at this period, this time in a letter from the Earl of Shrewsbury, again to William Cecil who was always anxious for information about what Mary was getting up to: this account describes Mary and Elizabeth Shrewsbury doing their needlework together, 'This Queen continueth daily to resort unto my wife's chamber where with the Lady Lewiston and Mrs Seton she useth to sit working with the needle in which she much delighteth and in devising works; and her talk is altogether of indifferent trifling matters.'[5] There can be no doubt that these descriptions confirm what the 1570 date suggests on the Shrewsbury Hanging, namely that it is to the early years of Mary's English exile in the custody of George Talbot and his wife, who we know as Bess of Hardwick, that the majority of the extant embroideries should be dated.

when one considers the sheer amount of needlework which these otherwise very busy women completed, it seems not unlikely.

When Mary first arrived in England she was received into protective custody at Carlisle Castle, and it was not until after the 1568 York Conference, set up to enquire into Scottish allegations of her complicity in Darnley's murder, that she was transferred, in 1569, to the custody of George Talbot, Earl of Shrewsbury. Shrewsbury and his wife owned numerous properties in England, and Mary was variously held at Tutbury Castle in Staffordshire, Wingfield and Chatsworth in Derbyshire, and Sheffield Castle in Yorkshire. We know that she sometimes complained about the inconvenience of these enforced removals and about the coldness and discomfort of her lodgings. She nevertheless retained a sufficiently large number of servants for their expenses to annoy the earl, although he was a very wealthy man, and it appears that she had enough of her own furnishings for the embroideries which she created to play their part in enriching her surroundings, including her Bed of State. Nicholas White reported to William Cecil on his visit to Tutbury in February 1569 that he asked how Queen Mary passed her time when bad weather prevented her from going outside.

It was during these years, when Mary was still under investigation by the York Conference (reconvened at

Westminster in November 1568), that the suggestion was made that she should marry the Duke of Norfolk. Although Mary's complicity in the murder of Darnley was not proven, her proposed marriage to Norfolk aroused the 1569 rebellion of the northern earls, who planned to restore Catholicism to England by deposing Elizabeth and placing Mary on the throne. The quashing of the rebellion did not produce evidence of Mary's complicity, but Norfolk's involvement in the Ridolfi plot in 1571 led to his arrest and execution the following year. The evidence against him included the embroidery that now forms the centrepiece to the Marian Hanging at Oxburgh, whose emblem of a hand holding a pruning hook and cutting back a vine to make it more fruitful was seen as offering encouragement to the duke in his treasonable intentions. Mary's supporter John Leslie, Bishop of Ross, confessed under interrogation that Mary had sent it to Norfolk as a gift in the form of a cushion cover, and although its precise message remains unclear it is only one of a number of allegedly incriminating emblems executed in her needlework which were cited as evidence of Mary's complicity in the Catholic plots to unseat Elizabeth. Mary's defence, that she was not guilty by association with plots that she herself did not plan or approve, led Elizabeth to pass the 1584 Act of Association, which provided the death penalty for anyone implicated, even unknowingly, in plots against the English throne. Accusations that Mary had been allowed to have undue contact with her supporters in their plotting, and Bess's malicious charge that Mary was actually having an affair with her husband Shrewsbury, led to a change of guardian when she was moved briefly into the care of the elderly Sir Ralph Sadler at Wingfield Manor, and in 1585 she was placed in the custody of the sternly Puritan Sir Amyas Paulet at Tutbury where she was held under a much stricter regime than hitherto. Paulet, for instance, removed the embroidered cloth of state beneath which she was entitled to sit when entertaining visitors or dining in state. In December 1585 she was moved to the manor house at Chartley, not far from Tutbury, where she was to make a final inventory of her personal possessions, including the embroideries, as she settled her affairs following her trial in the fallout from the Babington plot of 1586. On 8 February 1587 she was beheaded at Fotheringhay Castle near Peterborough.

The Chartley inventory

The inventory of Mary's possessions compiled shortly before her death remains the fullest account of her furnishings and the place which some of these embroideries held among her personal effects.[6] Known as the Chartley inventory from the place of its compilation on 13 June 1586, the list includes clothing from Mary's wardrobe, jewellery, various portraits in precious mounts, curiosities such as a unicorn horn and a bezoar stone, and furniture of various kinds which is of interest for what it reveals about the type of objects that much of her embroidery would have been used to decorate. Indeed the inventory begins with a list of 'pieces of work' (*besognes et pièces d'ouvrages*) transferred at this time by Mary to the safekeeping of her maidservant Renée de Rallay, née Beauregard.[7] The inventory was evidently Mary's own attempt to list her personal belongings and distribute them among her friends and servants prior to her execution. It is interesting that she should begin by listing objects and items which were, presumably, her own work. Thus Mary's bed is described as having six large needlework valances enriched with gold and silver, while a large number of separate panels from unspecified furnishings are described as decorated with flowers; the arms of France, Scotland, Spain and England in *petit point* (i.e. in cross-stitch embroidery); roses and thistles; the seven planets in cross stitch; four term figures; seven figures in embroidery showing ladies playing various musical instruments; and two tigers with various *fleurons* described as ready to be attached to a bed hanging that had already been started. This remark confirms that suggested by many of the other entries, namely that most of these pieces, described as *carreaux*, or square panels, were unattached embroidery squares (*pièces de cannevas, ouvrés de compartiments de soye au gros point*, p. 240), which had not always been finished or, if they were, had not always been attached to the bed hangings or other furnishings for which they had been planned. Some at least must have been Mary's own work, though one small panel is described as 'worked by the aged Lady Lennox whilst she was in the Tower'.[8]

Most suggestive for our purposes is the record of a truly remarkable number of animals, birds, fish and flowers that are not described as forming part of any particular furnishings but which were evidently embroideries (the flowers are described as embroidered in *petit point*) of exactly the type found on so many of the canvas panels that have survived and which constitute the larger part of the corpus of embroidery, the subject of this book. The Chartley inventory specifies 52 'diverse flowers' of which 32 are said to be 'uncut', and the rest each cut in its square.[9] It then specifies 24 birds of various kinds, 16 types of four-footed beasts including a lion attacking a boar, 52 fishes of various kinds, and no fewer than 116 other unspecified panels 'which have started to be cut out' (*commencé à couper*). The total comes to no fewer than 236 such panels of needlework with an identical type of plant slip ('slip' meaning a twig or shoot used in grafting or planting) or animal decoration as is found on the Oxburgh Hangings and the similar detached panels that make up the greater part of the surviving embroidery. The fact that these are only a part of the *besognes et pièces d'ouvrages* listed in the Chartley inventory and compiled 'in the presence of her Majesty' (p. 241) gives us some idea of the sheer amount of time and work that must have gone into their manufacture.

The Chartley inventory is substantiated by a slightly later inventory compiled not in Mary's presence but at Fotheringhay by Amyas Paulet immediately following her execution in 1587. Paulet lists Mary's belongings which particular servants claimed they had received as gifts, doubtless when Mary was distributing her bequests at Chartley six months earlier.[10] The pieces of work that she had assigned to the safekeeping of Renée de Beauregard are not listed, but many of the remaining pieces listed at Chartley can be found again here. They include furniture for a bed decorated with silk needlework showing various devices and arms 'not thoroughly finished' which Paulet signals is 'To be delivered to the King of Scots' along with a 'cloth of estate'. This is almost certainly the Bed of State which, in 1616, King James ordered to be brought from Edinburgh to London for repairs and which William Drummond describes in the letter to Ben Jonson (discussed later). A separate list details the belongings which the late queen appointed to be sold 'and the money thereof to be employed towards the expenses of the whole company in their journey homewards': in her final days Mary evidently went to the trouble of trying to ensure that her faithful servants had the means to pick up the threads of their former lives. The list includes items of some value, including valances, tester, and bed curtains of velvet; six pieces of tapestry depicting the history of Ravenna, and another six showing the story of Meleager; and three further rich cloths of state.

If these inventories suggest at least something of the richness and diversity of the furnishings and personal possessions that Mary managed to hold onto during her years of exile, they also confirm the important place occupied by the various textiles and embroideries worked by Mary herself among her personal possessions. It is clear that many were intended to decorate bed hangings, though they may well have also been designed as cushion covers, table carpets or wall hangings, and it is evident that many remained either unfinished or uncut. Moreover, regardless of whatever form they took originally, it is apparent that they were always liable to be cut up and reused, just like the ecclesiastical vestments that Mary ordered to be 'brokin and cuttit in her awin presence' to make a 'bed for the King' in 1562. The surviving needlework shows clear signs of such adaptation and improvisation, and we cannot say for certain for which furnishings most of the embroideries were actually made. Quite a number had evidently never actually been used on whatever furnishings they were designed originally to enrich.

The French background

Although amateur needlework was becoming a fairly popular pastime among noblewomen, both in Britain and in Europe, more generally at this period, the surviving work that Mary Queen of Scots completed with Bess of Hardwick has a number of distinctive characteristics.[11] These all derive from what Patricia Wardle (1981) calls their 'French background'. Wardle shows conclusively how these smallish panels of silk embroidery on canvas were inspired directly by the French needlework of Catherine de Medici. Although none of Catherine's own needlework is known to have survived, it is recorded in a number of inventories which, Wardle shows, leaves little doubt that it resembled the Oxburgh Hangings more closely than anything else that has actually come down to us in the needlework of this period. Inventories of Catherine de Medici's work make it clear that much of her embroidery for bed hangings, valances and other applications consisted of squares (*carrés*) of canvas work embroidered in silk with birds, animals, flowers and fruits, and often mounted, like the Oxburgh Hangings, on velvet. Furthermore, some of these are identified explicitly as *octogones de petit point*, as in the 'tapisserie remplie d'octogones de petit point, représentant des emblèmes et des fleurons' [tapestry filled with octagons in cross stitch, representing emblems and flower-shaped ornaments] or the 'teinture de tapisserie de petit point relevée d'or et de soye, représentant des fables, des métamorphoses, en trois piéces, compose chacune d'un tableau octogone dans le milieu' [tapestry design in cross stitch realised in gold and silk, showing fables, and metamorphoses, in three pieces, each made up of an octagonal picture in the middle], both of which are listed in the inventory of Catherine's possessions after her death in 1589.[12]

The similarity of these *octogones* with the octagonal panels from Oxburgh showing plants or monograms is almost certainly no accident, and we are surely right to conclude that 'Mary was following a French fashion in working the motifs for application in panels of various shapes' (Wardle 1981, p. 9). Among the emblems identified more than once on Catherine's embroideries is the salamander device of François I with the motto *Nutrisco et extinguo*, which was shown at the foot of a laurel tree in the embroidery. On the embroidery depicting fables and Ovidian metamorphoses there were interlinked branches of laurel and ivy which might perhaps recall the linked roses, thistles and lilies on Mary's two Hardwick cushion covers. The most significant entry is that for the whole set of furnishings for a bed, enriched with several octagonal pictures in *petit point* showing birds, animals, flowers together with fruits, salamanders and other needlework pictures, all of which originated in 'old furnishings from the royal furniture-store' (*d'anciens meubles du garde-meuble de la couronne*). As Wardle says, it is 'one of the small ironies of history' that this is among the pieces that are also recorded in a second, much later, inventory which includes the same embroideries – in 1689 a number of these pieces were brought out of storage to refurbish St-Germain-en-Laye for the reception of another Catholic exile, James II of England, following his flight from England in the revolution that put William of Orange on the throne to secure the Protestant succession. In his years of exile at St-Germain-en-Laye, James was thus surrounded by some of the same embroideries that had inspired the work of his great-grandmother during her own years of exile in England more than a century earlier. As Wardle puts it:

> The idea for the embroideries was of French inspiration and … with their emblems, plants, birds, animals and fish they fit completely into the tradition current at the French court during Mary's childhood and youth. It might well be, too, that some design for mounting the canvas-work panels had been worked out by Mary and Bess of Hardwick together in the days when they were still on friendly terms. It hardly seems likely that they would have made so many pieces of similar types without some plan in mind. And we can be sure they will have discussed hangings of a mixture of rich materials and canvas-work embroidery, just as they did other French modes which Bess set herself to emulate. (1981, p. 10)

Embroidered emblems

There is no evidence, however, that these French embroideries of Catherine de Medici used emblems. As we shall see, emblems were a specific type of symbolic imagery that had developed in distinctive ways during the sixteenth century, not only in a new genre of printed 'emblem books' illustrated with woodcuts, but also in a variety of applied and decorative arts, including embroidery. Typically, an emblem consists of a symbolic image and an accompanying motto, and it challenges the viewer to work out the relationship of one to the other, of image to adage. In the emblem books that relationship was often explained or 'moralised' in an explanatory verse-epigram, though in the decorative arts it was seldom possible to include quite so much text. Emblems in the decorative arts of this period – including painting, plasterwork and tapestries, as well as jewellery, costume and pageantry – are likely to include no more than a symbolic image and a brief motto, or sometimes just the symbolic image alone. Emblems certainly feature in early embroideries, though they were less popular than other decorative design types such as plant slips, biblical, mythological or pastoral scenes, perhaps for obvious reasons since emblems are comparatively difficult to invent and, often, to understand. They are puzzling.

Few embroideries, apart from these, have yet been identified as using emblems, though there are a couple of early examples in the Burrell Collection, Glasgow, which are surely not unique.[13] To see how such emblems work we might take the panel on the Marian Hanging showing three marigolds beneath a radiant sun and, in the border, the motto, NON INFERIORA SECVTVS (Not having followed lower things). The sunflower that follows the sun's course had been adopted in the French court as the personal *impresa* of Marguerite de Navarre, sister of François I, and the device plays on her name, since marguerite is the name of a flower, the marigold, ox-eye daisy (Chaucerian 'day's-eye') that follows the sun – there is no need to worry too much about species differentiation. Such name play was ubiquitous at court, where François called her his 'Marguerite des marguerites' and Ronsard wrote about 'La Royne Marguerite/ La plus belle fleur d'élite'. Queen of Navarre, Marguerite found the motto from Virgil, *Non inferiora secutus*, to signal, as French chronicler Brantome puts it 'how she directed all her thoughts, will, and affections towards that great Sun which is God'. The only thing Mary has added on her embroidery to this device of her royal relative is the cipher containing the letters of her own name, though whether this should be read as a personalisation of the device, with Mary laying claim to the heavenly aspiration that it expresses, or whether it should be seen as a simple signing of her work as embroiderer, remains an open question. As will become apparent, Mary uses quite a number of the personal *imprese* belonging to her own kith and kin, with whose values and aspirations she appears to be identifying herself. Indeed this same device is echoed in the MARIE STVART octagon on the same hanging, where the anagram on her name is spelled out in the border, SA VERTV MATIRE [Its strength draws me], implying the attractive power of the sun on the sunflower even though no sunflower is represented. It was surely the visual pun on Marguerite's name that suggested and sanctioned the way this favourite anagram played on Mary's own. One could always vary the device and Mary apparently reused the same anagram on her name, but with a different image, on her Bed of State, according to William Drummond, who tells us that it included an embroidery showing 'her Majesty's name turned into an anagram, *Maria Stuart, Sa vertu m'attire*' but with the image of a loadstone (i.e. a magnetic compass)

Figure 1.4 Marian Hanging, panel E, showing the *impresa* of Marguerite de Navarre, sunflowers following the sun with the motto 'Not having followed lower things'. Oxburgh Hall, Norfolk.

Figure 1.5 Marian Hanging, panel A, with anagrams on Mary's name; although no sunflower is depicted the border inscription implies it: SA VERTV MATIRE [Its strength draws me]. Latin *virtus* can also mean moral perfection, virtue, strength of character and is a keyword in Mary's emblematic vocabulary. Oxburgh Hall, Norfolk.

turning towards the pole star. That variation of details – an old motto with a new image, or a new motto for an inherited device – is absolutely characteristic of the way emblems were invented in a *bricolage* of received ideas at this period. Indeed Mary also had the device of the mariner's compass, pole star and the same motto, *Sa vertu m'attire*, engraved on her silver pocket watch. In the light of such inventive variation and reduplication, we can hardly doubt that she has made these various devices, figuring the power of heavenly bodies to draw earthly things after them, her own.

The surviving corpus: what and where?

The surviving corpus of embroideries consists of a variety of pieces which can be difficult to visualise or locate. A full inventory – the first since Francis Zulueta wrote his account of the embroideries at Oxburgh Hall in 1923 – can be found in the appendices, but since I shall be referring to individual pieces in the chapters which follow it is important to have a preliminary overview of the corpus. By far the greater number of surviving embroideries were preserved at Oxburgh Hall in Norfolk, where the so-called 'Oxburgh Hangings' are still displayed, though other pieces from Oxburgh are now conserved or displayed in the Victoria and Albert Museum, London. The three hangings, and a valance, mounted on the same green velvet, together with 38 detached, unmounted panels – the property of the Bedingfeld family since 1761 – were bought from Oxburgh Hall in 1953 by the National Art Collections Fund. Although gifted as a whole by the Fund in 1955 to the Victoria and Albert Museum, a condition of the sale was that, after due conservation work and temporary exhibition in London, the embroideries should be returned on permanent loan to Oxburgh, where they would be in the care of the National Trust, Oxburgh Hall having become a National Trust property some years earlier. Following their six-month exhibition in London, it was nonetheless agreed that all the unmounted panels should remain in the Victoria and Albert Museum, while the three great mounted hangings, along with the similarly mounted valance, should be returned for display at Oxburgh. The assumption behind this distribution seems to have been that the mounted hangings and valance were historic furnishings, and hence appropriate for use in their historic surroundings, whereas it was unclear what purpose the detached and unmounted panels could serve in any furnishing scheme, and therefore would be better displayed in a museum. However, after some discussion with the museum about the difficulties and dangers of using these very fragile textiles among the actual furnishings at Oxburgh, the three great hangings were eventually moved into their present display cases, while the valance portions were consigned to the storeroom, where they can only now be seen by special arrangement. As we shall see, the distinction between mounted and unmounted panels is not, perhaps, the most useful way of distinguishing these various artefacts, or their iconography and intended uses. Moreover, the question of just when the mounted hangings were assembled in their present format, by whom, and for what purpose, remains in doubt. Three further detached panels from Oxburgh were bought at Sothebys in 1957 by the Friends of the Palace of Holyroodhouse, Edinburgh, and it remains somewhat puzzling and unclear why these pieces were not included in the 1953 sale to the National Art Collections Fund, but that is why these panels are displayed at Holyroodhouse – the only examples of Mary's embroidery that can now be seen in her native Scotland. Two further detached cruciform panels showing animals (a 'Falcon' and 'A Cockle Crab') were preserved not at Oxburgh but at Hardwick Hall where they are now on display. Along with 30 octagonal embroideries with plant slips and Latin adages, closely resembling those on the Oxburgh Hangings though all signed by Bess of Hardwick, these unmounted panels at Hardwick are the only part of the whole corpus to have a different provenance from the Oxburgh embroideries: all the surviving embroideries thus appear to have come down to us in the Oxburgh or Hardwick collections.

Each of the three great hangings comprises 20 or 30 panels, embroidered in silk on canvas, which have been mounted on green velvet, itself decorated with elaborate scrollwork in silver thread. It is uncertain whether these were designed as wall hangings rather than bed curtains, although the four detached sections of very similar embroidery mounted on the same green velvet with its scrollwork are commonly referred to as the 'Oxburgh Valance' because of their size and shape: valances were drapery borders hung round the canopy of a bed, and if these four strips were really designed as a valance it may well be that the hangings were also made to serve as matching bed curtains.[14] The current assumption is that they were probably made up not long after Mary and Bess had executed the actual embroideries which they display, and the most telling evidence for this is to be found in the list of goods which were claimed by the Earl of Shrewsbury in 1586 in settlement of the dispute over matrimonial property following the breakdown of his marriage. Although the list of goods and chattels claimed by him includes such trifles as porringers, basins, trenchers and candlesticks, it specifically excludes 'Certain utensils of household made in the Earl's house, which the Earl will not demand', namely 'hangings of green velvet, birds and fowles and needlework set upon the velvet'.[15] Both the subject matter – 'birds and fowles' – and the mention of green velvet on which they were hung, besides the fact that they were 'made in the Earl's house', leave little room for doubt that these hangings must have been very similar to those now at Oxburgh, which means that they must have been assembled at least a year before Mary's death in 1587 when, as we have already seen from the Chartley inventory, similar pieces on green velvet were passed by Mary into the safekeeping of Renée de Beauregard. Moreover the Earl of Shrewsbury's reference also associates them with certain 'Rich hangings made by Thomas Lane Ambrose, William Barlow, and Henry, Mr. Henry Cavendish's man' who allegedly 'had copes of tissue cloth of gold and other things towards the making thereof; meat and drink and wages paid to the embroiderers by the Earl during the working of them', to which Bess responded that the copes were bought not by Shrewsbury but by her second husband, Sir William St Loe, while she was at Chatsworth where 'some of the Countess's grooms, women, and some boys she kept wrought the most part of them'. Furthermore, she 'Never had but one embroiderer at one time that wrought on them' and his lordship never paid more than £5 towards their making.[16]

If these are indeed the same as the present Oxburgh Hangings, however, then Bess's claim that they were made up at Chatsworth before her third marriage in 1567 to the Earl of Shrewsbury cannot be credited, since the present hangings include embroidery signed by Mary, who only came to England the following year. Shrewsbury evidently believed that the hangings had been executed by the three embroiderers whom he names, on rich velvet or 'copes' which he had supplied, and that their wages had been paid out of his own pocket. It was presumably the fact that they incorporated some of Bess's own needlework, though he does not say so, which nevertheless persuaded him to allow Bess to keep them in this acrimonious share-out of matrimonial goods. If the present Oxburgh Hangings were owned by Bess, rather than by Mary, it is rather surprising that they were preserved, not as part of the larger inheritance of Bess's textiles at Hardwick, but rather at Oxburgh Hall in Norfolk. The Oxburgh provenance of these hangings assumes, as will become apparent, a transmission through various Catholic families – the Howards, Montagus and Bedingfelds – directly from Mary, and not from Bess of Hardwick.

Although this evidence supports an early dating for the Oxburgh Hangings in their present form, there is some new evidence which now casts doubt on it, and we shall be returning to this evidence repeatedly in the course of this study. At least two of the panels that survive in the present Oxburgh Hangings are recorded in some early seventeenth-century descriptions of the embroideries that embellished Mary's Bed of State. Those bed hangings have since disappeared without trace, but if any parts of the present Oxburgh Hangings were still part of the Bed of State in 1603, almost 20 years after Mary's death, then it follows that the hangings cannot have been made up as they now are before this date. The earl's description of these as 'hangings' suggests that they were indeed wall hangings rather than bed curtains or valances.

Each of the present Oxburgh Hangings is made up of various pieces which are assembled in a very similar format. At the centre is a large square embroidery panel with an emblematic picture and a Latin motto in a scroll, and on each of the four sides of this are octagonal panels featuring either plant slips or monograms made up of the initials of Elizabeth Shrewsbury, Marie Stuart, George Shrewsbury, or in one case Elizabeth's and Mary's names together. Each of these octagonal panels has a Latin inscription in its border which does not, in most cases, appear to have any relevance to the plant shown. By far the greater number of embroidery panels on each of the hangings, however, are cross-shaped (a circle with four segments cut out), and they are filled with different species of animals, birds and fishes, each with its name on a label. There are 28 such cruciform animal panels on the Marian Hanging, 20 on the Shrewsbury Hanging, and 22 on the Cavendish Hanging. It will be clear that the two women must have worked out a peculiar convention of shape coding which, although it may well be indebted to the use of similar shapes in the embroidery of Catherine de Medici, is unique to their work. Thus the large emblematic centrepieces are all square panels, the personal monograms and plant slips with Latin inscriptions are invariably octagonal, and the animal embroideries are all cruciform. This shape coding for different types of subject matter is not found in any other embroidery of this period but is, rather, a unique signature of the work of these two women and one of the clearest signs of the remarkable community of taste that characterises their work.

The Oxburgh Hangings and the similar valance are not, however, the only surviving examples of their work to follow this particular shape coding as there is a large number of detached panels: at least 47 separate panels of cruciform animals, birds and fishes, eight octagons of plants or monograms, and the large square emblem-

Figure 1.6 'Elephant', detached panel showing corners filled with other details; when mounted on the surviving hangings such corner details were apparently cut off to leave just the cruciform centre panel. The elephant is copied from Conrad Gessner's *Historia animalium*. London, Victoria and Albert Museum.

atic *Las pennas passan* panel. Nearly all of these were preserved at Oxburgh (and are now in the Victoria and Albert Museum, London), though two such panels were discovered at Hardwick, where they are now displayed. A further 30 octagonal panels of plant slips, all embroidered by Bess alone, were discovered at Hardwick in the 1930s, when they were mounted on the present wooden screen. The detached panels from Oxburgh show clear signs of expediency and improvisation as some are mounted on pieces of the same green velvet as the Oxburgh Hangings and Valance, suggesting that they must once have been part of the same suite of furnishings, while some of the 'cruciform' animal panels have not had the corner segments cut out to make them cross-shaped – they are square pieces containing the cruciform design with its animal, the corner segments between the arms of the cross often being filled with other embroidered detail. When, in the case of several of the pieces, these corner segments have been cut off – as in all those on the hangings – the panel has then been finished off with a plain raised border. Several of the panels are damaged, not through normal wear and tear but because someone has taken scissors to a panel and cut it in half.

Provenance and transmission

So how did the Oxburgh Hangings (and 50 or more further panels) end up at Oxburgh Hall in Norfolk? The best explanation is still Margaret Swain's, who records that the Oxburgh panels were said to have been brought there in 1761 from Cowdray Park in Sussex, when the daughter of Viscount Montagu of Cowdray married Sir Richard Bedingfeld of Oxburgh.[17] The Montagus of Cowdray were related to the Howards by marriage, and it is through the Howard connection that any bequest of embroideries from Mary Queen of Scots is likely to have reached Cowdray in the seventeenth century. Swain notes that Mary bequeathed several of her specifically Catholic and most personal possessions to Anne Dacre, wife of Philip Howard, son and heir to the same Duke of Norfolk whose execution in 1572 put an end to any hopes Mary had of marrying again. We shall hear more of Philip Howard and his wife Anne Dacre later as Mary executed some embroidery for Anne that used emblems in some timely marriage counselling (see Chapter 2). Mary certainly bequeathed her rosary, her prayer book

Figure 1.7 Rowland Lockey, *Lady Arbella Stuart aged 13*, 1589. Daughter of the Earl of Lennox and Elizabeth Cavendish, she was brought up by her grandmother Bess of Hardwick. In 1611 she sold a number of pieces of needlework made by the late Queen of Scots (her aunt) to Mary Talbot (who was also her aunt). The Devonshire Collection, Hardwick Hall, Derbyshire.

and the white veil she wore at her execution to Anne Dacre, but these personal and devotional objects were surely meant to identify and encourage the Catholicism of a friend whose husband was at this very time imprisoned in the Tower of London because of his faith.

Anne Dacre's son Thomas inherited the Arundel rather than the Norfolk title through his father, and married Bess's granddaughter, Alethea Talbot, daughter of Gilbert Talbot (son of George, Earl of Shrewsbury) and of Mary Cavendish (who was Bess's youngest daughter by her second husband, Sir William Cavendish). This marriage united a great English Catholic family, associated with Mary, with the Shrewsbury and Cavendish families, in direct descent from Bess, in a union which might well have facilitated any transfer of Marian relics or bequests to their descendants. Thomas Howard was to become, as Earl of Arundel, one of the great collectors and connoisseurs of European art in the seventeenth century. Margaret Swain's theory is that Alethea Talbot would have found the unmounted embroideries at Arundel which her mother-in-law Anne Howard (née Dacre) had been bequeathed by Mary Queen of Scots, and that it would have been Alethea who 'decided to have them mounted on green velvet and made into hangings, either for Arundel Castle or Arundel House in the Strand'.[18] The panels would then have found their way from Arundel to Cowdray, following a later marriage between the first Viscount Montagu and an aunt of Anne Howard's which united the two families.

It is certainly true that in 1611 Alethea's mother, Mary Talbot, bought a number of pieces of needlework made by the late Queen of Scots from her niece, Arbella Stuart, for which she paid £850, money which helped to fund Arbella's escape overseas from the political restrictions and confinement in which she had been held for most of her life by her grandmother, Bess of Hardwick. So how and when might Arbella Stuart have acquired any embroideries created by Mary Queen of Scots? Arbella was closely related to Mary Stuart and to Bess, who had brought her up following the death of her father, Charles Stuart, Earl of Lennox and brother of Darnley, closely followed in 1578 by the death of her mother Elizabeth (née Cavendish). Bess of Hardwick, as widow of William Cavendish, was thus Arbella's maternal grandmother. If embroideries had indeed

Figure 1.8 The Marian Hanging. Oxburgh Hall, Norfolk.

EMBLEMS FOR A QUEEN

been given to Anne, Countess of Arundel, along with devotional relics, by Mary Queen of Scots in 1587, then Anne's daughter-in-law Alethea could well have inherited them, along with those which her mother, Mary Talbot, bought in May 1511, from Alethea's cousin Arbella.[19] The dates are now problematic, however, since if the embroideries that Anne's daughter-in-law Mary Talbot bought from Arbella as late as 1611 included the present Oxburgh Hangings, we now have to explain how William Fowler (and he is not the only witness) could have seen several of the panels that feature on those hangings, notably the *Virescit vulnere virtus* centrepiece to the Marian Hanging, on the royal Bed of State which he claims he saw in Edinburgh in 1603.

All the evidence is in favour of the Oxburgh Hangings being in Bess's possession not long after Mary's execution, whatever instructions Mary might have given Renée de Beauregard concerning the destination of pieces and uncut panels among her own possessions. That these pieces were the very ones we

Figure 1.9 The Shrewsbury Hanging. Oxburgh Hall, Norfolk.

now see on the Oxburgh Hangings is in no doubt once one recognises that one of the pieces described in the Chartley inventory as entrusted to Renée is identical, as Margaret Swain notes, with what we know as the *Las pennas passan* panel. Mary's inventory describes it as a panel (*quarreau* – i.e. square) in *petit point* with 'a single device in the centre and several others around it, the arms of France, Scotland, Spain and England in the four corners'.[20] In other words, the *Las pennas passan* panel must have been Mary's property at the time of her death, and cannot have been among any similar embroideries that the Earl of Shrewsbury had allowed his wife to retain when they separated in 1586. These, as we have seen, are described as mounted on green velvet backing. It seems at least possible that the unmounted panels, which Mary left in the safekeeping of her servant Renée, were acquired from her under some pretext and possibly for cash, by Bess, Countess of Shrewsbury, who wanted them to join the pieces of her own workmanship, mostly fully mounted, which she had obtained

Figure 1.10 The Cavendish Hanging. Oxburgh Hall, Norfolk.

Figure 1.11 Pinkie House, Musselburgh, long gallery painted ceiling c.1613 by an unknown artist. These were almost certainly the 'inscriptions' which Ben Jonson asked William Drummond to send him in 1619 when, instead, Drummond sent Jonson the emblems and mottoes on Queen Mary's embroidered Bed of State.

from her husband's estate only the year before. She would have been quite capable of enquiring after her late companion's embroideries and persuading Renée de Beauregard to part with them.[21] The 1587 inventory of 'goods found in the custody of the several servants of the late Queen' makes it clear that at least some of these, namely those left in the custody of Andrew Melvin and the queen's physician, Bourgoigne, were to be sold 'and the money thereof to be imployed towards the expenses of the whole companye in their journey homewardes' (p. 274). The possibility that many of the other bequests might also have been sold by her servants to meet their immediate necessities seems highly likely.

The embroideries from Oxburgh are not, however, the only examples which we need to consider as part of this corpus, and it remains to identify several other pieces that I shall discuss or refer to from time to time. Two very similar pieces from Hardwick have already been mentioned, but the many different Hardwick textiles, which have largely been excluded from this study for reasons given above, include several further pieces which do need to be taken into account. Most interesting of these are the two cushion covers illustrating fables from Faerno and copying emblems from two different emblem books, which are certainly the work of Mary since they have her personal cipher together with the three flowers – rose, lily and thistle – of the nations over which she had claims to sovereignty. Since the way her embroidery uses emblems (and fables) is a key concern, the Hardwick cushion covers are therefore artefacts of great interest. Also at Hardwick are 30 octagons embroidered with plant slips and Latin mottoes, now mounted on hinged wooden panels to form screens. Discovered in the 1930s by the Duchess of Devonshire, they resemble the octagonal panels on the Oxburgh Hangings so closely that they clearly need to be included in this study, representing as they do a significant part of the corpus, even though most of them carry Bess's initials and all were probably her own work.

The non-extant embroideries: Mary's Bed of State

In 1618 playwright Ben Jonson walked all the way from London to Edinburgh and back. Jonson was no lightweight – indeed in his poem *My Picture Left in Scotland* he jokes about 'My mountain belly'. We do not know why Jonson walked all the way though we do know that he got as far as Darlington before he stopped to buy a new pair of boots. In Scotland he had some famous literary 'Conversations' with poet William Drummond while staying in Drummond's house at Hawthornden, and on his return he wrote a thank-you letter dated 10 May 1619, recording that King James himself had welcomed him back to London and expressed an interest in a book Jonson proposed to write about his majesty's native land.[22] Drummond had promised to send him further information about various Scottish matters for this book, such as 'things concerning the Loch of Lomound', and the differences in teaching methods at various Scottish universities. 'I most earnestly sollicit you,' he also writes, 'for your promise of the inscriptions at Pinky.' This is the earliest reference to the painted ceiling which Chancellor Seton, Earl of Dunfermline, had installed in the remarkable long gallery at Pinkie House in Musselburgh in 1613, a ceiling full of emblems and Latin inscriptions.[23] Among the people Jonson met in Edinburgh, to whom he asks to be remembered in his letter, is a certain James Raith, an Edinburgh lawyer who was married to Drummond's cousin, Elizabeth Fowler, and who is also recorded as 'servitor' to Alexander Seton: the connection may well explain how the subject of this ceiling with its 'inscriptions' came up in conversation with Drummond. We shall hear more of the Fowler family later.

In his reply, dated 1 July 1619, Drummond makes no mention of the emblems or inscriptions in Seton's neo-Stoic gallery; instead he sends him a long account of 'the Impressaes and Emblemes on a Bed of State wrought and embroidered all with gold and silk by the late Queen Mary mother to our sacred Sovereign, which will embellish greatly some pages of your Book'. Evidently Drummond thought that these 'Impressaes and Emblemes' were similar to those at Pinkie and would serve equally well for Jonson's intended book. He identifies 30 devices on the bed hangings, quoting the Latin motto and describing the emblematic picture. In a few cases he also offers an interpretation of its meaning, or likely application to Mary's circumstances: 'Two women upon the wheels of Fortune, the one holding a lance, the other a cornucopia; which impressa seemeth to glaunce at Queen Elizabeth and her self, the word *Fortuna Comites*' [Companions of Fortuna]. We can see from such a comment that in their day these emblematic devices on her furnishings were open to a political interpretation, which is why the political implications of much of Mary's other embroidery will be examined. As we shall discover, the emblems displayed on these innocent-looking bed hangings and soft furnishings were keenly scrutinised as evidence of Mary's political views and intentions: these are potentially incriminating emblems, which is why they were collected by the English secret services under Elizabeth's chief spymaster, Sir Francis Walsingham. Indeed the only record of some of these embroideries that have not survived, or of their associated iconography, is to be found in precisely such intelligence records gathered for potential use against Mary by the Elizabethan secret services. Moreover, one of the reasons that William Drummond was able to describe the emblems embroidered on Mary's Bed of State was because he had inherited a description of these very same hangings from his uncle, William Fowler, who had himself been recruited many years earlier by Walsingham, at a time when the latter was busy gathering intelligence in the 1580s concerning Mary's political aims and intentions in England.

Until recently Drummond's 1619 letter to Ben Jonson remained the only known record of these emblematic embroideries sewn by Mary for her Bed of State, and

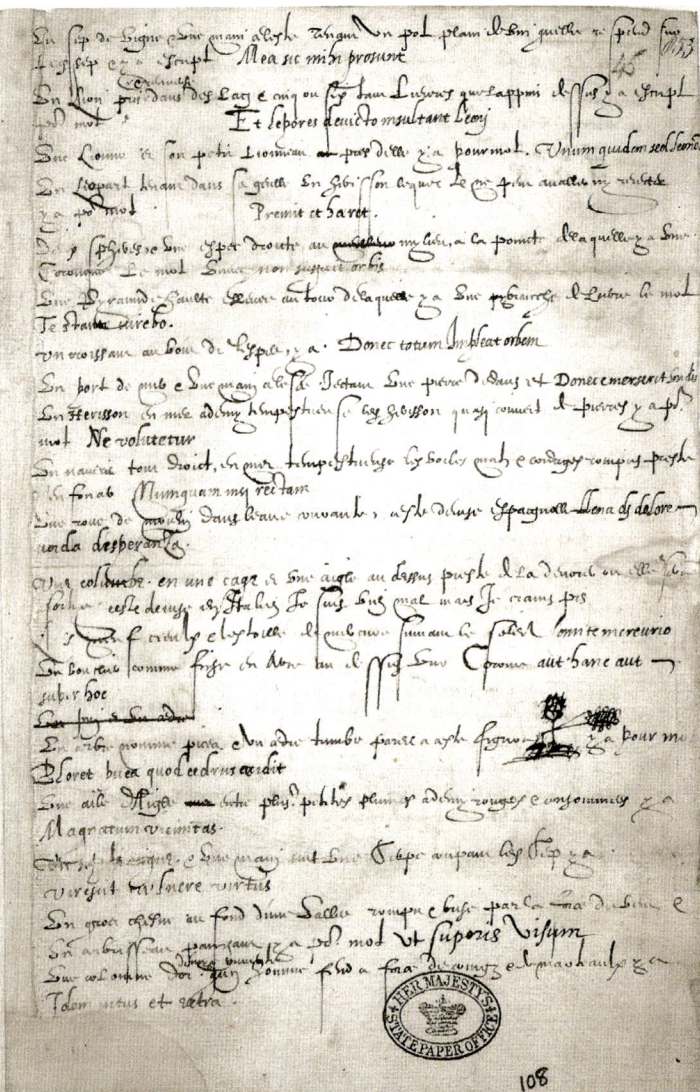

Figure 1.12 Unsigned French inventory, compiled sometime between September 1586 and October 1587, of devices embroidered on Mary's Bed of State. National Archives, SP 53/21, fol. 108r.

it has been often cited in the existing literature on her needlework.[24] However, no fewer than three further descriptions of these same bed hangings have recently come to light in documents that not only help us to realise their make-up and iconography but, more worryingly, force us to reconsider much of the received wisdom on the embroideries which, unlike the Bed of State itself, have actually survived. This new evidence will be examined in some detail in the following chapters, but for now all we need is a preliminary description of these three new documents.

The earliest is a French inventory preserved in the Public Record Office (now the National Archives) in England, consisting of three pages listing 49 devices, the last seven on a separate sheet and in a different hand with the date '9 Sept 1586' in the margin. A translation, headed 'Devices on the Queen of Scots Bed' and dated October 1587 was printed in the *Calendar of State Papers Relating to Scotland and Mary Queen of Scots* (vol. IX, 1547–1603), as long ago as 1915, but seems to have escaped the notice of all previous writers on the needlework. The dates (if they can be trusted), and the fact that these documents are in French, means that they must have been written by one of Mary's own servants either a few months before or a few months after her execution. Mary was beheaded 8 February

1587, and the Chartley inventory of her possessions, which she herself compiled as previously mentioned in June 1586, was also written in French and is preserved among the papers of French ambassador, Guillaume de l'Aubépine, Baron de Châteauneuf, in what is now the Bibliothèque nationale de France. The English authorities had long been collecting intelligence of Mary's personal possessions as these passed through the embassy in London, and it seems likely that it was one of these documents describing the devices on her Bed of State that ended up among English state papers from some such source.

Two further listings of the devices embroidered on Mary's Bed of State are preserved not in England but in Scotland, where they are to be found among the Hawthornden papers in the National Library of Scotland that were presented in 1782 to the Society of Antiquaries of Scotland by one of William Drummond's actual descendants at Hawthornden. In 1827 antiquarian David Laing assembled these loose papers into 15 volumes, of which volumes XI and XII consist of manuscripts left by Drummond's maternal uncle, William Fowler, one of James VI's 'Castalian Band' of court poets and, eventually, secretary to Queen Anna. Fowler had, indeed, travelled with King James to bring Queen Anna from Denmark in 1590. Fowler's papers, which Drummond inherited following his uncle's death in 1612, include two lists of the devices on the Bed of State, one written and signed by Fowler himself. Its header reads: '5 April 1603 after the King's departure I did observe these devyses upon the queens his mother's bed'. This numbered list includes 31 devices, and can easily be shown to have been Drummond's source for many of those he describes 16 years later in his letter to Jonson. Thus Fowler's list includes 'Thrie crownes two opposite and another above in the sky' with the motto *Aliamque moratur* [And awaits another]. This is a highly interesting device which had been adopted by Henri III of France to symbolise the fact that, although he was king of both France and Poland, a higher crown awaited him in heaven (see Chapter 2). Fowler's handwriting is not easy to read, and the word 'sky' looks very much like 'sea' because of the way the long 's' is carried down to form the upstroke of the 'k'; I first transcribed it thus, as did Drummond in the version of this letter he printed in his *History of Scotland* in 1655 and 1680.[25] I am convinced we both made this mistake because we were transcribing the same document. A crown 'in the sea' makes no sense, and the editors of Drummond's posthumous folio (*The Works*, 1711, p. 137) make the required correction. As will be discussed later (Chapter 2), Henri III's device was much talked about in the 1580s, when the identity of the third crown was given a particular political orientation following the breakdown of the Anjou marriage negotiations with Elizabeth, in circles that included the Italian philosopher, Giordano Bruno, who was in England at the time. Indeed Fowler was frequenting the French embassy in London at precisely the same time that Bruno was residing there with the ambassador, Michel de Castelnau.

Similarly, another device (also discussed further in Chapter 2) showed an eclipse with the motto *Ipsa sibi lumen quod invidet aufert* [She takes from herself the light which she envies] to which Drummond adds the interpretive comment 'glancing, as may appear at Queen Elizabeth'. This can now be shown to have been anticipated by his uncle, who also writes 'Glancing as I think at Queene Elizabeth' after this example. Although Drummond certainly consulted Fowler's description when writing his own for Ben Jonson, he nevertheless includes eight devices that are not mentioned by Fowler and his list appears to be somewhat selective, since there are 11 devices mentioned by Fowler that he does not bother to include. Fowler's header assures us that what he is describing are the devices he had actually observed on the bed in 1603, shortly after the king's departure for London following the Union of Crowns. Drummond must have had a different source for the eight emblems not described by his uncle, though we cannot be sure that he himself ever saw the actual bed hangings, even though they were certainly in Edinburgh in 1617 at the time of James's one and only return visit to his native kingdom.

Four of the devices described by Drummond that are not included in Fowler's list he may well have known of from the third of these new documents, an anonymous, undated inventory listing 43 'Devyces' on three leaves, preserved among Fowler's papers though not in his hand and using spellings which suggest a regional or provincial pronunciation ('devayce' for device; 'vayne' for vine; 'layon' for lion). There is no way of knowing any more at present about who might have compiled this description of the embroideries, or for what purpose, or how Fowler might have acquired it. I shall refer to it hereinafter as 'Hawthornden Anonymous'. Fowler does not copy its wording, and although all his devices are also in the Hawthornden Anonymous inventory, it describes 12 further ones that Fowler ignores.

It should be clear from this comparison that we cannot be sure which of these descriptions is the most complete and accurate. The earliest (1586/87) inventory, which also happens to be the longest (listing 49 devices compared to Drummond's 31), is almost certainly describing the actual bed. Although the four inventories vary in the total number, in the ordering, and in the particular devices included, this does not necessarily mean that the bed itself had been altered between the various dates when the different descriptions were compiled. It would have been easy enough, after all, to have missed out a valance. Of the four descriptions, only Hawthornden Anonymous offers any information about the actual make-up of the bed itself, telling us that an indefinite number of the devices were 'for the thrie first valances', whereas

> The Rufe of the bed att the four noukes hath the four armories half painted the armories of Scotland and France att the one end of the rufe half painted at another nuke Scotland and England half painted att the third nuke with Scotland and Lorayne half paynted and at the fourth nouke Lorayne and Bourbon half paynted. The first device that is in the rufe of the bed is the quines ma^tie pertrayd knieling before the cros and hir crowne and hire scepture laying at hir fite and haulding hir hands to heaven the word is *Vndique*.

I have deliberately not supplied the missing punctuation, since that would involve some guesswork as to exactly what went where. However clearly this writer is describing the actual bed, mentioning not only valances and roof but also at one point 'A devayce in the sete of the chayer the Bayrer of the heavens with vii starres aboufe the word is *divinae Vindicta*', a device unrecorded elsewhere, and, finally, 'Another devayce on the backe of the chayer'. This chair is not part of the bed hangings, and can only have been a similarly embroidered side chair, or possibly a Chair of State, located somewhere close to the bed itself. We might conclude from this that Hawthornden Anonymous was describing Mary's Bed of State in its actual surroundings when made up and in use. That makes it a potentially good witness.

This is certainly the same Bed of State which is identified in Paulet's list of goods found in the custody of her servants at Fotheringhay as 'Furniture for a bedd wrought with needle woorke of silke, silver and golde, with divers devices and armes, not throughlye finished', and in the custody of Andrew Melvin, which a note in the margin says is 'To be delivred by him to the Kinge of Scottes'.[26] That it was indeed delivered to James VI is confirmed by an entry in the Register of the Privy Council of Scotland dated 1616, which directs that four royal beds were to be sent from Edinburgh to London to be repaired and refurbished in time to be sent back to Scotland in preparation for the royal visit of 1617. The four beds are identified as 'ane bed of the labouris of Hercules'; a bed of crimson velvet and gold; a bed of embroidered work of gold, silver and silk; and a bed 'incompleete, sewit be his Majesties mother, of gold, silver, and silk'. John Auchmowtie, Master of the King's wardrobe, is ordered to deliver the four beds to a certain Mr Nicholls who will bring them to London 'and bring the same back agane accordinglie'.[27] Since the revamped bed was thus brought to Scotland for the king's visit of 1617, it is quite possible that William Drummond might have seen it then and that this is where it ended up. His uncle William Fowler would certainly, as a member of the royal household, have had access to the royal furniture if he wished, but he was already deceased by this date. Fowler had moved with the court to London, as Queen Anna's secretary, shortly after 1603, though some years before his death in 1612 he drifted back to Edinburgh where he lived in Dean House, another house like Pinkie with some interesting painted ceilings.[28] According to Fowler, he saw the bed in 1603 'after the King departure', which refers to his departure from Edinburgh, meaning that this is where the bed was then located.

And that is the last we hear of Queen Mary's embroidered bed. Whether it disappeared during the general plundering of royal loot during the civil wars is uncertain, though quite possible: it is certainly likely to have remained in Scotland after the royal visit of 1617. It is the only artefact using embroideries executed by Mary to be at all extensively documented in early records, and it is probably worth stressing that King James was not intent on getting these beds refurbished just so that he would be able to sleep comfortably on his visit to Scotland. What is at stake, rather, is their public appearance. The royal furnishings needed to reflect the status of their royal owner: made of luxurious materials and curiously wrought, the emblematic decoration of the Bed of State would be expected to make a statement about the qualities of kingship and the inherent values and aspirations of its owner. These are not just private and personal household goods but fashion statements that send public signals, both for James in 1617 and for his mother in her years of exile 40 years earlier. For that reason the particular messages which they transmit call for an emblematic reading and it does make sense to refer to them as 'emblems for a queen'. Let us now therefore try to work out what these emblems are saying.

2

Emblems

Source hunting

Although the emblems displayed on Mary's embroideries often look like original inventions, designed to express her personal values or her current situation, several of them use devices that can also be found in printed emblem books. Mary may well therefore have copied these, or adapted them to her own purposes. The most consistently emblematic of the embroideries are those that William Drummond described in 1619 on the embroidered Bed of State, and the fact that sources and analogues for many of these can now be identified is particularly fortunate, since it enables us plausibly to reconstruct the bed's iconography and appearance. For this reason the missing Bed of State is the focus of this chapter. It is important to bear in mind, however, that although this genre of illustrated book was eventually to generate several thousands of different titles, by the time the embroideries were being sewn in the 1570s or 1580s only 20 or so emblem books, strictly speaking, had been published. The first emblem book, Andrea Alciato's *Emblematum liber*, appeared in 1531 with its mottoes and epigrams all in Latin, but the earliest English emblem book, Geffrey Whitney's *A Choice of Emblemes*, would not be printed until 1586, only months before Mary died. Emblem books may have been better known on the continent, which is where they were all published at the time the embroideries were being sewn, and she might certainly have acquired some knowledge of them during her upbringing in France, though by 1561, when she returned to Scotland, only a dozen or so such books had been published anywhere. Emblem books are known to have circulated in Scotland, however – indeed one of the most important of the editions of Alciato's *Emblematum liber* had been dedicated to the Earl of Arran, Regent of Scotland, as early as 1549.[1]

Just four printed emblem books can be shown to have provided direct patterns for Mary's embroideries. Chief among these are the 118 devices collected by Claude Paradin and first published in Paris in 1551 under the title *Devises heroïques*. Paradin's book became one of the most popular sources for emblems in the applied arts: in needlework it provided the pattern for emblems on the Shepherd Buss embroidery in the Victoria and Albert Museum, and, in Scotland, for painted ceilings at Rossend, at Nunraw, and in a house in Edinburgh known as 'Mary of Guise's House'.[2] But Paradin's heroical devices might be expected to appeal to Mary for more personal reasons since they nearly all belonged to royal or noble persons, including quite a few of her own relatives. Thus when Mary sewed the famous salamander device of François I, with its familiar motto *Nutrisco et extinguo* [I nourish and extinguish] on her Bed of State, she hardly needed a printed emblem book to supply the pattern since she would have been familiar with this device on public monuments and courtly decorations all around her during her childhood in France. The salamander is a lizard that was thought to live amidst flames which it extinguished by the chill of its body. Since the actual bed hangings have not survived, there is no way of knowing whether her embroidered salamander copied Paradin's woodcut directly.[3] In 1559 Paradin's courtly devices were followed by a very similar collection, Gabriele Simeoni's *Le imprese heroiche et morali*, and in 1561 these were reprinted in the first of a number of joint Paradin/Simeoni editions published in France containing a total of 216 devices.

It is important to stress that neither of these authors invented the *imprese* they were illustrating or describing – they were merely providing an anthology of the most elegant or celebrated courtly devices. Mary did not need to learn about those from books since they were part of the courtly fashioning into which she was born and bred. It is not surprising, therefore, that quite a number of the devices she included in her embroideries should also be found in Paradin or Simeoni. The only other emblem books Mary can be shown to have copied from directly are the *Dialogo dell'imprese* of Paolo Giovio and the *Emblemata* of Hadrianus Junius. Giovio's *Dialogo* (Rome, 1555) is a prose treatise on the art of the *impresa* which set the precedent for such theoretical works on their composition, and was unillustrated until 1559 when publisher Guillaume Rouille in Lyon provided 102 woodcuts to illustrate Giovio's examples. The following year Rouille brought out an expanded edition containing 126 of Giovio's devices along with Simeoni's in a joint edition, though with separate pagination and title pages, and in place of Giovio's prose treatise there are verse 'testrastichi morali' beneath his pictures. This expanded edition includes the emblem *Los llenos de dolor* that Mary used for one of her Bed of State embroideries, and it follows that she must have used this expanded edition, or one of its successors. As an anthology of existing *imprese* the illustrated Giovio belongs with Paradin and Simeoni, and these three anthologies of emblematic devices were often issued, from 1561 onwards, in joint editions. If Mary used one of these, a single volume might well have included all three of her principal emblem sources, though there is no record in surviving inventories of her owning any particular emblem books.[4] The only other emblem book she is known to have used, the *Emblemata* by Hadrianus Junius (Adriaan de Jonge), was first printed in Antwerp by Plantin in 1565 in Latin, with a French translation in 1567. These are full tripartite emblems, composed by Junius himself, with not only a motto and picture for each but also an explanatory verse epigram. Although we can certainly find analogues in the printed emblem books for a few more of the devices in her embroideries,

Figure 2.1 *Nutrisco et extinguo* [I nurture and destroy], the salamander device of François I (Claude Paradin, *Devises heroïques*, 1557, p. 16).

they are not direct copies and it is important to stress that what all these sources and analogues illustrate is the richness of the courtly and cultural contexts within which such emblematic forms were circulating at the time. Mary would have had various motives for choosing particular devices for her embroidery: perhaps the bearer was known or related to her, or maybe the device had a moral which spoke to her own condition and could now be used in furnishings that would express her values, aspirations and principles.

The devices recorded on her Bed of State include at least ten that belonged to Mary's relatives. Not only Drummond but also Fowler and, especially, the anonymous English description of the embroidered Bed of State (though not the 1586 French description) identify the bearer of the *impresa* whenever possible. The bed hangings evidently included more or less well-known devices of François I and of her father-in-law Henri II; her mother-in-law Catherine de Medici; her husband François II; her brother-in-law Henri III; her mother Mary of Lorraine; her uncle Charles, Cardinal of Lorraine; and also of Godfrey of Bouillon, legendary ancestor of the Lorraine dynasty from which Mary was descended through her mother. The portcullis device which Drummond identifies as 'The Impresa of Henry VIII' might surprise us, but this heraldic badge had been first adopted by Henry VII of England, whose daughter Margaret Tudor had married first James IV of Scotland and second the Earl of Angus and was thus not only Mary's grandfather but also Darnley's.[5] In putting this 'English' badge on her embroideries, Mary was merely adding to the list of devices on her bed hangings that belonged to those to whom she was closely related. When the various accounts of her Bed of State cannot identify any other bearer, they are likely to ascribe the device to Mary herself or to her son, James VI of Scotland. For instance, the device showing a 'hedgehog' (almost certainly a sea urchin) being rolled about among rocks in the sea, with the motto *Ne volutetur* [Lest it be rolled about] is identified as 'Another for her Majestie', while two trees, a fallen cedar and a standing pine tree with a motto which means 'The pitch pine weeps because the cedar has fallen' is described as 'A devayce for the kings Majestie and his mother'. Their authority for making these direct ascriptions of the *impresa* to its bearer is unclear, however, and it may have involved some guesswork.

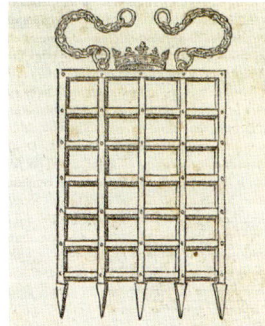

Figure 2.2 *Securitas altera* [Another safeguard], device of Henry VIII (Claude Paradin, *Devises heroïques*, 1557, p. 36).

Figure 2.3 *Te stante virebo* [Whilst you stand I shall flourish], the *impresa* of the Cardinal of Lorraine (Claude Paradin, *Devises heroïques*, 1557, p. 72).

Mary is nevertheless likely to have identified with the values that these devices advertise as those of her kith and kin. One of these is a device that Drummond describes as: 'The *impresa* of the Cardinal of Lorrain, her Uncle, a pyramid overgrown with ivy, the vulgar word, *Te stante virebo*' [Whilst you stand, I shall flourish]. Paradin shows this as an obelisk entwined with ivy and surmounted by a crescent moon, with the same motto. He tells us that the cardinal erected the device at the entrance to his abbey at Cluny, where its meaning was explained in a French verse *subscriptio* which interpreted the obelisk as representing the majesty of the king ('Soit notre Roy la grande pyramide') whose firmness supports the flourishing ivy of the *prince prelat* himself in upholding the shining light of the crescent moon, which is understood as the spreading light of the true faith, 'Laquelle va (tant qu'elle soit entiere/ En sa rondeur) tousiours tousiours croissant' [Which goes on and on growing until it becomes whole in its roundness]. The significance of this emblem, as an expression of the importance of a stable monarchy in allowing officers of the (Catholic) Church to uphold the expanding light of faith, would not have been lost on Mary, and it was certainly this meaning which motivated its appropriation when it was taken over in the rather different context of Protestant England, where we find it represented in one of the very earliest illustrations of tournament *imprese*, a manuscript in the College of Arms showing eight mounted knights jousting beneath a representation of their *impresa* shields.[6] Here the device of an obelisk entwined with ivy can be confidently assigned to Robert Dudley, the future Earl of Leicester – indeed Alan Young (1987) has shown that the only years on which tournaments were held in which the knights depicted in the College of Arms manuscript participated were 1559 and 1560, allowing us to date Dudley's appropriation of the cardinal's *impresa* with some confidence.[7] What motivated this appropriation is unclear, though it finds some explanation 25 years later, when it features as the opening emblem in the first English emblem book, Whitney's *A Choice of Emblemes and other Devises* (Leiden, 1586), which was dedicated to the Earl of Leicester. Whitney's verse *subscriptio* echoes Paradin's explanation of its iconography: 'The Pillar great, our gratious Princes is: / The

Figure 2.4 Armorial manuscript showing knights jousting, each surmounted by a shield showing his *impresa*, including the *Te stante virebo* obelisk entwined with ivy. The Earl of Leicester's association with the *Te stante virebo* shield is suggested by the Dudley device of the ragged staff on his horse bard. London, College of Arms.

braunche, the Churche ...', but the gracious princess in this case is Queen Elizabeth and the church is the reformed Church of England,

> ... that of late with stormes was almoste spent,
> And bruised sore with Tirants bluddie bloes,
> Whome fire, and sworde, with persecution rent.
>
> (1586, p.1)

There can be little doubt that this prominent opening emblem is designed to describe the precise role which, by 1586, Leicester was defining for himself in the Netherlands as upholder of the true (Protestant) faith with the support of his sovereign, support which he was, somewhat ironically, to lose precisely because of the ambitious role he assigned himself in this very campaign. Although the application of the emblem has changed, the meaning is the same as we saw in Paradin. The College of Arms manuscript offers sufficient justification for assuming that Leicester had taken over this *impresa* as early as 1559, although as already mentioned its original bearer had been the Cardinal of Lorraine, and such an appropriation of someone else's *impresa* is akin to the process we have witnessed in Mary's own appropriation of devices used by her relatives. The *Te stante virebo* device is likely to have appealed to Mary because, as already noted, it echoes the relationship between the monarch and the church – as long as the sovereign stands firm and upright, true religion will flourish. That moral was as relevant to her own status as it would have been to any other ruler at this period. Moreover the verb *vireo* [I flourish] is the same as that used in the motto of her *Virescit vulnere virtus* vine-pruning emblem.

Several of the emblems recorded on the Bed of State allude to Mary's imprisonment and her hope of resurgence under oppression. The apple tree bound to a thorn assumes this moral once it is read in the light of its motto, *Per vincula crescit* [It grows taller through chains], which identifies the horticultural symbolism as the grafting of fertile stems onto barren stock and, like the *Virescit vulnere virtus* emblem, offers the hope of a fruitful outcome to Mary's own confinement. It is surely inconceivable that references to binding in these emblems can refer to anything other than Mary's imprisonment in England. The tree most commonly identified by emblem writers as the symbol of such growth under oppression was, however, the palm tree, since classical writers authorised the belief that this grows taller if you rest or hang weights on its branches. Mary's Bed of State, Drummond tells us, had just such a palm tree with the motto *Ponderibus virtus innata resistit* [Innate virtue resists oppression]. Equally horticultural is the garden herb camomile which gives out greater fragrance when trampled on: *Fructus calcata dat amplos* [It is more fruitful when trampled on]. Out of her own oppression, Mary must have hoped, there might come some fruitfulness.

Another emblem of imprisonment is that showing a bird in a cage, above which flies a hawk; the motto is Italian: *Il mal me preme et me spaventa Peggio* [It is ill with me now, and I fear worse to come]. To see what this embroidery must have looked like we have only to turn to the *Emblemata* of Hadrianus Junius (1565, p. 45), where we find an emblem showing a pet dove in a cage above which hovers an eagle with pointed beak and exposed talons. Junius's Latin motto is *Malo oppressus, deterius formidat* [Oppressed with one evil, it dreads a worse one], but the Italian version of this which Mary quotes is inscribed on a scroll encircling

Figure 2.5 *Te stante, virebo* emblem (Geffrey Whitney, *A Choice of Emblemes*, 1586, p. 1).

the dove's cage in Junius's picture, and its use of the first rather than third person (not 'it fears worse' but 'I fear worse) may well have been what determined Mary's choice of the Italian rather than the Latin motto. She would have needed little prompting to apply this emblem to her own situation, where the recurrent efforts of her friends to secure her release threatened to deliver her into the predatory claws of her enemies: a case of out of the frying pan into the fire.

Base and cowardly opponents only exploit the weakness of their superiors when they have them at a disadvantage, or so the emblem would have us believe which Drummond describes as showing a lion (i.e. the king of beasts) caught in a net while hares (considered timid and cowardly) jump all over it. Mary's motto *Et lepores devicto insultant leoni* [Even hares insult the conquered lion] goes back to a classical proverb which Erasmus cites as *Mortuo leoni et lepores insultant* [Even hares insult a dead lion], based on the point in Homer's *Iliad* when Hector's dead body is surrounded by jeering Greeks, none of whom would have dared to insult him while living.⁸ The adage had already been turned into an emblem by Alciato, though with a different motto (also based on an expression used by Homer at this point), *Cum larvis non luctandum* [There is no wrestling with ghosts]. However Alciato's picture shows what the Erasmian adage describes, namely a dead lion, and not what Drummond describes on Mary's embroidery, which is 'a lyon taken in a net'. This, and the form of the motto – *devicto … Leoni* [the conquered lion] rather than Erasmus's *mortuo leoni* [the dead lion] – reflects her own situation and confirms the preoccupation with imprisonment which can be identified as a recurrent *leitmotiv* in these emblems. Mary may now be mocked by weaklings who would not have dared to insult her majesty in better times, but she is not yet a dead lion, only one in fetters. Although we do not have Mary's actual embroidery, Drummond's description is sufficiently vivid, I suggest, for us to reconstruct pretty accurately how this emblem reworked its source. Although Mary's emblem certainly goes back to the classical adage on which Alciato's emblem was also based, Alciato only echoes the *et lepores insultant* formula very weakly, though Drummond's description of the way the hares cavort over the lion in the embroidery certainly suggests that it must have resembled the way this was pictured

Figure 2.6 *Malo oppressus, deterius formidat* [Oppressed with one evil, it dreads a worse one], the captive dove fears a greater evil if it escapes into the talons of the predatory eagle (Hadrianus Junius, *Emblemata*, 1565, no. 39).

in the numerous Lyon Rouille/Bonhomme Alciato editions published in Lyon with engravings by Pierre Vase; the embroidery may well have copied this engraving. As the Fowler Anonymous description puts it 'hares romb and sitt apon him', which is just what can be seen in Pierre Vase's engraving.

Mary's ingenuity and inventiveness in adapting her sources can be demonstrated in another of these emblems, one that has provoked some comment and puzzlement beginning with Drummond himself. He describes an emblem showing 'A wheel rolled from a mountain into the sea, *Piena di dolor voda de speranza*: which appeareth to be her own, and it should be *Precipitio senza speranza*.' Drummond's suggested change of motto was evidently provoked by his inability, in this case, to make it fit the picture. There is indeed no easy way of understanding why a Spanish motto meaning 'Full of grief, empty of hope' should be associated with a wheel rolling into the sea. We should nevertheless resist his emendation, for something very like this Spanish motto is recorded as part of an *impresa* in Paolo Giovio's *Dialogo dell' imprese*, and looking at the woodcut for this emblem in the editions that began to include illustrations, from 1559 onwards, we almost certainly see what Mary's embroidery actually showed. This was not, as Drummond thought, a wheel rolling downhill, but rather a wheel with buckets designed to draw up water and empty it into an irrigation trench. As Samuel Daniel's English translation, which appeared in 1585, explains, 'And for that half the buckets are full receiving in the water, and half are empty casting it forth, he adjoined this mot *Los llenos de dolor y Los vazios de speranza* [Those that are full are full of sorrow, those that are empty, of hope]'.⁹ The *impresa* was invented, we learn, when a lover found his mistress unresponsive, and according to Daniel, 'This was esteemed an *Impresa* most subtile invention, and almost singulare in outward viewe, because the water and the wheele gave the beholders great light unto the subject, and seemed to inferre this, that his griefe was without hope of any remedie.' Looking at his illustration it is easy to see why anyone without the benefit of Giovio's commentary might have some difficulty working out just what this wheel was doing or how it illustrated the motto: its likely appearance when represented in needle and thread makes Drummond's failure to recognise this as 'a wheele with buckets which draw up water and cast

Figure 2.7 Andrea Alciato, *Cum larvis non luctandum* [There is no contest with the dead] (*Emblemata*, 1551, p. 166, with engravings by Pierre Vase).

Figure 2.8 *Los plenos de dolor y Los vazios de speranza* [Those that are full are full of sorrow, those that are empty, of hope] (Paolo Giovio, *Dialogo dell'imprese*, 1560, p. 28).

it forth againe' entirely understandable. Even Giovio's illustrator shows an image that looks more like an overshot water wheel than a wheel for raising water into an irrigation trench.[10]

Recognising the sources that supplied Mary's patterns not only helps us to reconstruct her motives and meanings in these emblematic embroideries, but also allows us sometimes to see things more clearly than early viewers who, despite having the object in front of them, failed to recognise the relevant sources and the received iconology. The way early readers interpreted emblems or *imprese* such as these certainly provides us with historical precedents and models for our own interpretation, but early witnesses also sometimes made mistakes. They may not always have understood what they were looking at, particularly when this was sewn in embroidery on bed hangings which they may have had to record in less than ideal surroundings and circumstances. It is precisely because emblems rework heavily coded materials into new structures and new meanings that they demand iconological source hunting. For this very reason they offered Mary a way of expressing herself either, as her enemies thought, when seeking others' support for her treacherous causes or, as we might think, in more private acts of self-reflection or renaissance self-fashioning.

Maritime messages: *Las pennas passan*

Not only her vanished Bed of State but also the surviving Oxburgh embroideries display devices belonging to Mary's relatives. The most family-focused of these is the detached square centrepiece, almost certainly once part of the Oxburgh Hangings, which is known as the *Las pennas passan* panel (Victoria and Albert Museum, normally on permanent display). It is a square panel consisting of an emblematic device and motto within a double border. The centre shows an armillary sphere from which feathers are falling, with the Spanish motto in a scroll: LAS PENNAS PASSAN Y QUEDA LA SPERANZA [Sorrows pass but hope survives]. The background shows stylised waves on which float various boats, birds or fishes. This central emblem is not easy to interpret, though the motto is evidently punning on 'pennas' as both 'sorrows' and 'feathers' – pains and pens – while alluding, presumably, to the armillary sphere as an instrument of navigation (hence the marine setting) which can give sailors some hope of safe arrival despite the pains of the voyage. The falling feathers we may take as those of a migrating bird, which will also find its way even if it loses its plumes. This large central emblem can hardly belong to anyone but Mary and it certainly does not represent any *impresa* belonging to her relatives. It is not copied from any printed emblem book, nor is it used anywhere else in the visual arts as far as we know. This is as close as one ever gets to a wholly 'original' emblem.

The inner border, however, is filled with four heraldic shields at the corners and eight heroic devices. Although the panel is unsigned, it has to be ascribed to Mary and not to Bess of Hardwick on heraldic grounds. The four corners show the royal arms of Scotland and England together with those of France and Spain; though not impossible for the Countess of Shrewsbury to use, they represent the four nations with which Mary had the closest ties of birth or alliance – indeed she had claims to sovereignty over three of them. Perhaps most telling in this context is the one detail on the inner border which has not been shown to copy a printed emblem: the device just below the top left corner shows two intertwined columns surmounted by a crown, and a scroll with the motto: PIETATE ET JUSTICIA. Not copied from Paradin or Simeoni, this was nevertheless the device of Charles IX, who adapted it from that of his godfather, Emperor Charles V, who had displayed the columns of Hercules with the motto *Plus ultra* [More beyond], making it one of the most famous of renaissance *imprese*, referring to the conquest of new worlds beyond the Pillars of Hercules.[11] The twin columns of Piety and Justice, however, had long featured in French royal iconography, and were sometimes identified with the pillars known as Jachin and Boaz from the biblical description of the Temple of Solomon.[12] Charles IX was Mary's brother-in-law, succeeding François II to the throne of France in 1560. In 1570 he married Elisabeth of Austria, daughter of Emperor Maximilian II, and his device of the twin columns was used, for instance, in the 1571 ceremonial entry into Paris to symbolise not only the union of the two houses of France and Austria but also the reconciliation of religious differences following the Peace of St-Germain-en-Laye. The strange intertwining of the traditional columns of Piety and Justice represents his most distinctive personalisation

Figure 2.9 The *Las pennas passan* panel, with the motto *Las pennas passan y queda la speranza* [Sorrows pass but hope survives]. London, Victoria and Albert Museum.

of this device, though it is a feature which only seems to have become standardised in the latter years of his reign (hence the pillars are not shown as twisted together in the pageant decorations for the 1571 royal entry).¹³

All the remaining devices on this panel are *imprese* which had been reproduced in the published anthologies of heroical devices. Seven of the eight devices copy woodcuts from Paradin or Simeoni:

- The top left *impresa* showing a crowned five-pointed star, with the motto MONSTRANT REGIBVS ASTRA VIAM [The stars show the way to kings], copying Paradin (p. 18), who identifies this as the device of the Knights of the Star founded by King Jean II of France in 1351, to express how, for French monarchs at least, the piety and persistence of the Magi could be relied upon to bring divine help and direction.

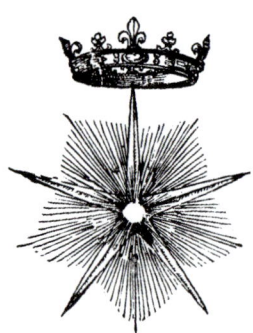

Figure 2.10 *Monstrant Regibus astra viam* [The stars show the way to kings], device of the Order of the Star founded by Jean de France in 1351 (Claude Paradin, *Devises heroïques*, 1557, p. 18).

- The top right has an *impresa* showing an eagle perched on the antlered skull of a stag, with the motto, ARDVA DETVRBANS VIS ANIMOSA QVATIT [The strength of courage shatters higher things], and copies Paradin (p. 87) who does not identify any bearer of this *impresa* but explains that it is based on a description in Pliny's *Natural History* of the way an eagle will land on a stag's head and scatter dust in its eyes until the stag hurls itself blindly from a cliff.

Figure 2.11 *Ardua deturbans, vis animosa quatit* [The strength of courage shatters higher things], device not ascribed to any bearer (Claude Paradin, *Devises heroïques*, 1557, p. 87).

- The upper right shows a disembodied hand holding a scimitar with which it cuts a knotted rope that hangs from a cloud, with the motto NODOS VIRTUTE RESOLVO [By my strength/virtue I untie knots]. This is Paradin (p. 214), who identifies it as the *impresa* of Jacques d'Albon, Mareschal de St André, who died in 1561, and explains that it represents the Gordian knot which Alexander the Great cut in fulfilment of the prophecy that whosoever untied it would rule over Asia, another device of French provenance offering the hope of answers to knotty problems.

Figure 2.12 *Nodos virtute resolvo*, *impresa* of Jacques d'Albon, Mareschal de St André (Claude Paradin, *Devises heroïques*, 1557, p. 214).

- In the lower right is a marigold, or marguerite, turning towards the sun in splendour, with the motto NON INFERIORA SECVTVS [Not having followed lower things], corresponding to Paradin (p. 41), who identifies it as the *impresa* of Marguerite de Navarre, sister of François I. As noted in Chapter 1, this *impresa* is also used on the Marian Hanging with the same motto, a favourite device not only because it belonged to one of Mary's French relatives by marriage but also because it could express her own aspirations.

Figure 2.13 *Non inferiora sequutus* [Not having followed lower things], *impresa* of Marguerite de Navarre (Claude Paradin, *Devises heroïques*, 1557, p. 41).

- At the bottom right is another disembodied hand holding a snake over a fire of sticks, with the motto QVIS CONTRA NOS [Who is against us?], copied from Paradin (p. 187), who does not identify any bearer but explains its basis in Acts 28 where St Paul suffers no harm from a viper that bites his finger as he is laying sticks on a fire but shakes it into the flames, thus demonstrating to unbelievers that God is on his side. This emblem was cited in evidence at the trial of the Earl of Arundel in 1589 (discussed in Chapter 3).

Figure 2.16 *Vias tuas domine demonstra mihi* [Show me your ways, O Lord], imperial device displayed on the ship of Admiral Andrea Doria (Claude Paradin, *Devises heroïques*, 1557, p. 88).

Figure 2.14 *Quis contra nos?* [Who is against us?], biblical device not ascribed to any bearer (Claude Paradin, *Devises heroïques*, 1557, p. 187).

- At the bottom left can be seen two disembodied hands clasped round a cornucopia full of plants, with the motto, DITAT SERVATA FIDES [Loyalty makes one rich], copied from Simeoni (1560, p. 31), who does not identify a bearer.

Figure 2.15 *Ditat servata fides* [Loyalty makes one rich], device not ascribed to any bearer (Gabriele Simeoni, *Le imprese heroiche et morali*, 1560, p. 31).

- The lower left shows a five-pointed star with arrows shooting out from it and the motto in an encircling banderole, the upper loop of which is damaged but almost certainly contains the first two words of VIAS TVAS DOMINE DEMONSTRA [Show me your ways, O Lord], copied from Paradin (p. 88), where it is the *impresa* displayed on a ship belonging to Emperor Charles V as a reminder of the need to pray for divine directions; the motto quotes Psalm 25, verse 4.

This last emblem is very close to MONSTRANT REGIBUS ASTRA VIAM in both its star symbol and its sentiment, and also chimes with the astrolabe device of the central and dominant device. For all the richness and complexity of detail in this embroidery, therefore, what emerges is a certain coherence and unity to the design. The devices belonging to her forebears or relatives are incorporated into an ensemble which reaffirms the power of virtue, if it holds true to its course, to overcome its enemies and win through. As for the wonderful aquarium of sea creatures that sport in the waves, their like is seen again in Mary's embroideries of animals, birds and fishes, while the ships find an echo in the storm-battered vessel of the *Nunquam nisi rectam* [Never if not upright] device that Mary sewed on her Bed of State, a device which also features on the reverse of a medal of 1579. Robert Southwell probably knew of this device, for an autograph fragment in the Stonyhurst archive has the title '*Amenomon*: I goe', with the lines:

> The shippe that from the port dothe sayle
> and lanceth in the tyde
> Must many a billows boystous brunt
> and stormy blast abyde.[14]

As we shall see in Chapter 3, Southwell was familiar with the iconography of Mary's medals and embroideries. It seems likely that, for Mary, the image of the perilous voyage to prosperity held a particular moral, recalling as it must have done the voyages she had undertaken between Scotland and France at key moments in her life, and also the boat ride across the Solway Firth that had, fatally, brought her to England. Sorrows pass, but hope abides.

Figure 2.17 Jetton of Mary Queen of Scots dated 1579, a ship with a broken mast in a storm and the motto *Nunquam nisi rectam* [Never if not upright]. Mary sewed this device with the same motto on her Bed of State embroideries. Edinburgh, National Museum of Scotland.

The Oxburgh centrepieces

All three of the large square centrepieces to the Oxburgh Hangings are strongly emblematic, whether executed by Mary or by the Countess of Shrewsbury. The centrepiece of the Shrewsbury Hanging, for instance, uses another emblem copied from Paradin's *Devises heroïques*, which in this case goes back to a fable from Aesop. The panel has to be Bess's work since it carries her initials and those of her husband. It shows the thirsty crow, or raven, that ingeniously solves the problem of how to reach the water in a deep vase by filling the vessel with pebbles and raising the water level until it can drink; the motto is *Ingenii largitor* [Bestower of talent] and the moral is that necessity is the mother of invention. It is not easy to see what application such a moral might have to Bess's own situation, particularly when linked, as it is here, to her initials and those of her long-suffering husband. The border to this centrepiece is filled with fine grotesque detail from a different print source: the two caryatids copy Hans Vredeman de Vries's set of *Caryatidum* engravings first published in Antwerp, c.1565, and the nude figure standing on his plinth in the bottom two corners is copied from one of Vredeman's *Grottesco* prints; he is being prayed to by a kneeling figure while the rear view of another figure retreats through the door behind him. Both these sets of ornament prints by Vredeman – and indeed this very detail from the *Grottesco* – were also used in the decoration of the ceiling which Mark Kerr painted at his house at Prestongrange near Edinburgh in 1581.[15] None of this surrounding detail is emblematic, however.

The centrepiece to the Cavendish Hanging has an emblem showing tears falling from the sky upon what is, in fact, a ground of quicklime from which clouds of steam or smoke arise; in a scroll is the motto EXTINCTAM LACHRIMAE TESTANTVR VIVERE FLAMMAM [Tears witness that the quenched flame lives]. We can be sure that this is quicklime and not, as some previous viewers have thought, smouldering coals or ashes, because this was a device of Catherine de Medici. Lime for use in mortar or plaster is prepared by burning limestone in kilns to produce quicklime; when water is then added the lime crumbles away and becomes very hot, and it is these properties which Catherine interprets emblematically as symbolising the power of tears to express the hidden flames of her love. Queen of Henri II and mother of a succession of French kings, including Mary's first husband François, Catherine adopted this device after the death of Henri in the fatal tournament of 1559 as an expression of her enduring love for her late husband, whose death in the tilting accident was, of course, the event that made Mary of Scotland, Queen of France. Why on earth should Elizabeth of Shrewsbury have appropriated this device of Mary's mother-in-law, and where might she have found Catherine's device? She would not have found it reproduced in any of the printed emblem books published at this date, and it seems more than likely that she would have learned about it from Mary. It is at least suggestive that one of the newly discovered descriptions of Mary's Bed of State, Hawthornden Anonymous, includes this device, which it accurately assigns to 'the queen mother of France' and describes as tears falling on quicklime with the motto *Ardorem extincta testantur flamma* [The extinguished flame shows passion]. The motto on the bed is, as it happens, closer to that which Catherine de Medici herself used than is the motto on the Cavendish Hanging centrepiece. Catherine's motto was *Ardorem extincta testantur vivere flamma* [The extinguished flame shows that passion lives], and these differences make it unlikely that the embroidery on the bed was the actual surviving centre panel to the Cavendish Hanging, which means that it must have been a very similar embroidery sewed by Mary and showing, like so many of the other emblems on her bed hangings,

Figure 2.18 Shrewsbury Hanging centrepiece, modelled on Claude Paradin's Aesopic fable of the thirsting crow; the grotesque-work border uses motifs copied from ornament prints by Hans Vredeman de Vries. Oxburgh Hall, Norfolk.

the *impresa* of one of her close relatives. It seems more likely that Bess of Hardwick appropriated this device for her own *Extinctam lachrimae* emblem following Mary's example.

A tapestry bearing this device hung in the Louvre in Paris and the device also found its way into portraits of Catherine de Medici such as the print, after François Clouet, depicting her in an oval frame supported by allegorical figures; the frame holds her *impresa*, much as is seen on the Cavendish Hanging, with teardrops falling onto what has to be understood as a heap of quicklime and with the same motto. In 1589 a medal showing the bust of Catherine dressed as a widow used the same device. The device was also satirised by Agrippa d'Aubigny in *Les tragiques*, a Protestant attack, begun in the 1570s though not

Figure 2.19 *Ingenii largitor* [Bestower of talent], device not ascribed to any bearer (Claude Paradin, *Devises heroïques*, 1557, p. 141).

Figure 2.20 Lucas or Johannes Duetecum after Hans Vredeman de Vries, engraving from the *Caryatidum* series (Antwerp, *c*.1565). The Shrewsbury Hanging centrepiece copies the second and the sixth of these architectural ornament figures from Vredeman's print.

Figure 2.21 Lucas or Johannes Duetecum after Hans Vredeman de Vries, *Hercules and the Centaur*, engraving from the *Grottesco* series (Antwerp, 1565). The frame details, bottom right and left, are copied on the Shrewsbury Hanging centrepiece and also at Prestongrange. Stedelijk Prentenkabinet, Antwerp.

Figure 2.22 Painted ceiling, Prestongrange, Lothian, using a detail from Vredeman's *Hercules and the Centaur* print that is also copied on the Shrewsbury Hanging.

published until 1616, on Catholic evils afflicting the kingdom of France in which Catherine de Medici figures prominently.[16] Catherine's responsibility for the St Bartholomew's Day massacre transformed her into a leading hate figure in Protestant martyrology, and d'Aubigny not only describes the tapestry he had seen in the Louvre with this device but ironically reassigns its properties to refer to the flames that consumed the Protestant martyrs and the tears evoked in the faithful by their sufferings. It is unlikely that any of this religious polemic inflects Elizabeth of Shrewsbury's use of the device in her embroidery, though one might still wonder about her wisdom in appropriating at this date in England a device that belonged to this persecutor of French Protestants.

Looking more closely at the centrepiece as a whole, however, it is clear that Bess is using the device as a testimony to her particular affection for William Cavendish, second of her four husbands and father of her four children. The border is filled with monograms of Elizabeth

Figure 2.23 Cavendish Hanging centrepiece showing tears falling on quicklime with the motto *Extinctam lachrimae testantur vivere flammam* [Tears witness that the quenched flame lives]. Oxburgh Hall, Norfolk.

Shrewsbury and William Cavendish, along with further emblematic or heraldic motifs: a broken fetter and a broken mirror; the Cavendish arms; three rings, interlaced and broken, with the 'ES' monogram below a coronet; a knotted and broken girdle; a torn gauntlet; a fan with falling feathers; a knotted serpent; and the Cavendish motto CAVENDO TVTVS [Secure through being cautious] – the motto puns on the Cavendish name. The date 1570 (top left) confirms that these tears testifying to her undying flame were still falling 13 years after the death of William Cavendish and is the firmest evidence we have for dating any of these embroideries. The repeated Cavendish and Shrewsbury monograms and the succession of broken love tokens in the border leave little doubt that we should read the panel as a whole: the liminary details comment on the central *impresa* and in this they might recall what has already been said about the relation of surrounding emblems to the central motif in the *Las pennas passan* panel. All of these details might be seen as reinforcing the personal nature of the *impresa*, confirming its status as an expression of Elizabeth Cavendish alias Shrewsbury's sense

Figure 2.24 François Clouet, *Catherine de Medici*, engraving combining her portrait with her *impresa*. Paris, Bibliothèque nationale.

of her own marriage(s): this was a woman who had, after all, perfected the art of making a good marriage. Quicklime is an essential ingredient which can be found on any building site and Bess of Hardwick was also, of course, a great builder.

The Marian Hanging centrepiece showing the vine being pruned with its *Virescit vulnere virtus* motto is, perhaps, the most distinctive and famous of these emblematic centrepieces on the Oxburgh Hangings, but because it was cited in one of the most important state trials of the Elizabethan period, discussion of it is postponed to the following chapter, where its various applications and transformations will be fully explored.

Octagonal emblems

Although it is these large square centrepieces that are most evidently emblems, the octagonal panels immediately surrounding them on the Oxburgh Hangings are filled either with slip decoration (single stems of plants) or with monograms spelling out the names of Marie Stuart or Elizabeth Shrewsbury; some of these include Latin mottoes which are indistinguishable from those found in emblems. To function as emblems, however, there needs to be some intelligible connection between word and image, and in some cases there is such a connection, but not in others. The octagon on the Marian Hanging showing a plant with conventionalised foliage and a snake coiled out from its stem with the motto SVB HERBA LATET ANGVIS [A snake lurks under the grass] is based on Paradin's *Latet anguis in herba* device, though the picture does not copy Paradin's woodcut. This is more like a moral emblem than a personal *impresa* since Paradin does not identify any bearer and explains the moral in general terms: when reading pleasant books we must beware of dangerous doctrines lurking behind their specious arguments. We have no way of knowing who or what Mary or Bess thought the snake might be that lay in their particular grass, or whether indeed the emblem had any such personal application.

Octagon C on the Marian Hanging shows a crowned monogram spelling ELIZABETH/MARY flanked by a lily and a rose, and with a thistle that lies as if bent or crushed beneath it. The fact that the monogram is crowned leaves no room for doubt that the names are those of the two queens, while the lily and rose are the

Figure 2.25 Medal of 1589, reverse with Catherine de Medici's quicklime device showing tears falling on quicklime with the motto *Ardorem extincta testantur vivere flamma* [Though extinguished, the flame shows that love endures]. Edinburgh, National Museum of Scotland.

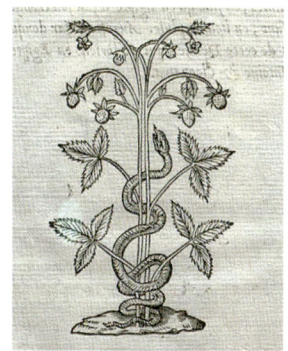

Figure 2.26 *Latet anguis in herba* [A snake lurks in the grass] (Claude Paradin, *Devises heroïques*, 1557, p. 70).

Figure 2.27 Marian Hanging, panel C, crowned monogram spelling the names MARIA/ELIZABETH with flowers symbolising the three kingdoms of France, England and Scotland. The motto means 'The bonds of virtue are lighter than those of blood'. Oxburgh Hall, Norfolk.

two kingdoms of France and England, and the thistle is of course Scotland. We might well hesitate before reading this allegorically or emblematically – it could, after all, have merely been lack of space that forced Mary to display the thistle lying on its side. However, when we read the motto we can hardly avoid seeing the whole of this panel as symbolic, for ARCTIORA SVNT VIRTVTIS VINCULA QVAM SANGVINIS means 'The bonds of virtue are tighter than those of blood', and can only be read as referring to the bloodline linking Mary and her cousin Elizabeth. 'Virtus' is a complex keyword in many of Mary's mottoes, untranslatable but signifying both moral integrity and/or physical strength, and it would be difficult not to take the motto as a reference to Mary's sense of the ties of blood, status and power that ought to have joined the three kingdoms and their two queens, ties which she had assumed would support her in her troubles. If we are indeed justified in seeing the thistle as bent or crushed (and I believe we are since there is absolutely no heraldic precedent for displaying the national flower in this way) then we should be struck by the extraordinary pointedness and power of this embroidery. Although its combination of monogram, motto and floral motifs is not characteristic of renaissance emblems, it works totally emblematically.

Do tortoises climb trees?

With the octagon on the same Marian Hanging showing a tortoise climbing a crowned palm tree, however, we have a real emblem, with the motto DAT GLORIA VIRES [Glory gives strength] which quotes Ovid, *Tristia*, V, 12. Moreover in this case is a device which, rather like the *Virescit vulnere virtus* centrepiece, Mary had used elsewhere. In 1565 an Act of the Privy Council issued instructions for a new silver coin to be minted, known as the Mary *ryal*. The instructions are remarkably explicit as to the design, whose reverse is specified in detail:

> Ane penny ... havand on the one syde ane palme tre crownit, ane schell padocke [i.e. tortoise, lit. 'shelled frog'] crepand up the schank of the samyn, ane bill about the tre writtin thairin DAT GLORIA VIRES, the dait of the yeir thairundir .... (*Reg. Privy C.* I, 413)

The obverse of the coin shows the royal arms of Scotland with the inscription MARIA ET HENRICVS R[EGINA] ET R[EX] SCOTORVM commemorating Mary's marriage to Darnley in July of that year. The rim inscription on the reverse, EXVRGAT DEVS ET DISSIPENTVR INIMICI EIVS [May God arise and his enemies be scattered] quotes Psalms, 68, 1, and might seem to be signalling a strongly religious, and hence potentially controversial, direction to the new reign, although the same inscription had already been used on pre-Reformation gold coins of James III, IV and V at a time when any sectarian bias could not have been implied or foreseen. The form of the obverse inscription, identifying Henry Darnley as King of Scots rather than as mere consort to the queen, has attracted some comment and, if seen as a coin commemorating the marriage, then the changes made to the motto might offer some help in interpreting the emblem. In July 1565, the very month of the marriage, a commemorative coin had been struck showing their two heads facing each other with an inscription which not only proclaims Darnley King of Scots but also places his name ahead of Mary's: HENRICVS ET MARIA D[EI] GRAT[IA] R[EX] ET R[EGINA] SCOTORVM. The occasion of the royal marriage was even more strongly signalled by the reverse inscription: QVOD DEVS CONIVNXIT HOMO NON SEPARET [Whom God hath joined together let no man put asunder], quoting the marriage service. We know that this styling of Darnley as king and the precedence given to him over Mary caused some disquiet at the time, and the change to the inscription on the Mary *ryals* minted in 1565 and 1566 must reflect the privy council's response to such disquiet. On later issues of the *ryal* in 1567, Darnley's name disappears from the

Figure 2.28 Marian Hanging, panel F, tortoise climbs a crowned palm tree with the motto *Dat gloria vires* [Glory gives strength]. Oxburgh Hall, Norfolk.

Figure 2.29 Mary *ryal*, coin first minted in 1565, the year of her marriage to Darnley, showing a tortoise climbing a crowned palm tree marked with a scroll: *Dat gloria vires* [Glory gives strength]. Edinburgh, National Museum of Scotland.

was certainly becoming fashionable on medal reverses, and there can be no doubt that whoever designed the Mary *ryal*, with its tortoise and palm tree, was familiar with the contemporary art of the medal.[17] The device is not copied directly from any existing medal or printed source, however, and although the Italian *impresa* theorists were fond of pointing out that a well-composed device might allegorise the properties and habits of animals, there is nothing in Pliny or any of the medieval bestiaries about tortoises climbing trees: this is a habit quite unknown to natural history. But although this emblem is certainly original, there are nevertheless a couple of parallels and anticipations of its iconography which, I suggest, allow us plausibly to reconstruct how it was put together and what it actually means.

The closest analogues for this curious image are to be found, interestingly, in two printed books with which we know Mary was familiar and which, indeed, eventually supplied many of the patterns for her other embroideries. In 1525 Hans Holbein had designed a printer's mark for Christoph Froschauer, the first printer ever to set up shop in Zürich, which shows frogs, not tortoises, climbing a tree trunk. The tree is not a palm tree and it is difficult to know what motivated this design or what its emblematic point might have been: there is no motto, the only inscription being Froschauer's name on a banderole around the trunk. First used in 1525 in a book by the great reformer Ulrich Zwingli, some time later Froschauer published a variant showing the same frogs mounting a similar tree with the addition of a putto beside the trunk. We might hazard a guess that the ambitious creatures scaling a tree were now to be read as symbols of a lover's aspiration (hence the putto), though how that would relate to Froschauer's values as a printer – or if indeed this printer's mark has any symbolic and emblematic intention at all – remains unclear. This redesigned printer's mark was used in 1555 on the title pages of all but the first volume of Froschauer's edition of Conrad Gessner's great *Historia animalium*,

coin altogether, although this has to be because he was murdered in February of that year, and not from any continuing resolve to demote him on existing coinage. These amendments to the motto, and the changing marital circumstances, have nevertheless been seen as offering some clue to the significance of the tortoise and palm tree device, for the palm is a traditional symbol of glory which, the motto implies, gives even the lowliest of creatures the strength needed to climb. Hence the device has been taken to show the ambitious Darnley climbing the royal trunk. If so the device can only be seen as a direct intervention by the queen herself, through her privy council, to signal a difference in the royal status of husband and wife, reflecting the revision to the obverse inscription, and highly ironic given the pious celebration of the royal marriage which this coin and its immediate predecessor of July 1565 were designed to celebrate.

Can we really believe that a coin of the realm might have any such complexity, any such irony? It is certainly a very unusual coin, and quite exceptional in the history not only of Scottish, but of European, coinage. Its emblematic reverse, using a symbolic device with its own motto, is much closer to that found on the reverse of medals than it is to a conventional coin of the realm, doubtless reflecting its commemorative function in the year of the royal marriage. The use of courtly *imprese*

Figure 2.30 *Invidia integritatis assecla* [Envy pursues the upright] (Hadrianus Junius, *Emblemata*, 1565, no. 9).

the very book which Mary used as her principal design source for the large majority of her embroideries of animals. Mary must, at least by the time she started making those, have been thoroughly familiar with this printer's mark that featured on title pages of three of the four volumes which made up Gessner's book. Since there is no other source that shows frogs, or tortoises, climbing a tree (and we might recall that the Scots word for tortoise, 'shell-paddock' means shelled frog), it is more than likely that this rare image commissioned by Mary's privy council for her coinage in 1565 must go back to this source.

Moreover in that same year, an emblem book was published in Antwerp which contains another precedent or analogue for this strange image. Hadrianus Junius's *Emblemata* has an emblem with the motto *Invidia integritatis assecla* [Envy pursues the upright]. The picture shows no tortoise climbing, but rather a nest of toads and snakes pushing up against the trunk of a palm tree. The epigram explains that this illustrates how envious but worthless men will oppose those who are rightfully above them. Could Junius's book, only printed in 1565, have reached Scotland in time for whoever designed the Mary *ryal* to have adapted its iconography on a coin of the realm first minted the same year? If so, the reversal of precedence given to the two royal names on the inscription that had appeared on the commemorative coin in that same marital year in Scotland might well supply the motive for using a medallic device symbolising the tendency of worthless people to envy the illustrious. However, Mary was certainly living dangerously if she deliberately placed this insult to her new husband on coinage in the first year of her marriage. It also begs the question as to why she did not remove the insult in 1567, when her husband had been brutally murdered and the coin was being reminted to reflect her second widowhood. The new obverse inscription: MARIA DEI GRA[TIA] SCOTORVM REGINA at that date reflects the fact that all such questions of royal precedence had by then disappeared.

Junius's *Emblemata* was, as we have seen, one of the few emblem books that supplied Mary with patterns for the later embroideries, so this too was a book with which we know she was familiar. The iconography of emblem and coin, though not identical, is nevertheless quite similar, and the substitution of the climbing tortoise for Junius's snakes and toads might be seen as no more than the normal process of adaptation and reinvention of *topoi* that was an accepted way of composing emblems, an adaptation that might well have been suggested in this case by a prior familiarity with Froschauer's printer's mark. The tortoise was a well-known symbol for domesticity, because it carries its 'house' on its back, as in Alciato's emblem 'Mulieris famam non formam vulgata esse oportere' [A woman should be celebrated for her fame, not her form], which argues that girls should stay at home and be silent, but it is not easy to apply this moral to Darnley.[18] Junius's emblem takes its hint from a passage in Plutarch (*Orac. Pyth.* 12), and it had an afterlife, for Whitney includes it in his *Choice of Emblemes* in 1586 (p. 118), as does Joachim Camerarius in *Symbolorum et emblematum ex re herbaria* that, in 1590, began his great output of emblems based on natural history. In 1617, Peter Isselburg and Georg

Figure 2.31 Printer's mark of Christoph Froschauer, Zürich, showing frogs climbing a tree. Based on a design by Hans Holbein in 1526, this version is the one used on the title page to volumes II, III and IV of Gessner's *Historia animalium* (1554–1560).

Rem included it in their *Emblemata politica* published in Nuremberg, but all these successors acknowledge Hadrianus Junius as their source, and if Junius was not also the direct inspiration for this emblem on the Mary *ryal* of 1565, then we have the rather remarkable coincidence of two emblems in the very same year, and in different places, inventing a new symbolism involving palm trees and climbing amphibians for which, apart from Froschauer's printer's mark, there was no precedent. We therefore have to conclude that Hadrianus Junius's emblem of 1565 was most probably Mary's source for this device, and if the notable similarity between this and Froschauer's printer's mark is not pure coincidence, then I suggest we have to surmise that the design of the Mary *ryal* was almost certainly determined by Mary herself and that she was already familiar with both of these books at this date. She must have adapted both sources by making Hadrianus Junius's ambitious frogs, symbolising envious and worthless men, climb the trunk of their tree just as they were shown doing in another book she evidently owned, Froschauer's edition of Gessner. Junius would have supplied the rationale for seeing this as a palm tree, while his interpretation might well have suggested the potential application to Mary's young husband, whose ambitions in marrying her were already a cause for concern, whatever her other feelings about him, even in the first year of her marriage. When she sewed the device on her furnishings in later years, it would have had a range of associations that reflected her sense of her status and the recurrent challenges to that status to which she had to respond. Whether her subjects who saw the device on coinage in the 1560s would have associated its moral with Darnley, or recognised it as an insult to her husband, is entirely unclear. Certainly none commented on its iconography, as far as we know, and it may well be that the moral would have been read in an altogether more innocent sense as a general reflection on human glory and aspiration.

Perhaps the most significant detail on the coin is the introduction of the royal crown placed above the tree. This alone makes it impossible to read the ambition that climbs to glory in the emblem as anything other than monarchical. Only those, like Mary, who knew their Junius would be aware of the insulting inflection that his precedent puts on this extraordinary device with its reference to the way unworthy or ignoble (*degeneres*) ambition assails those who are truly illustrious (*proceres*). That ability of a courtly device, or personal *impresa*, to mean something specific to those in the know, while remaining conveniently general and obscure to the unlearned, was a quality which the Italian writers on the art of the *impresa* sometimes commented on as one of its advantages.

Another world: *Manet ultima caelo*

It should now be becoming clear how important it is to put these emblems into context if we are to understand what they mean on the embroideries. That context includes their wider iconology as it was understood at the time. My approach so far has been preoccupied with the identification of sources and analogues: what existing iconographic motifs and materials are these emblems reusing? This assumes that Mary's emblems are derivative. However, in devising her emblems Mary was not simply a passive imitator of continental materials and models, she was also an active player in their circulation: not just a borrower but also a lender of devices. This can most clearly be seen when exploring the context and the iconology of one of the most interesting and significant of the emblems of her Bed of State, the device showing three crowns, two on earth and a third in the sky, with the motto *Manet ultima caelo* [The last awaits in heaven]. At first sight this looks

Figure 2.32 Medal of Mary Queen of Scots, 1560, showing two earthly crowns beneath a star-filled sky with the motto *Aliamque moratur* [And awaits another]. This is certainly the original of the device which Henri III inherited or adapted from his sister-in-law Mary in 1574. Edinburgh, National Museum of Scotland.

quite simple, expressing the queen's pious recognition that, although she had worn two earthly crowns – those of Scotland and France – the last and greatest was the crown she aspired to wear in heaven.

When we start to explore the contexts or antecedents for this emblem we certainly find some increasingly familiar characteristics. For a start, we discover that, like so many of these emblems, this one also belonged to one of her relatives, Henri III of France, brother to her late husband, François. Henri, however, only came to the French throne in 1574, when he used this device to signal the union of the crowns of France and Poland, having only just been elected to the Polish throne in the previous year on the death of his brother Charles. We might therefore conclude that Mary cannot have sewn this embroidery for her Bed of State any earlier than 1574. That conclusion would be challenged, however, by our next discovery, namely that this is one of several devices on the embroideries which were also used on coins or medals. A medal survives in the National Museum of Scotland which shows something very similar to this device, but with the date 1560, more than ten years before the device was adopted by Mary's brother-in-law, Henri. Clearly, Mary is not simply borrowing one of her relative's *imprese* for this detail on her bed. The devices are, admittedly, not identical, though as we shall see they are closely related. The medal (actually a jetton; the surviving examples are all minted in base metal) has two crowns not three, with the inscription *Aliamque moratur* [And awaits another]. The two crowns are shown one above the other and above them is a cloudy sky full of stars, which has to be seen as the location of the 'other' crown which, the motto suggests, is to be awaited.

Whatever the differences, Mary's 1560 jetton is certainly the source and original of Henri III's famous royal device, a device which was hailed in its day by writers on the art of the emblem as the very model of a perfect *impresa*. We can be quite sure that this was the order of events when we uncover what Adrien d'Amboise has to say about the *Manet ultima caelo* device in his book *Devises royales*. Although the book was not published until 1621, Adrien was the son of François d'Amboise, who had been with Henri III in the 1570s at the time when the French king was crowned King of Poland in Cracow. The book draws on his father's knowledge of the devices used by royalty, and he tells us that *Manet ultima caelo* was borrowed by Henri from a similar device used by Marie Stuart, dowager Queen of France,

Figure 2.33 *Manet ultima caelo* [The last awaits in heaven], device of Henri III (Adrien d'Amboise, *Devises royales*, 1621, p. 42). Henri inherited the two crowns of France and Poland, but would earn the heavenly crown only through his wise policies in the cause of religious reconciliation. According to Amboise, Henri borrowed the device from a very similar one borne by Mary Queen of Scots.

which showed just two crowns with the motto *Aliamque moratur*, to indicate that besides Scotland and France she was also heir apparent to the crown of England, a destiny that was only fulfilled when her royal son, James VI, succeeded to it so peacefully.[19] According to Amboise it was a Scotsman named Gordon who had bestowed Mary's device, which he describes as 'the finest and most perfect of its century', on King Henri. Amboise gives an accurate description of the *Aliamque moratur* device, with its two crowns rather than three, precisely as is seen on Mary's jetton, and it provides the explanation needed for the different dates; Mary's device is the original, and Henri's is a copy whose details – three crowns and a change of motto – represent exactly the kind of adaptation and variation already witnessed in the circulation of such devices at this period.

Any doubts we might have about these two being versions of the same device are clearly overcome by Amboise's account. The relationship between the two versions is further clarified by the earliest of the descriptions of the Bed of State, for whereas Drummond, following Fowler, describes three crowns with the *Aliamque moratur* motto, the 1586 French description, preserved among the English state papers, describes two different emblems, the first corresponding to Mary's device as represented on her 1560 jetton, and the second, which follows, described as *quasi pareille* [almost the same] but with three crowns not two, and the *Manet ultima caelo* motto.

Deux couronnes en terre et une au ciel compose d'estoiles les flambes de feu y deroulant *Manet ultima caelo*. Une aultre quasi pareille horsmis icelle d'en hault semblable a celles qui sont en terre

Giordano Bruno: a *politique* interpretation

It is now also possible to show that, rather like the *Te stante, virebo* device, this is an emblem that was not unique to Mary but famous in a number of different applications, playing its part in some of the most important political issues of its time. Moreover, in 1584, this very emblem crowned the allegorical design of one of the most sophisticated books by the Italian philosopher, Giordano Bruno. Written during his two-year stay in England (1583–85), Bruno's *Lo spaccio della bestia trionfante* [The Expulsion of the Triumphant Beast] is dedicated to Sir Philip Sidney, and takes the form of an elaborate and allegorical *gigantomachia*, or fight to expel the false gods of religious bigotry, schism and intolerance from the European heavens. It is a truly cosmic reformation that seeks to define the philosophical and political grounds upon which European intellectuals, such as Sidney, could unite across national and sectarian frontiers around a philosophical and cultural programme which might guide princes in the paths of humane wisdom and enlightenment. The prince who stands poised to win this crowning achievement will win the 'third' crown of peace.

> This ... is that crown which, not without the lofty disposition of Fate, not without the instinct of divine spirit, and not without very great merit, awaits the most invincible Henry III, king of magnanimous, potent, and warlike France. After having obtained the crown of France and that of Poland, he promised himself, as he declared at the beginning of his reign, this other Crown, and in order to strengthen the two lowly crowns with another more eminent and beautiful one, he ordered that to that so celebrated emblem of his there should be added for encouragement this motto: *Tertia coelo manet* [The third awaits in heaven]. This most Christian, holy, religious, and pure king can surely say: '*Tertio coelo manet*,' because he very well knows that it is written: 'Blessed are the meek, blessed are the silent, blessed are the pure of heart, for theirs is the kingdom of heaven.' He loves peace and, as much as is possible, maintains in tranquillity and devotion his beloved people. He does not like the noises, the boisterousness, and the clashing of martial instruments that administer to the blind acquisition of unstable tyrannies and principalities of the earth,

Figure 2.34 Medals of François II (Jacques de Bie, *La France métallique*, 1636, fol. 61). The device showing two globes with a crown on the point of a sword and the motto *Unus non sufficit orbis* [One world is not enough] can be seen top right.

y a *Aliamque moratur*. [Two crowns on earth and one in heaven composed of stars with flames of fire issuing from them: The last one remains in heaven. Another almost like it, except that the one above is like those that are on the earth; there is: And awaits another.]

Clearly, the Bed of State in 1586 included both devices, the only differences being between the mottoes and the appearance of the heavenly crown, which was composed in one case of stars and what are taken to be flames (I see them as clouds), just as is seen on the 1560 jetton. With the jetton in front of us, it is possible to see just how closely the embroidery must have copied its medallic model, and make sense of these variant details.

but loves all acts of justice and blessedness that point out the direct path to the eternal realm.[20]

Bruno thus identifies Henri III as the hero of this anticipated expulsion of religious intolerance and persecution from the world. Bruno had arrived in Paris in 1561, when enthusiastic reports of his intellectual abilities led Henri to encourage him to remain in France, and Bruno accordingly dedicated his works on the art of memory to the king. The revival of religious conflict in France, however, led him to seek a letter of recommendation to the French ambassador in London, Michel de Castelnau, Sieur de Mauvissière, at whose house in London Bruno arrived in June 1583 after a couple of months spent lecturing on philosophy in Oxford. He remained as tutor and companion to Mauvissière for another two years, making the acquaintance of leading English intellectuals and people of note, including the Earl of Leicester and, indeed, Queen Elizabeth herself, frequently accompanying the French ambassador on his visits to the English court. Treated as a European intellectual and celebrity, Bruno brought some of the leading ideas which we associate with an Italianate, neo-Platonic renaissance to Britain, where they played their part in the literature and philosophy of the Elizabethan cultural renaissance associated with such writers as Sidney, Spenser, and Florio, if not Shakespeare.

Bruno's project in England, and in the *Spaccio*, was however political as much as philosophical. Mauvissière's major preoccupation as ambassador at this period was to forge some kind of alliance in the wake of Elizabeth's refusal to marry the Duc d'Alençon, which might have consolidated power in the face of what was seen as the growing threat to both countries from Spain. The poker games of European politics did not, ultimately, favour these attempts, but Bruno, who stood outside all the religious differences that separated Protestant England from its Catholic neighbours, clearly realised the symbolic capital that could be made out of Henri III's device of the three crowns. Is the third crown heavenly or earthly? In a compelling essay on his use of this device, Nuccio Ordine (1999) shows that, although often interpreted in a non-political, otherworldly sense, the device was occasionally interpreted, along with its more famous analogues – such as the *Non sufficit orbis impresa* of Philip of Spain or the *Donec totum impleat orbem* of Henri II – as alluding to specific countries, including the kingdom of England, which Virgil had described in his *Bucolics* as a land beyond the edge of the known world: *Et penitus toto divisos orbe Britannos*.[21] The allusion appeared justified by the word *ultima* in the motto: Britain, according to the ancients was situated at the end of the world, and to acquire the English crown could thus, by a convenient conceit, be claimed as the conquest of another world. The Virgilian reference was validated by a couple of further *loci* in Catullus and in Horace which confirmed Virgil's marginalisation of the British Isles by describing the British as *ultimos*, the very same word that Henri's three-crowns emblem uses.[22] Bruno's misquotation of this as 'tertio' could have been mere oversight though it could equally well, as Ordine argues, have a more pointed and ironic political implication in the period immediately following the Anjou marriage negotiations, a marriage that would have united the crowns of both France and Poland with England. Elsewhere the three crowns of Henri's device were interpreted as the three sons of Catherine de Medici who had become successive kings of France: François, Charles and Henri. Whatever their identity, what all this evidence reveals is the extraordinary political capital which could be extracted, on different occasions, from this powerful device that King Henri of France had borrowed from Mary Stuart.

The conformity of this geographical ordering of the world with the imperial *Unus non sufficit orbis* [One world is not enough] device, which sees the New World beyond the Pillars of Hercules, should be clear enough – indeed we might well find parallels with modern usage suggestive, for it was the twentieth century, not the sixteenth, that came to refer to the undeveloped world beyond the assumed bounds of civilisation or empire as the 'Third World'. Mary used jettons and embroidered a panel for her Bed of State with precisely this imperial *impresa*. Jacques de Bie in his early seventeenth-century catalogue of commemorative French medals, *La France metallique*, illustrates a jetton showing two globes with a crown on the point of a sword and the motto *Unus non sufficit orbis*, which he says must go back to the time of Mary's marriage in 1558 to François when, he suggests, such jettons would probably have been distributed as *pièces de largesse* (p. 184). Cochran-Patrick's (1884) catalogue of Scottish medals records a similar jetton of Mary Queen of Scots dated 1559 with the same motto and showing only the sword with the crown on its point, but not the two spheres.

A version of this device can be seen on the magnificent sixteenth-century binding to the printed book of hours which was almost certainly given to Mary by

Figure 2.35 Book of hours printed in Paris in 1549 with luxurious binding showing the initial 'F' for François II with his dolphin motif as Dauphin of France, and an *impresa* panel showing the *Unus non sufficit orbis* emblem. Probably given to Mary by her husband, this book was left as a parting gift in 1561 with her aunt, who was abbess at Pierre-les-Dames where Mary stayed on her journey back to Scotland. Bibliothèque de Reims.

François at the time of their marriage. Printed in Paris by Renauld and Claude Chaudière in 1549, the stamped and gilded binding shows, on the front cover, an armillary sphere suspended from the heavens, with the *Unus non sufficit orbis* motto in a star-spangled, radiant heavenly sphere above a segment of the verdant terrestrial globe. The decorative strapwork surrounding this oval *impresa* carries the initial 'F' and the dolphin device, while the back cover displays the arms of François as Dauphin of France and King of Scotland crossed with those of Mary. On leaving France in 1561 Mary gave this book to her aunt, Renée, Abbess of St-Pierre-les-Dames, as a memento of her overnight stay en route to Calais, and it is now preserved in the Bibliothèque de Reims. It remains one of the most impressive historical book bindings, whose similarity with the other devices we have been looking at and their periodic reminders of earthly and heavenly crowns to be inherited or earned, begins to suggest the full value and associations which they would have held for Mary on her embroideries. If we bear in mind in looking at the various manifestations of the *Aliamque moratur* device that a similar and closely related device figured on the magnificent prayer book given to Mary by her late first husband, it will be suggestive. It will certainly supply the context and motivation that led her to embroider not only these on her bed hangings, but also the *Unus non sufficit orbis* embroidery showing two spheres (or according to the anonymous Hawthornden description, two pillars) and a sword between them, on the point of which is a crown.

So what did Mary get out of the *Manet ultima caelo* device? How much of the political content which we have now begun to unravel was known to her, and what does it tell us about the meaning of the embroidery with which she decorated her Bed of State? I do not believe, and am not claiming, that she had read Bruno. It is, however, rather curious that, at the very time when Bruno was residing at Mauvissière's French embassy at Salisbury Court in London, William Fowler, to whose papers we owe at least two of the surviving descriptions of this bed, was also frequenting Salisbury Court in pursuit of intelligence that might serve Walsingham in his surveillance of the Scottish queen. I have found no evidence that Fowler ever met Bruno, although it is suggested by the fact that some years later Fowler wrote a list of 'My Works' that includes 'An Art of Memory'. Indeed a note in Fowler's Hawthornden manuscripts records that he instructed James VI in the art of memory: 'Whilst I was teaching your majestie the art of memorye yow instructed me in poesie and imprese for so was yours.'[23] Fowler can hardly have been unaware that his compatriot, Alexander Dickson, had also, in 1584, produced a memory treatise, *De umbra rationis* that was a close imitation of Bruno's own *De umbris idearum*. Indeed it was Dickson who defended Bruno's work on the art of memory from its English critics, and Bruno himself refers to Dickson, a native of Errol in Scotland, as 'Arelio', describing him as his 'faithful friend'.[24] Dickson consequently became well known as a master of the art of memory in Scotland, where he served as secretary to the Catholic Earl of Errol. This did not prevent him acting as a spy for the English while he was in England at the same time that both Fowler and Bruno were also in London, and he too was also a double agent, offering intelligence of the Spanish Netherlands to the Catholic earls in Scotland. Fowler almost certainly knew Dickson, who had graduated from St Leonard's College of St Andrews University in 1577, a year before Fowler graduated from the same college.[25] How much Mary knew of these individuals, if anything, remains unclear.

What this context suggests is that, whatever she may or may not have known of Bruno, Mary's *Aliamque moratur* device had accumulated a wealth of cultural and political baggage by the mid-1580s. Its third crown was easily interpreted as a reference to the English throne, which would always have made it a politically sensitive device in English eyes. Its political implications could, however, be explained away by claiming that this heavenly crown was precisely that – heavenly. Or, if we take Bruno's example as indicative, it could be seen as an ultimate reward of the ruler who strove to overcome religious conflicts and differences, just as Mary had done in Scotland, as Elizabeth (through the Anjou marriage) had the option of doing in England, or as Henri III (in Bruno's opinion) had the power to do in France. All three of these interpretations were open to Mary, and I see no reason to exclude any of them from our understanding of the significance of the device that she sewed on her bed hangings. Or, perhaps, one should say 'devices', since if the earliest French description of these is to be credited, she sewed two versions of this device, one (*Aliamque moratur*) being her own original, which evidently conformed very closely to the device she had used on a jetton minted in 1565, and the other (*Manet ultima coelo*) representing the device as it had been borrowed and reinvented by her brother-in-law, Henri III of France. The existence of the two versions on her embroidered bed hangings suggests that she must have been quite well informed about its recent history. Finally, we should not underestimate the extent to which her courtly devices participated in an extended network of European royal iconography and emblematics. Despite her lack of a court, and despite the dispersal of her supporters, Mary was up there with the leaders in this style of courtly fashioning.

3

Incriminating Emblems

Courtly devices

In his *Remaines, Concerning Britaine* (1605), William Camden has a chapter on 'Impresses' in which he recalls that in 1579 Sir Philip Sidney took part in a tournament at which he entered the tiltyard with an *impresa*, probably painted on his shield, which consisted of the single word *Speravi* [I hoped] crossed out. Camden has no hesitation in interpreting the significance of this device:

> Sir Philip Sidney, who was long time heir apparent to the Earl of Leicester, after the said Earl had a son born to him, used at the next Tilt-day following 'Speravi' dashed through, to shew his hope therein was dashed.

Alan Young (1987) has clarified the background to this tournament *impresa*, reminding us how in 1578 Leicester, long-time suitor to Queen Elizabeth, had married his old love Lettice Knollys, and how the subsequent birth of a son completely dashed Sidney's hopes as heir apparent to his uncle.[1] This kind of public display of an *impresa* expressing one's attitude towards events that might be both personal and political normally took place at one of the Accession Day tilts held on 17 November to celebrate Elizabeth's accession to the throne. There is no such tilt recorded, however, for 1579, but whatever the occasion on which Sidney displayed his SPERAVI *impresa*, the English queen would certainly have been present and must have understood its hidden message. Indeed Leicester's marriage concerned her personally, and Sidney's disappointment at its implications would only have been exceeded by her own displeasure.

Although Camden's interpretation – and even his identification of the occasion on which this *impresa* was displayed – has since been questioned, what he makes of it can nevertheless be taken to illustrate historical attitudes towards *imprese* and the ways in which they were used. This helps to explain some otherwise rather puzzling aspects about similar devices found embroidered in Mary's needlework and the way these circulated and were interpreted in her own day. Camden assumes that such devices are invented in order to express some personal response or intention on the part of their bearer in relation to his or her own circumstances. Or as he puts it in the opening sentence of his chapter on 'Impresses',

> An Impress (as the Italians call it) is a device in picture with his motto, or word, born by noble and learned personages, to notifie some particular conceit of their own, as Emblems (that we may omit other differences) do propound some general instruction to all.

In other words, whereas emblems offer a general moral applicable to any viewer, *imprese* join together an image and a motto in order to express the mind or intention of their bearer towards his or her own particular circumstances. Clearly the meaning of Sidney's *impresa* on this occasion would only have been apparent to those viewers who had some knowledge of its relevance to

Sidney's situation at the time: his *impresa* is a riddle which requires a reader (or viewer) who can supply the missing context. This would be true even if, as Alan Young suggests, Camden is quite mistaken about the actual occasion when Sidney displayed this tiltyard device: the alternative hypothesis – that Sidney actually used this *impresa* to express his contrition after he had been forced to retire from court for advocating the Alençon marriage in 1580 – puts a construction on it that is equally personal, equally political, and equally circumstantial. Indeed everything Camden says in his *Remaines* about the various *imprese* used by 'noble and learned personages' on such occasions confirms the impression that such devices could only be properly interpreted by those who were privy to the particular circumstances of their bearers. Moreover it should also be apparent that in this case, and it is not alone, those circumstances had implications of a more public and political nature. To signal your attitude in such a way towards events which were public knowledge and of some political moment could have serious repercussions for your standing at court, your relations with your monarch, and what might be called your public self-fashioning.

Understanding some of these conventions surrounding the way *imprese* were used at court in England at the period when Mary was creating her embroideries in the custody of the Earl of Shrewsbury may help in understanding why her use of 'emblematic' devices in her needlework could have such telling political consequences, and why the imagery embroidered on some of her soft furnishings was not merely a matter of fashionable taste or the innocent arts of design. This was a material culture in which, as we shall see, the pictures Mary embroidered on her cushion covers or on her bed hangings could be cited as evidence in a court of law, evidence which might well influence life-or-death verdicts affecting men of considerable power and standing such as the Duke of Norfolk or his son, the Earl of Arundel. Although Mary's *imprese* were never displayed before the public in a tiltyard, they are nevertheless using a type of speaking picture whose hidden meanings were understood to hold messages concerning the attitude of the bearer towards circumstances which might be both personal and political. The fact that they were disclosed beneath an emblematic veil of word and image will explain their usefulness to someone in Mary's position, where communication of her aspirations and intentions was always subject to surveillance, but it might also explain why the decoding of such hidden messages was likely to attract the attention of a skilful lawyer looking for evidence to support his prosecution in a court of law. It is, indeed, difficult for us to imagine the conditions of a culture in which the pattern embroidered on a cushion cover sent to the Duke of Norfolk could be produced as evidence at his treason trial; however the assumptions which Camden brings to the interpretation of Sidney's tiltyard *impresa* might help us to leap over the horizon of expectation that separates our modern acts of interpretation from theirs.

Camden's *Remaines* (1605) consists, as its title suggests, of various leftovers – names, anagrams, coats of arms, proverbs, epitaphs, as well as *imprese* – which he had collected as part of his antiquarian researches for his great topographical description in *Britannia* (1586). Between 1615 and 1617, however, Camden rounded off his life's work on the historiography of Britain with his *Annales rerum anglicarum*, and it is here that Camden gives us an account of Mary's *imprese* which shows the relevance of his comments in *Remaines* to the devices found depicted in her embroideries. In 1584, Camden reports, an attempt was made to persuade Elizabeth that Mary should be removed from the Earl of Shrewsbury's custody into a stricter regime, and certain calumnies were fabricated which, it was thought, would tend to undermine his authority.

> Suspitions were laid hold on, as if there were a plot already laid to set her at liberty; and those raised upon occasion of certain emblemes sent unto her. The emblemes were these: Argus with his many eyes lull'd asleep by Mercury sweetly piping, with this short sentence: *Eloquium tot lumina clausit*, that is, So many eyes hath eloquence fast clos'd: Mercury cutting off Argus's head, who was Io's keeper: a scien [i.e. shoot] grafted into a stock, and bound about with bands, yet budding forth fresh, and this writing about, *Per vincula cresco*, that is to say, By bands I grow: A palmtree pressed down, yet rising up again, with this sentence, *Ponderibus virtus innata resistit*, that is, Gainst weights doth inbred virtue strive. This anagram also *Veritas armata*, that is, Truth armed, according to her name *Maria Steuarta*, the letters being transposed, was taken in an ill sense.[2]

Camden adds, 'Under pretence hereof she was removed from the Earl of Shrewsbury, who had many time earnestly desired the same, and committed to the custody of Sir Amias Powlet and Sir Drue Drury, and that purposely, (as some thought) that, being thereby driven to despair, she might be apt to take rash counsels and resolutions, and be more subject to be insnared.'

Devices about a watch dial

Camden does not make clear that these 'emblems' were embroideries, but it is notable that at least three of the four he mentions correspond to emblems on the embroidered Bed of State which William Drummond described in his letter to Ben Jonson: the two branches *Per vincula cresco* is Drummond no. 3; Mercury charming Argus is Drummond no. 7; the palm tree *Ponderibus virtus innata resistit* is Drummond no. 14. This coincidence might well suggest, therefore, that the embroideries were the source of this fabricated evidence. However these embroideries were not alone among her personal possessions to use these four *imprese*, as evidenced by a document in the (English) National Archives (formerly the Public Record Office (PRO)) at Kew that contains sketches of eight emblems which decorated a watch owned by Mary. According to the *Calendar of State Papers*, the document, consisting of two-and-a-half pages of pen-and-ink drawings, is endorsed: 'Janu. 23, 1575. Devices about a Diall of the Q. of Scottes'.[3] The fact that these sketches ended up with the English state papers suggests that they were almost certainly copied for similar reasons to those designs which Camden describes as being 'raised upon the occasion of certain emblems sent unto her' in 1584. Indeed the 'Devices about a Diall' include at least two of the four that Camden cites: we can therefore now see what these emblems actually looked like even though the embroidered bed hangings have disappeared without trace. For instance, one of the devices described in 1575 on her watch corresponds to the incriminating emblem that Camden records as 'a scien [i.e. shoot] grafted into a stock, and bound about with bands, yet budding forth fresh' with the motto *Per vincula cresco*. Drummond describes this device on the Bed of State as follows: 'The *impresa* of an apple tree growing in a thorn, the word *Per vincula crescit*.' Note the change of case ending in the motto here: *crescit* [it grows] on the bed hangings becomes *cresco* [I grow] on the 'designes for her delivery', which certainly makes it more incriminating: we might conclude that what Camden calls the 'mischievous counsels, and devices' of her enemies extended to changing the verb ending on a motto that had been secretly copied from her personal belongings, so as to make it more damaging.

Similarly we can also, for the first time, see the device on her bed hangings that Drummond tells us showed a palm tree growing taller under oppression. The oppressed palm tree became a well-known emblematic device in the sixteenth and seventeenth centuries, widely used with a variety of different mottoes and applications.[4] It is not difficult to see what political and personal implications might be read into both these devices as expressions of the Scottish prisoner's determination to resist oppression and to grow stronger and taller through her chains. Two further devices 'About the sides of the Diall' on the watch illustrated on the same page do not match any of Camden's incriminating emblems, but do correspond to

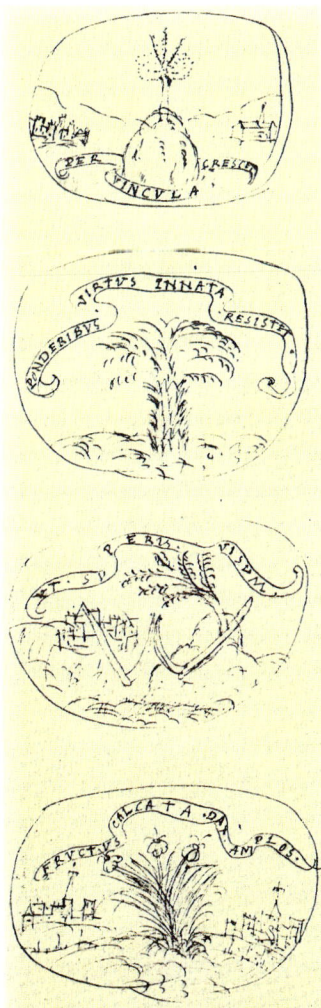

Figure 3.1 Sketches of devices on a watch owned by Mary in 1575. These four were engraved 'About the sides of the Diall'. National Archives (England) SP 53/10.

those recorded on the Bed of State embroideries. *Fructus calcata dat amplos* [It is more fruitful when trampled on] shows a plant flowering in a landscape, an emblem that hardly makes sense without Drummond's explanation that the plant is camomile, a herb that gives out more fragrance when crushed. We can easily, once again, apply the moral of this emblem to Mary's sense of her own situation in England. Another device with the motto *Ut superis visum* [As it seemed good to those above] shows a tree on a hilltop swayed by the wind, with what turn out to be two scythes at the foot. Drummond does not mention this in his letter to Ben Jonson, though the three other descriptions of the Bed of State do include it, with variations of detail that suggest that they all had difficulty making out exactly what it represented, thus the 1586 French inventory describes it as an oak tree with a smaller shrub at the foot of a hill, and does not mention the scythes. Hawthornden Anonymous also thinks he sees a tree trunk with a smaller branch springing up beside and supporting it, with a scythe mowing all the grass around, while William Fowler believes the two scythes are cutting a great tree. Not only these details, but also their relation to the motto and hence their emblematic point, remain obscure, though it is certainly referring to earthly downfall and heavenly judgement.

The anagram on Mary's name, VERITAS ARMATA, that Camden says was 'taken more badly' (*in peiorum partem acceptum*) corresponds to another emblem on her watch. Beneath 'the cover of the boxe opening over the hours', according to the 1575 sketches, was a device showing a mariner's compass with the motto *Sa vertu m'atire* [sic]. The mottoes are admittedly different, though both are anagrams on the name MARIA STEUARTA,[5] moreover we find Drummond bringing together the two anagrams in the first of the devices he describes on the Bed of State: 'The first is the loadstone turning towards the pole, the word her majesty's name turned into an anagram, *Maria Stuart, Sa vertu m'attire*, which is not much inferiour to *Veritas armata*.' Clearly there is a lot of overlap between these different devices on the various occasions and artefacts that used them. The second device on this page showing 'A Diall with a watche wherin upon the cover of the boxe opening over the houers was this figure' corresponds to that on the Bed of State described by Drummond as 'A tree planted in a Church-yard environed with dead mens bones, the word, *Pietas revocabit ab orco*' [Piety will recall them from the underworld].

The third emblem on this page of the 1575 manuscript shows the actual watch dial, with the position of the hours marked around its circumference, an hour hand, and the dial itself decorated with a moon in a starry sky above a castle and the motto QUAE CECIDERE RESURGUNT [Those that have fallen rise again]. Neither Drummond nor Fowler include this, but the French inventory of 1586 describes it thus: '*Le soleil levant pour mot Quae cecidere resurgunt*' [The rising sun, with the motto: Those that have fallen rise again]. Hawthornden Anonymous offers us: 'A devayce for the quines majestie wherin there is the sonne and the moun the word is *que ceder* [sic] *resurgent*.' The logic of placing such an emblem of daily resurrection (whether of the sun or the moon) on her watch dial should be clear enough, though the emblem might also offer the captive Scottish queen some assurance that, however low her fortunes appeared to have sunk, recovery was still possible.

Furthermore, there is another device among the four incriminating emblems that Camden claims were used against Mary in 1584, which can now be identified as engraved on her watch. The emblem he describes as 'Argus with his many eyes lull'd asleep by Mercury sweetly piping, with this short sentence: *Eloquium tot lumina clausit*, that is, So many eyes hath eloquence fast clos'd', although not illustrated in the eight surviving PRO sketches, is recorded in another document that copies it and requires some attention at this point.

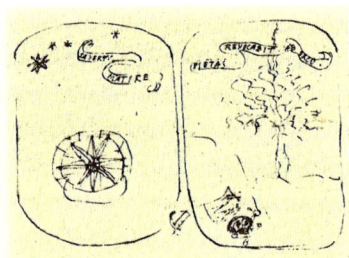

Figure 3.2 Devices on Mary's watch, with a header for this page recording 'A Diall wth a watche wherin upon the cover of the boxe opening over the houers was this figure'. National Archives (England) SP 53/10.

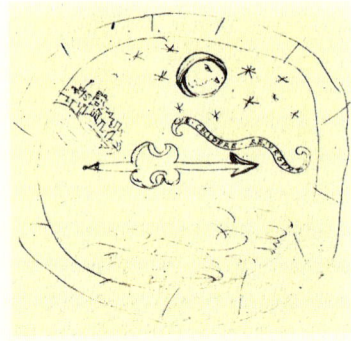

Figure 3.3 Sketch of the dial of Mary's watch showing 'The hande wth the howers'. National Archives (England) SP 53/10.

Sometime in the later seventeenth century, a London teacher of drawing and designer of engravings called John Dunstall copied this manuscript in 12 undated pen-and-ink sketches headed: 'Certaine Emblemes upon a clock of the Q. of Scotts'.[6] Dunstall's drawings include four that are no longer to be found in the earlier document, and among these is a picture of Mercury beguiling Argos, which corresponds to the Bed of State embroidery Drummond describes thus in his letter to Jonson: 'Mercurius charming Argos with his hundred eyes expressed by his caduceus, two flutes and a peacock, the word *Eloquium tot lumina clausit*'. Dunstall's sketch of the same device on Mary's watch shows the flutes, the caduceus and the peacock in a landscape with a church. Both Drummond and Camden have no trouble recognising the classical myth to which these details refer: Argus was the herdsman with a hundred eyes whom the goddess Juno set to guard Io, whom she had turned into a heifer after Zeus fell in love with her, and when Mercury killed the vigilant Argus, Juno placed his eyes on the peacock's tail. The application of this to the circumstances of Mary's imprisonment, or to designs to effect her release from her ever-watchful guardian, would not be difficult for any lawyer to spell out, though it requires competent interpretation of the iconography to identify the myth of Juno and the peacock to which the emblem alludes. This emblem is one of four (all on the same page) that are no longer to be found in the earlier manuscript – evidently the page has gone missing from the state papers since the time Dunstall copied it. Moreover the fact that two of these four can now be shown to correspond to emblems that Mary used in her embroideries also means that we should be in no doubt that Dunstall is not adding anything original to his source. It should also be noted that Drummond recognises the relevance of the peacock and the beheading of Argus to this emblem: it follows that Camden's allusion to 'Mercurius beheading Argus, keeper or watcher of Io' (*Mercurius Argo Io custodienti caput obtruncans*) is not a reference to a separate emblem for which no motto is cited in the *Annales*, as the original punctuation suggests and as some commentators have thought.[7] Rather, the Mercury references are all to a single emblem, and I suggest that Camden identifies just four, and not five, different emblems that were used in 1584 as part of the fraudulent attempt to fabricate evidence that would result in Mary's removal from the custody of the Earl of Shrewsbury. William Fowler says of this device representing Mercury charming Argus, which he saw on

Figure 3.4 John Dunstall's copy of the device alluding to the myth of Mercury charming Argos with his hundred eyes and the motto 'Eloquence has closed many eyes'. British Library, MS Cotton Calig. CV, fol. 73r.

the Bed of State in 1603, 'This is the best in my judgement of all.'

We can now therefore conclude that all four incriminating emblems described by Camden in his *Annales* were to be found on this elaborate (almost certainly engraved silver) pocket watch which, although it has since disappeared, was sketched in a document among the English state papers as early as 1575 (if the PRO dating is correct). It seems most likely, therefore, that this very document was Camden's source, and was quite possibly the same document used by Mary's enemies in 1584 to fabricate their evidence of her readiness to follow 'the dangerous advices of her friends'. Of the 12 emblems illustrated in Dunstall's seventeenth-century copy of the earlier PRO document, all but two correspond to emblems that can now also be identified as having been sewn by Mary for her Bed of State. They are therefore an invaluable witness to the actual appearance of those pieces of embroidery, none of which has survived. It thus makes sense to illustrate the remainder of these before investigating more fully the historical evidence that is beginning to emerge of the way these royal *imprese* were circulating and being interpreted at the time Mary was incorporating so many of them into her embroideries.

Looking at the only drawing that Dunstall has signed, showing a device on the watch, we see a terrestrial globe marked with cities and oceans that is bisected by a conical shadow representing diagrammatically a lunar and/or solar eclipse, with the radiant sun partially obscured below and the shadowed moon above. The Latin motto means 'She takes from herself the light which she envies'. This is the device that was described by Drummond as 'Ecclipses of the Sun and the Moon, the word, *Ipsa sibi lumen quod invidet aufert*' in Chapter 1, where I noted Drummond's interpretive comment: 'glauncing, as may appear, at Queen Elizabeth', a comment which, as we saw, echoed William Fowler's on the same emblem: '*Luna super umbram columnarem terra marique circumscripta cum hoc titulo. Ipsa sibi Lumen quod invidet aufert.* Glancing as I think at Queene Elizabeth' [The moon above a columnar shadow surrounding land and sea with this motto: She deprives herself of the light which she envies]. Fowler's description (the only one, incidentally, that he writes in Latin) confirms how closely the eclipse emblem on Mary's Bed of State must have resembled Dunstall's drawing, with its globe mapped with lands and seas – most probably because in selecting patterns for her embroideries during these final years of exile she sometimes resorted, naturally enough, to the decorative designs she found on jewellery and furniture that she already owned.[8] William Fowler was well placed to assess how any political content of these emblems might have been understood at the time since, in the 1580s, he had been one of Sir Francis Walsingham's spies against Mary Queen of Scots. We shall return to the whole subject of espionage in due course.

Finally, the watch emblem showing half-buried spears and helmets with the motto *Dabit Deus his quoque finem* [God will bring an end to these things also] corresponds to the Bed of State embroidery described in 1586 as 'A tilled field, producing instead of ears of corn points of spears and some helmets; the motto is, *Dabit Deus his quoque finem*'.[9] Drummond makes no mention of this, though it is included in both the Fowler and the Hawthornden Anonymous descriptions. Both are in no doubt that these weapons are growing out of the ground and not being buried, which means that they are most likely alluding to the legendary foundation of the city of Thebes by Cadmus, who sowed dragon's teeth which grew into armed warriors who fought and killed each other, except for the five winners who became, with Cadmus, founders of the city. The legend is not found in emblem books before the seventeenth century and its significance – as a reference to the foundation of a great city under divine guidance but only after a period of strife – is not easy to summarise, although the motto is clearly alluding to the resolution of such conflict.

Representations of this subject normally show the warriors emerging out of the earth, and may show the goddess Minerva directing events overhead. Mary's artist could well have made the mythological allusion more evident by following this iconography but, as with the Mercury and Argus emblem, he seems to have preferred to leave such allusions somewhat teasing and obscure.[10] This is one of two devices to which Fowler has added

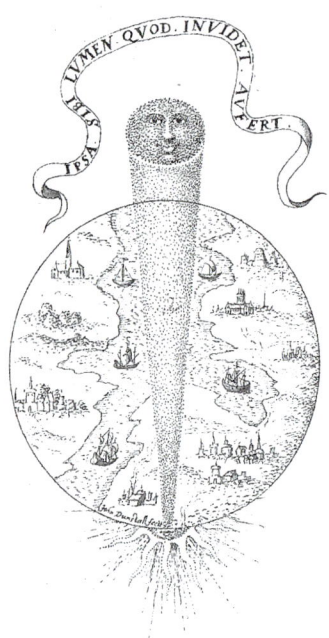

Figure 3.5 John Dunstall's copy of the device showing an eclipse and the motto 'She takes from herself the light that she envies'. British Library, MS Cotton Calig. CV, fol. 75r.

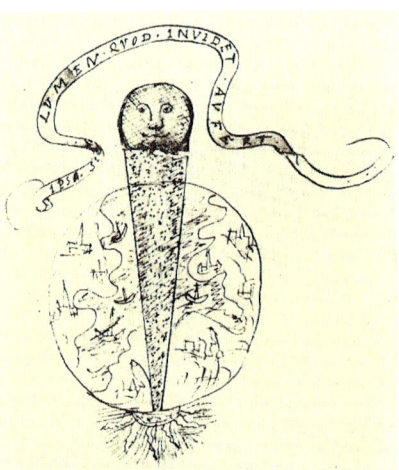

Figure 3.6 Sketch of the device on Mary's watch showing 'The botome of the Diall'. National Archives (England), SP 53/10.

Figure 3.7 Dunstall's copy of the device alluding to the myth of Cadmus's foundation of Thebes, showing weapons growing out of the ground and the motto 'God will put an end to these also'. British Library, MS Cotton Calig. CV, fol. 73r.

the Latin comment '*fatidicum*' [prophetic]. As with the *Aliamque moratur* emblem discussed in the previous chapter, it is a comment that appears to register his belief that at least some of these devices had anticipated historical outcomes by the date, 1603, when he was compiling his own description of the Bed of State.

Mary certainly owned several clocks and watches, but none of those listed in the various inventories is described in sufficient detail for us to make a positive identification, and Mary only acquired some of them later than 1575.[11] The inventory made up at Fotheringhay following her execution in 1587 includes a watch left to 'Melvin', a clock and a watch to her physician Burgoyne, and 'Two great watches and a little one' left with Elizabeth Curle, one of her chambermaids. An inventory dated 1 July 1579, of objects sent in a box to Mary from Jacques de Senlis, the valet responsible for her dowry in France, mentions 'A chased watch and an alarm-clock gilt and trimmed with its case, which cost forty-eight crowns' and 'Another chased watch which cost fifteen crowns'.[12] Since 'chased' means engraved, the implication is that one of these was the watch recorded in Dunstall's sketches, except that the dates (if they can be trusted) would rule this out. In 1564, which is certainly early enough, the exiled Earl of Lennox, who Elizabeth had persuaded Mary to receive back in Scotland, presented her with rich propitiatory gifts including 'a clock, and a dial curiously wrought and set with stones', described in a letter from the English ambassador Randolph to Cecil.[13] It is difficult to imagine, however, what the original point of these emblems would have been on such a propitiatory gift, and it seems unlikely that Mary would have later adopted on her Bed of State emblems associated with the man who became her father-in-law following her ill-fated marriage to Darnley in 1565. Mary certainly owned similar jewellery with engraved emblems: the silver hand bell that she used to summon her servants survives and is decorated, as we shall see, with one of the most politically telling and important of all the emblems on the embroideries. The *Calendar of State Papers (Scotland)* records further gifts sent to Mary which were embellished with emblems, for instance in 1576 when a ring was sent from King Philip of Spain, and another from the 'Duke of Feria, wherein was written these poyses, *Numero complera omnes* [These make up the full number], and *Presentibus fruor meliora spero* [I enjoy what I have and hope for better things]'. These gifts were brought by George Fitzwilliam, who had just returned from Spain, and the English state papers record that 'Her majesty was content that ... he should deliver both letters and rings to Queen Mary, who returned both letters and a book of gold to the King from Queen Mary, wherein was written *Absit michi gloriari*, etc.'[14] Such emblematic inscriptions on a ring were known as 'ring posies' – a 'posy' is a sententious motto that was seen in this period as much the same thing as an emblem.[15] What all this evidence suggests is that one of the places on which Mary would have found the kind of emblems and mottoes seen on her embroideries was her personal jewellery. We should, however, note how often the only surviving record of such artefacts is in the Elizabethan state papers, and the reason that they are recorded there is because they were thought to be politically sensitive, especially when they used emblems.

Philip Howard: the Arundel connection

The attempt in 1584 by her adversaries to remove Mary from Shrewsbury's custody was not the only occasion on which emblems or *imprese* such as those found on her embroideries were collected as evidence to support the case against her. Better known is the trial, a few years earlier, of the Duke of Norfolk – an event of major importance in the story of Mary Queen of Scots and to British history as a whole. Before we look at this, however, it will be instructive to examine a couple of less familiar accounts of the way Mary's emblems were cited and used, both of which are associated not with the Duke of Norfolk, as it happens, but with his eldest son and heir Philip Howard, variously Earl of Surrey and of Arundel. Some time in the 1570s Mary herself had used such *imprese* to bring comfort to Philip Howard's deserted wife. The young Howard was named after his godfather, Philip of Spain, who attended his christening with Mary Tudor in the chapel of Whitehall in 1557, the other godfather being his grandfather the Earl of Arundel, whose title he was to inherit when the latter died without issue in 1580. Philip Howard met Anne, daughter of Thomas, Lord Dacre, when her widowed mother remarried his father, the Duke of Norfolk, and brought her daughter Anne to live with them. The marriage of Philip and Anne was apparently celebrated 'without any noise or public solemnity by reason that the Duke at that time was in disgrace, and in trouble about the business of the Queen of Scots, for which not long after he lost his life being beheaded on Tower Hill 2. June 1572'.[16] Newly married, Philip went to court where, we are told, 'he neglected his wife in order to please the Queen'.

> Not long after his being at Court, he began first to neglect his wife, seldome comeing or sending to visit her: and after some time in a manner to reject her, by dignifying and saying unto some, that he knew not whether she were his wife or no, and so wholly absenting himself from her, as if really he had not so reputed her. The occasion of this was, a great desire he had to give contentment to the Queen: for having understood by some who had caus'd his Nativity to be calculated, that he should be in great danger to be overthrown by a woman (the which he interpreted to be no other than the Queen) he endeavor'd by all means to get and keep her favour: and because he well perceived she could not endure his Lady (nor indeed the wife to any one to whom she shew'd special grace) thereupon he neglected her.[17]

This account comes down to us in a manuscript of the lives of these two Catholic martyrs preserved in the family archives which, although not published until the mid-nineteenth century by the then Duke of Norfolk, was evidently written by Lady Anne's Catholic priest within her lifetime from information which she herself supplied ('his Lady has often told me', p. 11). It seems to be the only record of Mary's attempt to effect a reconciliation between the estranged couple through her gift of what can only have been a piece of emblematic embroidery. Hearing how bravely the countess bore up in the face of her husband's behaviour, 'partly to comfort, partly to shew the love she bore her', Mary sent Lady Anne 'a piece of work in silk and silver made and contriv'd by herself in this form'.

> There was a tree framed, whereon two turtles [i.e. doves] sate, on either side one, with this difference that, by that on the right hand, there were two or three leaves remaining: by that other none at all, the tree on that side being wholly bare: over the top of the tree were these words wrought in silver, *Amoris sorte pares* [Equal in the fortunes of love]. Signifying: that herself and the Countesse represented by those two turtles were alike in their affections to the two persons of the same family; the Duke of Norfolke, and the Earl of Surrey. At the bottom of the tree on that where the former turtle sate by the green leaves these words were also wrought in silver: *Haec ademptum* [This is taken away], with an anchor under them to shew that the Countesse whom she put on the right hand, might be in some hope because her Lord was yet alive, tho' by reason of his absence and unkindnes to her, she mourn'd as a turtle. On the other side of the tree under the other turtle were these words in like manner wrought: *Illa peremptum* [That is taken away], with certain pieces of broken boards, signifying that her own hopes were wholly wrack'd by the death of the Duke for whom she mourn'd as a solitary turtle without hope of comfort or redress. (pp. 266–7)

Mary's emblematic gift, which was evidently her own invention, is quite complex, expressing as it does not only Lady Anne's situation but also her own and inviting a comparison between the two. Lady Anne, we learn, sought refuge with her grandfather the aged Earl of Arundel, who tried to reconcile husband and wife. On his death in 1580, by which Anne became Countess of Arundel, Philip Howard returned to live with her, having failed to win royal favour despite his repudiation of his young wife. He converted to Catholicism and the couple had two children. Anne was imprisoned for her Catholicism in 1582–83, but although she was released the earl was himself imprisoned after years of struggling to maintain his position against the growing tide of anti-Catholic feeling. In 1585 he sought to sail into exile in one of the great Elizabethan escape stories: Walsingham's agents had prior knowledge of the voyage even if they had not actually set it up in a typical sting operation; his ship was intercepted and he was brought to London where he was tried in the Star Chamber for attempting to leave the country without permission. He was fined and imprisoned in the Tower, and in 1589 he was further charged with high treason, though it was not until 1595 that he fell ill after eating roasted teal, suspected poisoned, from which he died and was buried at Arundel Castle. His sufferings for his faith made him glorious in the Catholic Church – indeed the Norfolk manuscript, which is our only record of Mary's emblem of the two turtle doves, asks to be read as a justification of the claims to such reverence of this 'chief Earl of England' who, it concludes, 'died in durance of a glorious Confessor, yea a Martyr' (p. 162). After his conversion, Philip Howard repented his past misdeeds, and particularly his former treatment of his wife, 'as himself signify'd in a letter out of the Tower to Father Robert Southwell of the Society of Jesus, who then liv'd with his lady' (p. 12). At the moment of his arraignment, a nightingale sang in an eglantine tree at Arundel, and 'Another thing as strange did happen in the Tower soon after his death; for two tame stags which the Lieutenant kept there for his pleasure falling into a fury, never desisted knocking their horns against the walls till their brains being beaten out they dy'd' (p. 124).

It is in the *Complete Collection of State Trials* rather than in this Catholic martyrology that we are told of the part that emblems played in Philip, Lord Arundel's own trial: 'Then was produced an emblematical piece found in the earl's cabinet, which had on the one side a hand bitten with a serpent shaking the serpent into the fire, about which was written this poesie, *Quis contra nos?* and on the other side, a Lion Rampant, with his chops all bloody, with this poesie, *Tamen Leo*.'[18] The earl tried to play down the significance of these devices: 'To these charges the earl answer'd in the gross, That as for the picture, 'twas a trifle presented to him by his man.' The hand shaking a snake into the fire is an emblem which had been illustrated in Claude Paradin's collection of *Devises heroïques* (1551) with the motto *Quis contra nos?*, where it is explained as an illustration of the biblical account (Acts 28: 1–6) of St Paul's visit to Malta when a viper fastens onto his finger as he puts sticks on a fire, but which the apostle, unharmed, shakes off into the fire; the motto quotes Romans 8: 31, 'If God is with us, who can be against us?' Paradin does not identify any existing bearer of this *impresa*, though Mary had used it, as we have seen, along with other devices from Paradin, in the border to her *Las pennas passan* panel. The same device was also used, interestingly, on a medal signed by the Italian medallist Jacopo Primavera showing Queen Elizabeth I in profile and the reverse with the hand shaking a serpent into the fire and the motto NOCEBIT NIHIL CVI NON NOVISSE DEBET ACTO XXVII [Nothing will harm him whom nothing should harm, Acts xxviii].[19]

The other emblem cited in the prosecution of Philip Howard is interesting, among other things, because it goes back to a fable attributed to Aesop which had been cited in the sixteenth century as the basis for an Egyptian hieroglyphic. Fables and hieroglyphics were both high on the list of the means of informing the imagery and the morality of emblems. The fable of the lioness and the fox tells of a vixen, in conversation with a lioness, who congratulates herself on the fact that foxes invariably produce a good litter of cubs, whereas a lioness (as it was thought) never produces more than one; to this the lioness replies that although she only produces one cub, at least that one is a lion and not a fox. The late-classical *Hieroglyphica* of Horapollo Nilus sanctioned the idea that this was not just a fable but a symbol in the priestly writing of the Egyptians, where it signifies a woman who has conceived only once: 'When they wish to indicate a woman who has conceived once', Horapollo tells us, 'they draw a lioness. For the lioness is never pregnant twice.'[20] In 1543 the *Hieroglyphica* was printed by Jacques Kerver in Paris, for the first time with woodcut illustrations strongly resembling the emblems

Figure 3.8 *Quis contra nos?* [Who is against us?], St Paul shakes off the viper that bit his finger as he fuelled the fire: God will protect the faithful (Claude Paradin, *Devises heroïques*, 1557, p. 187).

Figure 3.9 Reverse of medal of Queen Elizabeth of England by Jacobo Primavera, c.1572. British Museum.

Figure 3.10 Hieroglyphic signifying a woman who has only given birth once (Horapollo Nilus, *De sacris notis* [= *Hieroglyphica*], 1551, p. 179).

the Howards had received from their fellow Catholic and former friend, the late Queen of Scots, there can be little doubt that this citing of an emblematic artefact as evidence in the state trial of a prominent member of the English Catholic nobility is of a piece with those former occasions on which emblems, including emblematic embroideries, were produced as evidence in state trials. The most famous of these, and quite probably the example which established the immediate precedent for this very curious Elizabethan legal practice, was the trial of Philip Howard's father and Mary's intended fourth husband, the Duke of Norfolk, in 1572.

The Norfolk trial

Mary, it will be recalled, had entertained the prospect of marriage to England's premier earl as a way out of her difficulties which might resolve the problems of her own exile if not the succession to the English and Scottish thrones. The historical and political implications of the match have been endlessly debated and discussed, and it is hardly necessary to rehearse them again here. Elizabeth had first suggested the possibility of a marriage to Norfolk before Mary opted to marry Darnley in 1565, but it was at the York conference in 1568, over which Norfolk himself presided to settle the vexed question of Mary's alleged complicity in the murder of Darnley, that serious plans for the match with Norfolk were initiated. Norfolk's suspected involvement in the 1569 rebellion of the northern earls however and, more disastrously, in the 1571 Ridolfi plot, led to his trial and execution in 1572. Mary never met her prospective bridegroom, though she exchanged presents and love letters, and it was one such embroidered gift which was cited in evidence against the duke at his trial. The *Virescit vulnere virtus* [Virtue flourishes from its wounds] embroidery has, for this reason, become probably the best-known and most frequently illustrated of the emblematic embroideries associated with Mary Queen of Scots.

in the newly emerging emblem books, on which hieroglyphics exercised an enormous influence. In order to determine what any artefact illustrating this fable might have looked like at this time, we have only to look at Kerver's woodcut. When Pierio Valeriano produced his hugely expanded and influential *Hieroglyphica seu de sacris Ægyptiorum ... literis* in 1556 he gave the image of the lion pride of place, Book I, at the head of his list of hieroglyphics using animals, and he takes Horapollo's hieroglyphic back to its fable, quoting the Aesopic moral which is summed up in the lioness's reply to the vixen: 'Leaenam respondisse, se quidem semel et unum parere, sed eum leonem' [The lioness replied that she did indeed give birth to only one cub, but that one was a lion].

The official records of the trial of Philip Howard do not reveal what form this 'emblematical piece' took, though apparently it had two 'sides' and was evidently not a piece of embroidery. Nor does the prosecution allege that these incriminating emblems had any connection with Mary Queen of Scots. However both of these correspond to emblems used on Mary's embroideries, which suggests this might well have been where the *imprese* had originated. William Drummond and all three of the other descriptions tell us that the emblematic embroideries on Mary's Bed of State included a lioness with her lion cub beside her, and the motto *Unum quidem sed leonem* [One only, but that one a lion], which Drummond has no hesitation in interpreting: 'This is for her self and her son'. Even though the prosecution, as far as is known, did not rest its case on the allegation that these were seditious emblems that

The embroidered cushion with its incriminating emblem is described in the official records of the examination of Mary's ambassador and supporter, John Leslie, Bishop of Ross, who had been active not only in the Ridolfi conspiracy but also in the Norfolk marriage negotiations. Leslie was a key prosecution witness whose evidence played a large part, despite his obligations to

Mary, in its fatal outcome. In November 1571, Leslie testified that he had been at Howard's house at Kenninghale when a member of Mary's household called 'Bortycke' brought a cushion to the Duke of Norfolk, 'wrought with the Scotts Queen's own armes, and a devyse upon it, with this sentence, VIRESCIT VULNERE VIRTUS, and a hand with a knife cutting down the vines, as they use in the sprynge tyme; al which work was made by the Scots Queen's own hand'.[21] A letter written to Lord Burghley immediately after this evidence was produced in court offers the following interpretation of the emblem, 'declarynge thereby her courage, and wyllinge the Duke by such a watch sentence, to take a good harte unto him'.[22] That sounds a fairly weak interpretation, and it would surely not have been difficult, in the circumstances, to put a more damaging inflection on the *impresa*. Susan Watkins (2000), for instance, makes it far more incriminating, 'The message to Norfolk was clear: the unfruitful royal branch of the Tudors (Elizabeth) was to be cut down, so that the vital branch (Mary) would flourish.'[23] To which a valid defence might have been that the clipped vine is a single plant and in pruning vines excessive leaf growth is cut off to stimulate fruiting: it is the wounded plant that bears fruit, and not some other; we flourish from our own wounds, not from someone else's and it is therefore Mary's own wounds that she hoped might bring recovery, not any injury that she planned to inflict on her sister queen. However we interpret it, this application of the device to the circumstances of its bearer is once again replicating the hermeneutic strategy already witnessed in the interpretation of all these devices, from Sidney's erased SPERAVI onwards. This emblem might well be seen as particularly appropriate to the duke since the Norfolk heraldic motto is *Solus virtus invicta* [Only virtue is invincible].

Moreover for this example we almost certainly have the actual embroidery. At the centre of the Marian Hanging at Oxburgh Hall is a square panel which corresponds exactly to the cushion cover Mary allegedly sent to Norfolk. A disembodied hand reaches down from the sky to prune the unfruitful branches of a vine which is growing between two fruit trees. The motto in a scroll reads VIRESCIT VVLNERE VIRTVS, and Mary's distinctive cipher/monogram is shown beside the tree on the left side, with the royal arms of Scotland, just as described in the Bishop of Ross's testimony, on the right. The identity of this panel from the Oxburgh Hangings with the cushion that John Leslie alleged the queen had sent to the Duke of Norfolk once again raises the whole question of what these embroideries were made for, what form they took, and how they might have been cut up and reused over the years. If the Oxburgh Hangings were put together soon after Mary and Bess embroidered the distinctive panels which they use, and if those panels were created for these very hangings, then any cushion cover that Mary sent to the duke must have been returned to her or to Bess before it could be sewn onto the surviving hangings.

Although the panel is certainly of a suitable size and shape to serve as a cushion cover, it is also very similar in size to the two other 'emblem' panels on the Oxburgh Hangings, and I have to say that the idea that the two needlewomen adapted three separate cushion covers (one at least of which had been cited in a criminal trial) to serve as centrepieces of some elaborate and splendid hangings into which they had put a great deal of other work, is not very convincing. The only evidence that a cushion cover corresponding to this panel ever existed is in the testimony of John Leslie, Bishop of Ross, a witness statement for the prosecution exacted under great pressure in 1572. If Leslie was fabricating stories about incriminating devices in response to leading questions from his interrogators in a type of sixteenth-century plea bargaining, then the strategy certainly worked, for his confession to involvement in the Ridolfi plot undoubtedly saved his life. Leslie would have had ample opportunity to see what Mary's embroideries looked like, and when pressed for incriminating evidence that might help save his skin, he may well have recalled this example. Drummond does not mention this panel in his letter to Jonson describing emblems on the Bed of State, but the 1586 description attests that, at that date, it included 'Un sep de vigne et une main avec une serpe coupant ledit sep y a Virescit vulnere virtus' [A vine stock and a hand with a pruning knife cutting the said stock, there is Virtue flourishes from its wounds]. It is highly unlikely that Mary could have retrieved the cushion cover that she had allegedly given to Norfolk, and which had been cited as evidence in the state trial a dozen years earlier, in order to sew it onto her bed curtains only a year before her own execution. Moreover William Fowler also describes it on the Bed of State furnishings he saw in 1603 as 'an aix upon a vine tree, Virescit vulnere virtus'. Clearly, if this embroidery was part of the bed hangings that Fowler saw as late as 1603 in Edinburgh, it cannot also have served as the centrepiece on one of the present Oxburgh Hangings at this date.

Figure 3.11 Marian Hanging, centrepiece; a vine is being pruned with the motto *Virescit vulnere virtus* [Virtue flourishes from its wounds], with Mary's monogram and the royal arms of Scotland. Oxburgh Hall, Norfolk.

The silver hand bell

The same inventories of her possessions compiled in 1586 that describe the various embroideries, including the bed furnishings, also include another object that now demands our attention. The June 1586 Chartley inventory records, 'Une clochette d'argent de sus la table de Sa Majesté' [A little silver bell on Her Majesty's table].[24] In 1886 an exhibition was mounted in Peterborough to commemorate the tercentenary of Mary's death, and it included, catalogue no. 81, 'Mary Stuart's Hand-Bell, of silver gilt' which is described as engraved with four figurative designs: the royal arms, a ChiRho monogram and two further emblematic devices. One of these showed her favourite crowned monogram with the Greek *phi* (for François II) and letter M (for Marie) that she also used on several of the Oxburgh embroideries, encircled by the anagram SA VERTV MATIRE which we have already encountered on the Bed of State as well as on her watch dial. Another

INCRIMINATING EMBLEMS

Figure 3.12 Silver hand bell engraved with emblematic devices of Mary Queen of Scots, possibly the *clochette d'argent de sus la table de Sa Majesté* recorded in the Chartley inventory in 1586, here showing the *Virescit vulnere virtus* emblem. Private collection.

Figure 3.13 The same silver hand bell, showing ChiRho monogram with the inscription IN HOC VINCE [Triumph in this].

device on the silver hand bell, however, showed a hand pruning a vine, one branch of which was leafless, with the motto *Virescit vulnere virtus*.[25] This exhibit had been 'preserved among the heirlooms of the family of Bruce, of Kennet', we are told, by the descendants of Sir James Balfour, who had been deputy governor of Edinburgh Castle during Mary's reign; the hand bell had been loaned for exhibition by Lord Balfour of Burleigh. It had already been described and illustrated by Albert Way in the *Archaeological Journal* in 1858, and was to be further illustrated in a book by William Gibb on Stuart memorabilia in 1890.[26] The hand bell survives, and although one should always be doubtful about the authenticity of such Marian memorabilia, the provenance and iconography in this case seem wholly reassuring.[27]

The ChiRho monogram on the hand bell, encircled with the inscription IN HOC VINCE 86 [Triumph in this], raises questions that are not easy to answer. Albert Way suggests (pp. 261–2) that this might be the Old Style way of dating Mary's death, 1586 for New Style February 1567 (Old Style began the New Year in March). There is something to be said for this suggestion – turning the otherwise obscure motto into a claim that to have died in the name of Christ was a triumph for religion. That would mean that this detail can only have been placed on the bell after 1587, a hypothesis which might be supported by the somewhat cruder execution of this engraving. We shall certainly see how quickly, following Mary's execution, some of these devices were being appropriated and adapted to express a view of Mary as Catholic martyr, and it is just possible that the details on the bell that 'appear to show ... appearances of later workmanship' may have been added, as Way suggests, 'subsequently to her death' (p. 262). It is, however, difficult to believe that the original decoration would have left two spaces free for later engravings on the outside of the bell and, if so, they are likely to have been on opposite sides, which means that the *Virescit vulnere virtus* emblem must also be a later, posthumous addition. This is an altogether more complex and intricate design than the ChiRho monogram, and it is not evident to me after close inspection that these two, when compared to the other two motifs on the bell, show any clear signs of later, inferior workmanship. Nor is it at all certain that the number '86' is a date. The case is complicated by one further engraved detail on this very curious and fascinating object, for besides the four figurative devices on the outside of the bell one finds engraved numbers and lettering inside the bell, where the clapper swings. The letters, spaced out in three concentric and segmented circles, have been plausibly interpreted as spelling out the phrase CLAMAT SVAS [She calls her own], but the placing of two numbers, 4 and 3, opposite each other in the second circle, makes no obvious sense, even though they are exactly half the number 86 which is engraved,

EMBLEMS FOR A QUEEN

Figure 3.14 Silver hand bell: engraving inside the bell with numbers and lettering that can be read as CLAMAT SVAS [She calls her own].

as we have seen, on the outside. The suggestion that they, too, might be a date, referring to her coronation in 1543, remains equally speculative, and equally difficult to relate to the Latin motto, unless this too was a posthumous insertion by some religious adherent, asserting that the coronation, like the martyrdom, of the Catholic queen was a call to all her co-religionists to follow her. It makes more sense, however, to see the inscription inside the hand bell as serving similar ends to those we have witnessed in the personal *imprese* and devices with which she surrounded herself in her years of exile. Resting on her table, as described in the 1586 inventory of Mary's possessions, the hand bell would doubtless have been used to summon her servants, while also giving the captive and exiled queen some assurance that, in the hour of her need, she could summon supporters to her assistance.

Virescit vulnere virtus: *medals and mottoes*

The likelihood that Mary might have wanted to put the *Virescit vulnere virtus* device on her personal hand bell is made more probable by the fact that this same device was also used on the reverse of a medal or jetton as early as 1557, a year before she married François II, showing the arms of Scotland on the obverse with the legend MARIA DEI G SCOTOR REGINA on the exergue.[28] Moreover, a few years later, following the death of François, the same jetton was reissued, with the dimidiated arms of Scotland and France encircled by the legend MARIA D G SCOTOR REGINA FRAN DOI [Mary by the grace of

God Queen of Scotland and Dowager of France]. Both of these have the *Virescit vulnere virtus* device on the reverse, and one has only to look at the way this is executed to recognise that the hand bell can only have been designed by someone who had already seen the jetton. Clearly the significance or application of this *impresa* to her own circumstances could have nothing to do at this early date with her designs on the English throne or with her hope to draw strength from her injuries. In reusing it as dowager Queen of France, following the untimely death of young François, the application might well have been to her hopes of recovery from bereavement. These jettons must have been minted in France, and would probably have been distributed to friends and supporters. Less valuable than medals, they differ not at all in their design: indeed true medals in gold or silver could easily be struck from the same dies.

The 1586 Chartley inventory, after describing Mary's writing desk, mentions 'purses of green velvet, furnished with silver jettons marked with Her Majesty's coat of arms'.[29] She would have used these as counters for adding up accounts or payments. It follows that if she sent the embroidery that can still be seen at the centre of the Marian Hanging at Oxburgh as a cushion cover to the Duke of Norfolk, Mary was sending him a highly personal *impresa* that she had adopted 20 years earlier, while she was still a young woman, whose original meaning could in no way be linked with the Babington plot or her alleged designs on the English throne.

Figure 3.15 Jetton of Mary Queen of Scots: reverse showing the *Virescit vulnere virtus* device. Edinburgh, National Museum of Scotland.

The *Virescit vulnere virtus* motto comes from the *Noctes Atticae* of second-century AD essayist Aulus Gellius, where he is discussing grammarians' objections to the nonce word *virescit* in an alliterative poem by a poet called Furius which used the whole phrase to describe a spring awakening of martial vigour.[30] This way of linking image to adage was the normal process when composing an *impresa*: you either had to make up your own motto or borrow a quotation from an ancient author, the inventive skill then lay largely in finding an appropriate image to illustrate the motto. There should ideally be something of a semiotic gap between the two, indeed according to the Italian writers on the art of the *impresa* the image should not show something already named in the motto – instead it should represent something different, posing a challenge or puzzle to the reader/viewer. In choosing a classical quotation there was always the risk that the same motto might also be chosen by others, and that certainly seems to have happened with Mary's *Virescit vulnere virtus*, for the same adage had long been the heraldic motto of the Stewart earls of Galloway, who inscribed it over their crest: a pelican pecking open its breast to feed its young with its lifeblood in a traditional emblem of Christian sacrifice. However, in the 1550s the Burnett family had already adopted the *Virescit vulnere virtus* motto with a different crest – a hand with a knife pruning a vine – just as we see it in Mary's embroidery. In 1550 there had been a famous case heard in the court of the Lyon King of Arms, Sir David Lindsay of the Mount, to decide which of two rival branches of the Burnett family had best title to this particular crest and motto. Lindsay was one of the most famous of Scotland's renaissance poets, active at the court of Mary's father, James V, where, among other things, he had devised the pageants to welcome Mary's mother, Mary of Guise, into Scotland in 1538, so we might well wonder if the 1557 jetton was simply copying the heraldic crest of the Burnetts. However, it seems unlikely that anyone inventing a jetton or medal for the 15-year-old Queen of Scots on the eve of her marriage to the Dauphin of France would have appropriated the motto and badge of one of her own subjects. It seems more likely that this easily moralised, lapidary phrase from a late-classical author was known to educated courtiers or scholars in both countries, where the inventive process of finding an image to illustrate the adage could quite easily have led both quite independently to associate the Latin poet's proverbial expression with the pruning of vines: a case of serendipity not sourcing.[31]

Moreover, it also seems likely – though I have found no contemporary witness to confirm this – that the vine pruning is a biblical image, alluding to John 15: 1–5, where Christ declares,

> I am the true vine, and my Father is the husbandman. Every branch in me that beareth not fruit he taketh away; and every branch that beareth fruit, he purgeth it, that it may brong forth more fruit … As the branch cannot bear fruit of itself, except it abide in the vine; no more can ye, except ye abide in me. I am the vine, ye are the branches: He that abideth in me, and I in him, the same bringeth forth much fruit; for without me ye can be nothing.

Although the Bible makes no specific mention of a pruning knife, its reference to the branch that is 'purged' (Vulgate *purgabit*) to produce more fruit would be sufficient to suggest what any 'husbandman' would have regarded as the normal and most practical means of making vines more fruitful, and its reference to the

Figure 3.16 Sketch of Mary's *Virescit vulnere virtus* device (J. Dorat, *Recueil de devises*, MS Bibliothèque de l'Arsenal Ms. 3184), owned by royal herald Hector le Breton who died in 1652. Paris, Bibliothèque nationale.

Figure 3.17 Arms of the earls of Galloway with their crest showing the 'Pelican in her Piety' who feeds her young with her own lifeblood and the *Virescit vulnere virtus* motto (Lyon Court, Edinburgh, MS 21, 'Kings and Nobilitys Arms', *c*.1638).

Figure 3.18 The vine-pruning emblem with the *Virescit vulnere virtus* motto also featured as the crest to the heraldic arms of Alexander Burnett of Leys, here shown on the sculptured panel *c*.1596, Crathes Castle, Aberdeenshire.

two branches – one barren, the other fruitful – corresponds exactly to that seen in the *impresa*. The biblical allusion opens up the possibility that, far from being primarily a political or even a personal and funerary emblem, Mary's *Virescit vulnere virtus* was originally and essentially religious. That religious inflection would certainly explain a common grounding of the two Scottish heraldic crests that use the motto, and we can easily see how the Burnetts might have found a different image to vary the Galloway earldom's 'Pelican in her Piety' if we bear in mind that both the pelican and the vine-pruning image were, basically, religious symbols.

This *impresa* is thus not copied from any printed emblem book, although like all emblems it is recycling received materials. The motto *Virescit vulnere virtus* certainly appears in the *Imprese heroiche et morali* of Gabriele Simeoni where, from the Lyon edition of 1560 onwards, it was illustrated with a woodcut showing not the hand pruning the vine but rather a man trampling on a plant, English sorrel, which, Simeoni explains, is a herb that grows stronger when it is crushed.[32] Mary evidently used a very similar image on her Bed of State hangings which, as we have seen, included an emblem showing what William Drummond takes to be a 'camomile' plant in a garden with the motto *Fructus calcata dat amplos* [It is more fruitful when trampled on]; though no human figure is mentioned the Latin *calcata*, 'trampled', leaves it strongly implied. The same device was also engraved, as we have seen, on her watch. This kind of reworking of received materials in a *bricolage*, or mosaic, of word and image is fundamental to emblematic invention, as Daniel Russell (1985) has argued.[33] That is, indeed, the name of the emblematic game since 'emblem' means insert and composing an emblem is largely a matter of inserting received images or familiar adages into new contexts and new combinations.

The *Virescit vulnere virtus* panel on the Marian Hanging at Oxburgh is not the only embroidery that turns out to be using devices which also feature on her medals or jettons. In 1579, ten years after she fled to England, at least three medals or jettons were minted of which two have emblematic reverses corresponding to devices Drummond describes on her bed hangings.[34] One of these shows a version of the same image, a vine stem of two branches, one flourishing the other withered; this time however, a hand in the sky holds not a pruning knife but a pot. The motto is *Mea sic mihi prosunt* [Thus are mine profitable to me]. It is only when reading Drummond's description that we can

INCRIMINATING EMBLEMS

Figure 3.19 *Virescit vulnere virtus*, emblem of the herb that gives out greater fragrance when trodden on (Gabriele Simeoni, *Imprese heroiche et morali*, 1560, p. 33).

Figure 3.20 Medal or jetton of Mary Queen of Scots, dated 1579: a vine being sprinkled from a watering can, one branch flourishing while the other is dead, and the motto *Mea sic mihi prosunt* [Thus are mine unto me]; we are expected to infer that the vine is being watered with wine, which will kill it. Edinburgh, National Museum of Scotland.

Figure 3.21 Marcus Gheeraerts the Younger, *The Persian Lady*, c.1600. The motto *Mea sic mihi* [Thus mine to me] can be seen on the tree trunk. Hampton Court, The Royal Collection, by gracious permission of H.M. Queen Elizabeth II.

understand the emblematic point of this: 'A vine tree watred with wine, which instead to make it spring and grow, maketh it fade, the word, *Mea sic mihi prosunt*'. Clearly the picture does not show whether the watering pot holds wine rather than water, and we have to conclude that not only Drummond but also Fowler and the 1586 description of the Bed of State had independent knowledge of the *topos* which informs this device, since all three describe it as a vine being watered with wine. Mary's motto can only be read as implying that, far from coming to her aid when called, the efforts of her servants to make her cause flourish would be more likely to destroy her, something that was true only too often in her history, alas! Mary was not alone in using this motto in such a context, for the Hampton Court painting by Marcus Gheeraerts, known as *The Persian Lady* and described by Roy Strong (1993) as 'the most extraordinary of all Elizabethan portraits'[35] shows a weeping stag standing before a tree whose trunk is marked with three inscriptions, of which the middle one reads *Mea sic mihi* [Thus to me my]. The motto has never made much sense hitherto, but if we now read it as a reflection on the tendency of one's friends to do one harm, it makes perfect sense in the context that Strong has convincingly identified for this portrait, executed as a plea for clemency by Lady Essex to Elizabeth during the period of Essex's imprisonment following his return from Ireland in 1599 in the lead-up to the rebellion which resulted in his execution in 1601.[36] The circumstances are closely analogous to those surrounding the state trials of the Earl of Arundel, or his father, the Duke of Norfolk, 20-odd years earlier when, as we have seen, similar mottoes and emblematic devices were used.

What I hope to have shown is how that process was working in the gradual evolution of a courtly iconography surrounding Mary Queen of Scots, an iconography that was both deeply personal and yet also a process of public self-fashioning. Mary undoubtedly played her part in that inventive process, though it is also clear that the design and production of these courtly artefacts must also have involved sympathisers and supporters at home and abroad. While Mary was quite capable of selecting or designing the devices that figure in her embroideries, she is unlikely to have designed the various medals that were struck during her years of exile. We do know that as early as 1553 two Scottish goldsmiths, John Acheson and Nicolas Emery, had been granted licenses to make dies in Paris with portraits of Queen Mary and jettons with her coat of arms.[37] I have not been able to discover who designed similar jettons and medals, almost certainly in France, as late as 1579 when Mary was in exile and could have played no role in their production. Nor is it easy to say how they circulated, or exactly what purpose they served. However, it does seem that they were designed, like her bed hangings, to construct a public image of the persecuted queen, her values, ambitions and intentions, that would outlast her, and that is doubtless why she and her supporters carried on producing them after any realistic prospect of regaining her own court and kingdom had effectively vanished.

That process was to continue even after her death in continuing efforts, in which the survival or manufacture of relics played its part, to construct her as a Catholic martyr. The developed iconography of her embroidered Bed of State played its part in that construction too, as evidenced by the opening stanzas of the poem which the Jesuit priest (indeed, saint) and poet, Robert Southwell, wrote immediately following her execution. Entitled 'Decease, Release', its Latin subtitle corresponds to the motto of an *impresa*: DUM MORIOR ORIOR [In dying I rise].[38]

> The pounded spice both tast and sent doth please
> In fading smoke the force doth incense shewe
> The perisht kernell springeth with encrease
> The lopped tree doth best and soonest growe.
> Gods spice I was and pounding was my due
> In fadinge breath my incense savored best
> Death was the meane my kyrnell to renewe
> By loppinge shott I upp to heavenly rest.
>
> (ll, 1–8)

I would suggest that we now know just where Robert Southwell's images of the 'pounded spice' that gives greater savour, and the 'lopped tree' that springs up afresh, are coming from: a developed iconography that Mary and her supporters incorporated into a variety of different artefacts and media in which emblematic composition played a central role. It is hardly surprising that they outlived her to play their part in the definition

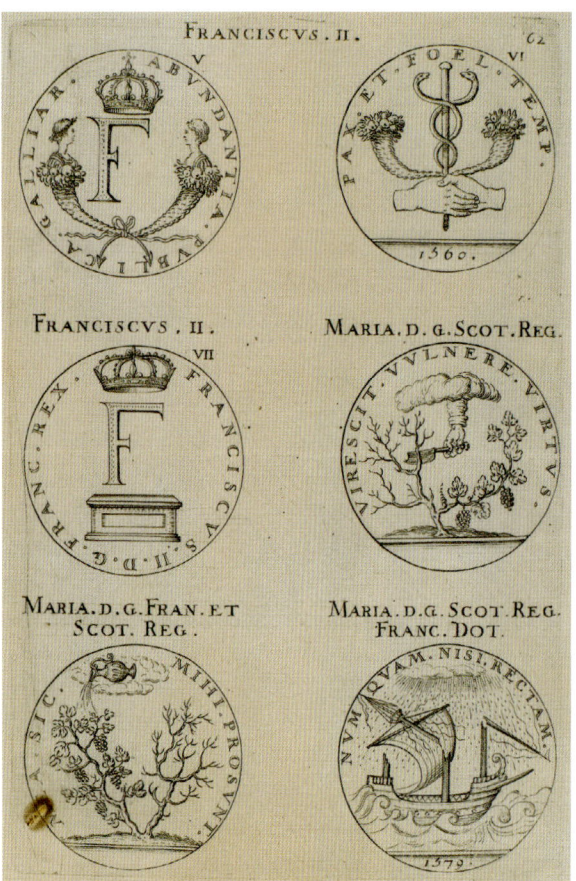

Figure 3.22 Illustrations of medals of François II and Mary (Jacques de Bie, *La France metallique*, 1636, fol. 62).

of her posthumous place in Catholic martyrology, or as Southwell expresses it in his poem:

> Alive a Queene now dead I am a Sainte
> Once M. calld my name nowe Martyr is
> From earthly raigne debarred by restraint
> In liew whereof I raigne in heavenly blisse.
> (ll, 13–16)

It is also not difficult to show where Southwell might have gained the knowledge and understanding of this set of Marian *imprese* that he needed in order to write his elegy on the martyred Queen of Scots, whose execution took place only ten months after he had arrived at the start of his Jesuit mission to England. We have seen how many of these Marian *imprese* were also associated in some way with the Earl and Countess of Arundel, and it was indeed Anne Dacre, wife of Philip Howard, who had asked Southwell in November or December 1586 to become her resident chaplain at Arundel House in The Strand, London, where Southwell spent the first period of his mission in a small secluded room with access to the countess's private apartments. Anne was on her own at this time, Philip Howard having been locked up in the Tower in 1585, which he was not to leave until his death ten years later, but the relationship between the countess and her hidden priest was evidently very close, for we are told that on her own deathbed she suddenly said 'Oh, Blessed Father Southwell', and asked for a priest.[39]

Southwell appears to have written 'Decease, Release' immediately after Mary's execution on 8 February 1587, since a manuscript copy of it among the papers of Anthony Bacon at Lambeth Palace is marked in French, 'Some verses by Mr Southwell on the Scottish Queen, received the month of February, 1586' (i.e. New Style 1587).[40] Bacon was a cousin of the Southwells, resident in France at this time, which is where he must have received and endorsed the document using the Old Style dating. If we can trust this annotation, as we almost certainly can, it means not only that there can be no doubt about 'Decease, Release' being an elegy to Mary Queen of Scots and not, as one or two earlier editors had thought, to some other person,[41] but we also have to conclude that Southwell wrote it within weeks of his appointment as the Countess of Arundel's chaplain and within days of Mary's execution. Clearly, if he was not already familiar with the evolving iconography surrounding Mary Stuart which we have been examining in this chapter before he arrived in England, he must have learned enough about it from the countess during their few hours of conversation in these weeks when he acted as her spiritual director. The knowledge they both shared of the iconography and significance of her personal *imprese* then found its way directly into his poem. The correspondences may extend, I suggest, still further in the poem, which continues:

> My life my griefe my death hath wrought my joye
> My frendes my foyle my foes my Weale procur'd.
> (ll, 17–18)

Although no emblematic *pictura* is suggested in this case, the sentiment in 'My frendes my foyle' is precisely that witnessed in the *Mea sic mihi prosunt* emblem showing the vine being watered with wine. Perhaps Southwell might have seen the medal with this device on its reverse even before he arrived in England; the medals were certainly circulating on the continent where Catholic, if not specifically Jesuit, involvement in their production or circulation is at least a possibility. Clearly the evidence we have seen in this chapter of the way these personal *imprese* were reduplicated in a variety of different artefacts, and the various records of their contemporary circulation and familiarity, defines the context within which, historically, we can begin to understand the significance they would have held both for Mary and for her associates – whether friend or foe. We can also discern their political, moral and religious significance in this context, a context in which their relevance to her actual situation could easily lead to the seemingly innocent designs on her embroidery being interpreted as potentially incriminating emblems.

4

Birds and Beasts

By far the greater number of embroidered panels sewn by Bess of Hardwick and Mary Queen of Scots shows pictures of animals. A total of 120 such panels has survived either on the various Oxburgh Hangings or as detached pieces, mostly preserved at Oxburgh and now in the Victoria and Albert Museum in London. These illustrations of animals, birds, fishes (and a few insects) are all executed on cruciform panels, generally measuring 27–28 cm, with the animal's name written on a scroll but with no further text of any kind. The lack of any moralising inscription, such as is found on the octagonal panels, suggests that these were not intended to function as symbolic pictures or emblems, even though many of the animals they depict came down to the sixteenth century with quite a large amount of potential symbolism from the way their supposed habits and characteristics had traditionally been moralised in fables, in heraldry, in emblems, or in the medieval bestiaries. As noted in Chapter 1, these cruciform panels show particularly clearly how difficult it can be to determine exactly what type of furnishings the panels were originally intended to decorate as quite a few of them have, at one time or another, been cut up and reused. Those that are sewn onto the green velvet of the Oxburgh Hangings all have narrow raised borders, though many of the unmounted panels are square pieces in which the four corners between the arms of the cruciform panel remain uncut and may be filled with further embroidered details such as plant slips, extra animals, or decorative motifs. Evidently when sewn onto hangings these corners, along with any embroidery they may have contained, were cut off to leave only the cruciform panel showing the animal and its label.[1] Occasionally the panel itself was brutally cut in half, and two such half panels with quite different animals have been joined together on the Marian Hanging where the 'She Dolphin' is joined to another unlabelled and as yet unidentified fish. Two half panels showing quite different creatures are joined equally awkwardly on a portion of the Oxburgh Valance, and the unmounted panels from Oxburgh that

Figure 4.1 'An Ape of Turky', unmounted panel from Oxburgh Hall, T33DD. Note how the corner segments of the centre roundel have not been cut off in these unmounted panels but are filled with further embroidered details, whereas on all the mounted panels they are invariably cut off to create a cruciform panel showing only the animal. London, Victoria and Albert Museum.

are now in the Victoria and Albert Museum include 12 similarly cut-up fragmentary pieces.

Animals feature quite commonly in the decorative arts at this period, often copied from the same print sources and pattern books as those used by Mary and Bess. Similar creatures are to be found, for instance, in costume or dress patterns such as the finely stitched blackwork of the Falkland bodice (Victoria and Albert Museum), or the sleeve from a similar jacket decorated with insects, snails, frogs and a spider,[2] or the skirt which Queen Elizabeth wears in the anonymous portrait at Hardwick, covered in birds and sea monsters painted on white satin (illustrated in Figure 4.28 below). Such animals were evidently part of an accepted design vocabulary for the decorative arts at this period, and available for a variety of uses and applications.

It is nevertheless possible to suggest Mary's, and possibly Bess's, motives for selecting at least a few of the creatures which are represented in these embroideries once their source in printed illustrations and pattern books has been established, and it is my aim in this chapter to illustrate those sources and what they suggest about Mary's likely reasons for selecting them. As we shall see, the beasts found in the embroideries include quite a few exotica: strange creatures and monsters which must have appealed precisely because their striking appearance would attract the attention and curiosity of any viewer who caught sight of them on furnishings. Closer to home than such exotica, however, is what we are told about the Scottish habitat of quite a few of these creatures in at least one of the sources used, and I suggest that Mary was drawn to a number of Conrad Gessner's illustrations because of the information contained in his *Historia animalium* about their Scottish connections. And finally, despite what has already been said about the purely decorative and non-symbolic nature of these images, we frequently find the authors who supplied her patterns identifying their received proverbial and emblematic significance in ways which, if she read them, can only have suggested their relevance to Mary's own situation: at least a few of these animals, therefore, may function as what might be called 'implicit emblems'.

Therefore the focus of this chapter is the identification of print sources and patterns for the actual embroideries, while taking the discussion some way beyond conventional source hunting in order to consider Mary's possible motivation for selecting the images she copies. I believe the books she used were not just design sources but also sources of information; indeed Mary can be shown to have read at least some of Conrad Gessner's and Pierre Belon's descriptions of the animals they illustrate since she follows their guidance on colours or plumage, and I suggest that it was often those descriptions that must have aroused her interest and influenced her choices. Obviously such speculation will sometimes be problematical due to uncertainty regarding the unsigned panels for which she was actually responsible.

Historia animalium

The most important by far of the print sources used as patterns for the embroideries of animals are the woodcuts which first appeared in the great *Historia animalium* written in the mid-sixteenth century by the Swiss scholar Conrad Gesner (or, more correctly, Gessner[3]), first printed in Zürich between 1551 and 1587. At least 60 of the surviving embroideries copy animals, birds or fishes from the 1,079 beautifully executed woodcuts

Figure 4.2 Tobias Stimmer, *Portrait of Conrad Gessner*, 1564. Schaffhausen, Switzerland, Museum zu Allerheiligen.

which illustrate this monumental work of more than 3,000 folio pages, published in five successive volumes, on quadrupeds (two volumes), birds, fishes and serpents respectively, between these dates. Although the Oxburgh embroideries represent a very early use of Gessner's woodcuts in the decorative arts, this was by no means the last time these woodcuts were used. For example, more than a dozen of Gessner's animals inhabit the Garden of Eden as depicted in the undated 'Adam and Eve' needlework picture in the Metropolitan Museum, New York, Untermeyer Collection.[4] Some time between 1620 and 1626, Gessner's animals supplied the patterns for a number of the stained glass panels that Sir Francis Bacon commissioned for the windows of his gallery at Gorhambury.[5] In Scotland, Gessner's illustrations supplied the patterns for many of the animals in the painted long gallery of 1620 at Earlshall near Leuchars in Fife,[6] and the Devonshire plasterer John Abbott was still copying these same woodcuts of animals into his pattern book in England as late as the 1660s.[7] In view of their importance as a design source, not only for these embroideries but also for the longer history of the decorative arts in Britain, it might therefore be interesting to learn more about Conrad Gessner and his work.

Born in 1516 to a family which had migrated to Switzerland from southern Germany, Conrad's father became a citizen of Zürich where he set up in business as a furrier, a trade that must have familiarised the young Gessner with the appearance of some of those animals he was later to describe in his *Historia animalium*. Indeed he adds an illustration of a jenet skin to his description of this valuable fur-bearing animal in his *Historia*, an illustration that is copied in the detached panel in the Victoria and Albert Museum with the label 'A Gene Skyn'.

Direct observation of the various species is closely allied in Gessner's writing, however, to an exhaustive knowledge of the literature of his subject, knowledge for which the ground was also being prepared by his early mastery, despite his family's impoverished circumstances, of the classical languages: he was fluent in Latin and Greek by the age of 15 and although he struggled throughout his life to earn a living either as a tutor at his former school, the Carolinum in Zürich, or from his writings, he quickly earned an international reputation for his scholarly publications, which include a revised Greek–Latin dictionary, editions of such classical writers as Marcus Aurelius, Martial and Aelianus, and in 1545 his magnum opus, the *Bibliotheca universalis*, a work which has been described as 'a huge bibliography of scholarly books in the three "classical" languages Greek, Latin, and Hebrew, the first of its kind and indeed in a sense the cornerstone for all subsequent bibliographical work'.[8] This comprehensive directory of classical and neo-classical writing spread his fame throughout Europe, earning him an enduring reputation as the father of bibliography.

These philological and humanist preoccupations might seem somewhat remote from the study of animals, which is what concerns us here, however it is important to recognise that there are vital continuities

Figure 4.3 'A Gene Skyn', unmounted panel from Oxburgh Hall, T33FF. London, Victoria and Albert Museum.

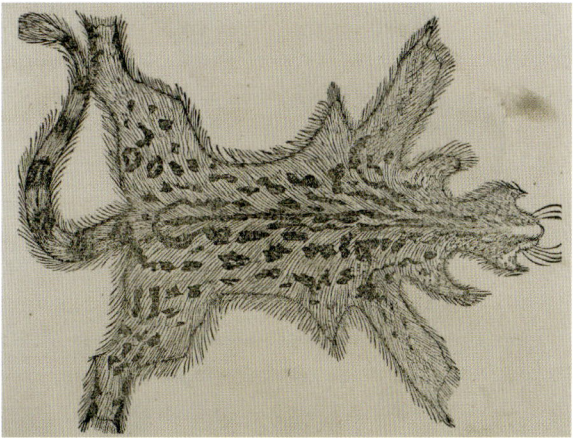

Figure 4.4 Skin of the jenet, woodcut (Conrad Gessner, *Historia animalium*, I, 1551, p. 1102).

that will help us to understand some of the things that are going on in these embroideries. Gessner stands as a great polymath or *doctor universalis*, a good example of that early modern assumption of the continuity of all knowledge which can be so difficult for modern readers to grasp. Gessner's writings on natural history are recognised as important documents in the history of science, but they are equally informed by his humanist, classical and philological interests; indeed the continuities between his philological and his 'scientific' writings are greater than any of the distinctions which more modern taxonomies of learning might assume, largely because Gessner, like most of his contemporaries, believed that advance in any science has to rest on an exhaustive knowledge of the existing literature of its subject, which necessarily includes the writings of the ancient authorities. That is why so much of the *Historia animalium* (and the *Historia* and *Catalogus plantarum* on which he was still working at the end of his life in 1565) consists of a compilation of passages from ancient and modern writers. Gessner's examination of actual specimens is as much motivated by a concern to fix the meaning of names which classical writers assign to various animals as it is by any sense of the need to advance empirical science for its own sake: the impulse is as much philological as scientific. The embroideries typically include the animals' names on the labels, and it will become apparent later how some of these labels reflect Gessner's fuss over names: the naming of beasts is a serious matter.

Gessner's move towards what we think of as 'scientific' subjects began with two medical treatises based on the second-century AD writings of Galen, and he later became a practising physician, supplementing his meagre income by treating patients, particularly during recurrent outbreaks of the plague in Zürich (eventually writing a book on the treatment of plague victims). He first encountered the classical writings of Aelianus on animals during his 1545 visit to Augsburg, at the invitation of Fuggers, its great merchant banker, where he discovered a manuscript on which he wrote a commentary that has become the basis of all subsequent work on this second-century AD Latin author. Finally, his interest in botany led to a book on the rare plants to be found in the Swiss mountains containing one of the earliest descriptions of mountain scenery on a walk up Mount Pilatus near Lucerne to look for specimens, a description which has been claimed to mark 'the very beginnings of Alpinism and the appreciation of nature for its own sake'.[9] It might also remind us that, for all his literary and philological approach to science, he was not averse to doing a bit of what we would call fieldwork.

Scotland in Gessner: monkfish and monsters

Writing a natural history of animals involved Gessner in the kind of scholarly networking through extensive correspondence with fellow enthusiasts, which is so characteristic of international neo-Latin learning at this period. His correspondents included such people as Pierre Belon, whose books on birds and fishes, published in the 1550s, were illustrated with woodcuts very similar to some of Gessner's own. Mary or Bess certainly had access to Belon's books, since several of the creatures in the embroideries that are not copied from Gessner have been shown to copy Belon's woodcuts.[10] Margaret Swain (1973), for instance, illustrates both the dolphin and the 'Sea Moonke' embroideries with woodcuts from Belon's *La nature et diversité des poissons* (1555), and there are several more panels that can now be shown to go back to Belon.[11] An examination of the possible sources for the rather striking 'Sea Moonke' will, indeed, serve to illustrate some of the consequences of this scholarly networking for our understanding of what is going on in these embroideries.

The 'Sea Moonke' on the Marian Hanging copies the creature which Gessner calls a 'Water Monk' and Belon calls 'A sea monster with the face of a monk': it shows an upright humanoid creature with finny arms and legs and a loose cowl covering its torso through which protrudes a tonsured human head. Gessner's woodcut of the creature is so close to Belon's as to leave little doubt that one of these illustrations must have copied the other, and it might be difficult to say categorically which of these the embroidery copied. There are differences, however, in the angle of the face and in the feathering of the fins that leave little doubt, as Margaret Swain notes, that it was Belon's illustration rather than Gessner's that supplied the embroidery pattern. Swain also notes that Belon describes various sightings of this creature, including an account of a female monkfish that was adopted as a pet by the women of Edam in Holland. Such tales would doubtless have appealed to our embroiderers, but what Gessner says about this creature is even more interesting, and although the needlework panel copies Belon's

Figure 4.5 'Sea Moonke' on the Marian Hanging, panel 20, Oxburgh Hall, Norfolk.

illustration and not Gessner's, I believe there are good grounds for supposing that Mary or Bess also knew Gessner's description of this creature when executing the embroidery.

Turning to Gessner's discussion of this strange creature, one of the things we notice is that he identifies a Scottish source for his knowledge of it, a source which demands our attention since, as we shall see, it is cited in connection with several of the other animals which Mary chose to include in these embroideries. According to Gessner, such creatures have been recorded within living memory both in Norwegian waters and in the Firth of Forth, with human faces and dressed up in what looks like the cowl of a monk. Wherever such fish are seen, Gessner says, they are immediately given the name 'Monk', though they are also called 'Bassinates' or in German *Wassermann* [Waterman] or *Wassermünch* [Watermonk].[12] Gessner's source for this Scottish information is given as: 'Hector Boëthius in Descriptione regni Scotiae' (Hector Boece in his description of the kingdom of Scotland). This is the learned author, sometime Professor of Philosophy in Paris and first Principal of King's College, Aberdeen, whose *Scotorum historia* was printed in Edinburgh in 1527. Boece's history of Scotland would certainly have been known to Mary, and it begins with a 'Description of the Kingdom of

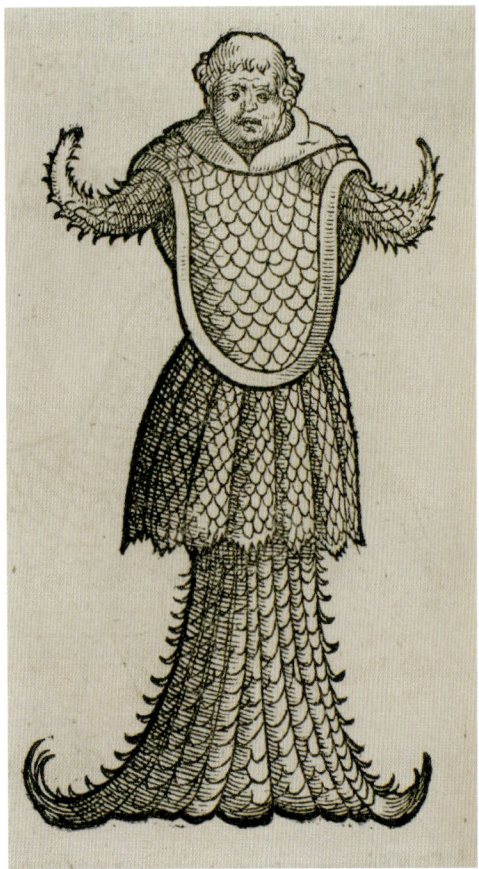

Figure 4.6 Monkfish, or genus of sea monster having a human face and monk's cowl sometimes seen in the Forth estuary, according to Conrad Gessner (*Historia animalium*, IV, 1560, p. 174).

Figure 4.7 Monkfish, woodcut (Pierre Belon, *La nature et diversite des poissons*, 1555, p. 33).

Scotland' (1527, fols iii–xvii), to which Gessner is here referring. Boece's opening account of the geography of Scotland includes information about its wildlife, which is evidently why it attracted Gessner's attention not only here but at various other places in his *Historia animalium*. Despite Gessner's reference, Boece's account of the monkfish is found not in this opening '*Descriptio*', but much later in his actual history where he describes the strange signs that marked the defeat of King Constantine at the hands of the Danes, notably the appearance of a multitude of peculiar fish in the Firth of Forth having the shape and figure of a man and, in John Bellenden's sixteenth-century translation, 'callit, be the pepil, Bassinatis. This fische hes blak skinnes hingand on thair bodyis with quhilk, sum time, that covir thair heid and thair cragis, evin to thair schulderis. Quhen this fische fletis in our seyes, thay signify gret unfortuniteis to mortall pepill.'[13]

This account of the monkfish or 'Bassinatis' is included in the section of Gessner's book devoted to what he calls 'Certain whale-like monsters, having a human appearance or that of terrestrial creatures' (p. 173). This section is likely to have attracted the embroiderers' attention not only because it shows some particularly striking and extraordinary creatures, but also because it contains further Scottish references to Hector Boece's 'Description of Scotland'. When Gessner came, in his 1558 *Pandectarum*, to write his *index locorum* to the subjects dealt with in his *Historia animalium*, he asked studious readers, wherever they might live, to send him further pictures of animals from remote places (*ex remotis regionibus*, p. 221), and it must have been Scotland's status as just such a remote region that had already drawn him to Boece's descriptions of some of the zoological exotica to be found there. Mary's attention would have been attracted to this section of his

Figure 4.8 'A Lion of the Sea' on the Oxburgh Valance, panel 13. Oxburgh Hall, Norfolk.

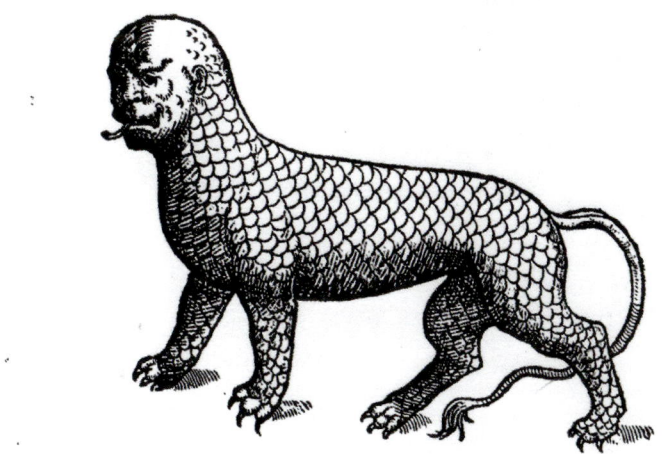

Figure 4.9 Sea lion, woodcut, first of the sequence of 'sea monsters having some sort of human appearance' (Conrad Gessner, *Icones animalium*, 1560, p. 173).

book by these very references; moreover much of the information he included about Scottish animals was supplied, as we shall see, by Scottish informants who had responded to a similar request, and some of these informants were certainly known to Mary.

The embroidered panel showing 'A Lion of the Sea' on the Oxburgh Valance is certainly copied from this section; shown as a feline quadruped covered in scales, Gessner describes it as being as big as a lion with four legs ending in feet divided into toes, a long

Figure 4.10 'Sea Hors', part of a detached, damaged panel from Oxburgh Hall. London, Victoria and Albert Museum.

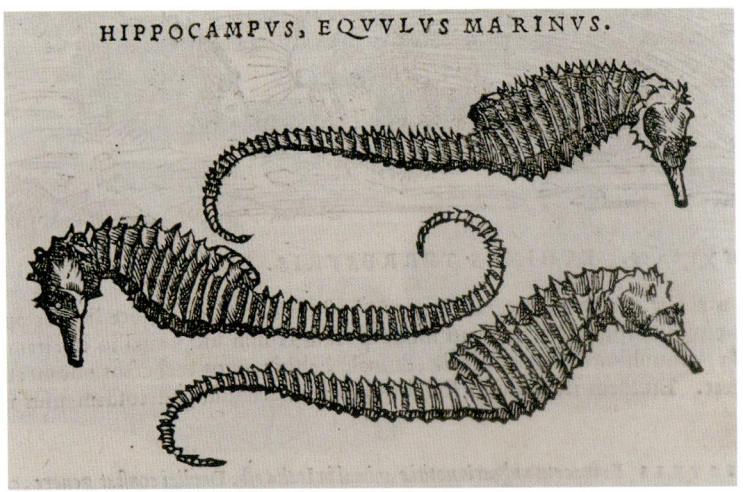

Figure 4.11 Sea horse, woodcut (Pietro Andrea Mattioli, *Commentarii in Dioscoridis*, 1558, p. 176).

tail, and scaly all over. Just as Mary's 'Sea Moonke' is not what we now call a monkfish, so her 'Lion of the Sea' is not what we would call a sea lion; both look more like marine parodies of the land animals which their names echo, reflecting that traditional assumption that came down through the Middle Ages that everything on land had its counterpart in the sea, which thus mirrored God's terrestrial creation in a *mundus alter et idem*. Such reflections are echoed in the embroideries that carry the labels 'A Rhinocerote of the Sea' (copying Gessner's 'Rhinocerotus cetus', *Historia*, p. 248) or 'A Sea Hors', which shows a hybrid creature with the front half of a horse joined to a serpentine fish tail.[14]

Such hybrids were already beginning to excite some scepticism at this period, and Gessner himself cites a correspondent who doubts that a creature such as the 'Lion of the Sea' could possibly swim. However he also cites an informant who told him that one was actually caught offshore in thirteenth-century Italy, when it was offered as a curiosity to the Pope, and it is this report of an actual specimen that leads him to again quote his Scottish source, for Hector Boece, he tells us, describes a very similar lion-shaped sea monster in his 'Description of Scotland', which Sir Duncan Campbell found on a lake called 'Garloil' in Argyll.[15] Gessner's citation of such witnesses is largely determined by his interest in establishing the written records for such exotic species, whereas Boece's inclusion of them is motivated by a more credulous interest in omens and wonders. As Bellenden (1821) translates, 'Sundry prudent men belevit gret trubill to follow in Scotland, be appering of this beist; for scho was sene afore, and ay trubil following thairefter'.[16] It seems hardly likely that in using several of Gessner's illustrations from this section as patterns, Mary would fail to notice the repeated references to Scotland or the citation of a well-known history of Scotland. Moreover, although neither panel is signed, it seems unlikely that Bess would not have mentioned to her companion such references to Scotland in any sources she was copying: either woman's use of these sea monsters in her embroidery designs can hardly have been unaffected by their Scottish associations.

Boece's Scottish beasts include birds and animals as well as fishes, and if Mary was alert to the Scottish provenance of some of these, then that may well have been what drew her attention to Gessner's illustration of the 'Solen Goose', which is copied in the Marian Hanging. Gessner describes this species as 'Goose found on the Bass Rock, or Scottish Goose, a sea bird; in Scots a Solend Goose; in German it can be called *Solendganz* or Scottish goose.'[17] He acknowledges a Scottish informant, Henry Sinclair, as the source of his picture, and the bird is what we now know as a gannet. 'Solan' is the Scots form of *sulan*, the Icelandic name for a gannet, but Gessner's Latin name, *Anser Bassanus*, reflects the fact that one of its most familiar nesting places is the Bass Rock in the Firth of Forth, indeed 'bassanus' means 'from Bass Rock'. If this is, as I believe, Gessner's own formulation, then it would be a good example of his readiness, which Hans Wellisch (1975) notes, 'to invent suitable names for animals in languages that had no names for them'.[18] Gessner would certainly have known of Boece's *Descriptio* of the Bass Rock and its geese that arrive in spring to build their nests: the keepers of the castle on the rock, says Boece, take not only young birds for food, from which they derive 'great profit', but also fish from the very mouths of the parents and sticks from their nests for use as firewood.[19] Descriptions of the gannet right down to the present day seldom fail to mention the Bass Rock as one of its principal nesting sites, which would of course have been familiar to Mary during her Edinburgh years. Indeed when Linnaeus came, 200 years later, to determine a more scientific basis for the classification of genera and species – the Linnaean taxonomy that we still accept – he decided to call the gannet *Sula bassanus*, and this remains its 'official' zoological name, whose Scottish origins we can now account for in a circle of correspondence which was, as already noted, very close to the origins of some of these embroideries. It must surely have been Gessner's comment on the various names of this bird: 'Scotice vulgo a Solendguse' [in the Scots tongue a Solen goose] that supplied Mary's label on her embroidery of the 'Solen Goose'.

Birds of America

If it was Scotland's remoteness from those parts of the world familiar to ancient writers that raised expectations that it would be home to some rather exotic creatures, for which new Latin names would have to be invented, then much the same was true of the New World. In 1555, Frenchman André Thevet joined the colonial expedition led by Nicolas de Villegagnon to Brazil. On his return he published an account of his travels under the title *Les singularitez de la France antarctique* (1558), with descriptions of the flora, fauna and the habits of the native peoples. It should not surprise us to discover that Mary took an interest in this voyage and its discoveries, for it was Nicolas de Villegagnon who had commanded the French ships which sailed to Scotland in 1548 to bring the five-year-old queen from Dunbarton to France. Since undertaking this important Scottish voyage, Villegagnon had been offered few duties by Henri II, perhaps because he was a Protestant: though granted the title 'Admiral of Britanny' he was only employed in minor offices at court. However, just three years later, in 1561, it would be Villegagnon who would again ferry Mary back to Scotland. The 16-year-old Mary would naturally have taken an interest

Figure 4.12 'Solen Goose' or gannet, Marian Hanging, panel 1. Oxburgh Hall, Norfolk.

Figure 4.13 'Bass-rock or Scottish Goose', Gessner's name for the gannet (*Historia animalium*, III, 1555, p. 158).

in Thevet's account of this expedition to Brazil, led by the very sea captain who had brought her to France, and we happen to know that three Scots who had sailed to France with Mary seven years earlier also joined the Brazilian expedition as bodyguards to the admiral. Mary must have owned, or had access to, a copy of Thevet's account of this expedition since four of her embroideries can be shown to copy the woodcut illustrations of exotic creatures that appeared in his book.

Margaret Swain suggests that the panel on the Marian Hanging labelled 'A Byrd of America' copies Gessner's picture of a toucan from his *Icones animalium* (1560), and she illustrates both.[20] However Gessner tells us in his commentary that he based his own illustration on the picture that had already appeared in Thevet. A glance at Thevet's picture is enough to confirm that Mary's embroidery copies Thevet's woodcut, with its toucan standing on a fallen tree branch, rather than Gessner's version of this, which lacks the branch. Gessner also says something interesting in his commentary about his other sources of information, that he obtained the beak of one of these birds from a certain Io[vanni] Ferrerius, 'a man of great erudition from Piedmont'. Ferrerio was an Italian (Piedmontese) immigrant in Scotland who had spent time at the court of James V and had taught the monks of Kinloss Abbey, of which he wrote a history. For some years he had been corresponding with Gessner in Geneva, using his Scottish contacts to put the great Swiss scientist in touch with informants who could send him details and, hopefully, specimens of the native fauna of Scotland, precisely such creatures as those which evidently attracted Mary's attention when selecting her subjects for embroidery. Indeed at the very time that Mary was executing these embroideries, Ferrerio was himself working on an expanded second edition of Boece's history of Scotland, taking it down to the reign of James III. Although not published until 1574, i.e. after Gessner's death, it may well have been Ferrerio who, in the course of this scholarly networking, first drew Gessner's attention to Boece's description of the Scottish animals.

Although Mary copied Thevet's illustration, and not Gessner's, for her 'Byrd of America' on the Marian Hanging, I suggest that it is more than likely that she also read Gessner's commentary in his *Icones animalium*, the book that she drew on for by far the greater number of her other animal embroideries. She almost certainly knew of Ferrerio by the time she created this embroidery and, as will become clear, she herself owned the beak of a toucan, possibly the very one sent to Gessner

Figure 4.14 'Byrd of America' or toucan, Marian Hanging, panel 6. Oxburgh Hall, Norfolk.

Figure 4.15 Toucan, woodcut (André Thevet, *Les singularitez de la France antarctique*, 1558, p. 91).

Figure 4.16 Toucan, or *Pica Bressillica*, woodcut (Conrad Gessner, *Icones animalium*, 1560, p. 130).

by Ferrerio. No wonder she was interested in birds of America – they turn out to have not only strong French, but also Scottish connections.

Mary sewed another embroidery with the same label, copied from one of Thevet's woodcuts. The 'Byrde of America' on the Cavendish Hanging is no toucan but copies an unnamed species that, according to Thevet, lives in a tree called the '*Peno absou*'. The bird has a large yellow crest, he tells us, and a black tail with the remainder of its plumage mixing both colours, which is exactly what Mary shows us on her embroidery, thus confirming that in working these panels she did not merely copy the printed pattern but also read the commentary. The English edition of Thevet, printed in London in 1568, translates Thevet's description of this bird:

Figure 4.17 'A Byrde of America', Cavendish Hanging, panel 15. Oxburgh Hall, Norfolk.

Figure 4.18 Unnamed fruit-eating and large-crested bird from Brazil, woodcut (André Thevet, *Les singularitez de la France antarctique*, 1558, p. 116).

Figure 4.19 'A Pye of Persia', Shrewsbury Hanging, panel 3. Oxburgh Hall, Norfolk.

Figure 4.20 Strange Brazilian bird called 'Pa, en Persien', woodcut (André Thevet, *Les singularitez de la France antarctique*, 1558, p. 45).

In this tree frequenteth a byrde, having a great bushe of feathers on his head as yealowe as fyne golde, the tail blacke, and the rest of his feathers yealowe and blacke, with some strikes of divers other colurs, redde about the chappes, between the byll and the eyes lyke scarlatte, and she keepeth this tree only for hir foode, whyche is littell wormes that she fyndeth in the sayde tree.[21]

We can recognise the traces of this description in the large yellow crest, the black tail, and the black and yellow body, of the bird in the embroidery.

The third American bird is on the Shrewsbury Hanging, labelled 'A Pye of Persia', showing us a parrot-like bird, again perched on a fallen log, but this time with a snake or worm in its beak and another on the log beneath its claw. In view of the name, it is hardly surprising that no one has hitherto sourced this image to Thevet's book about America, but once again the label on the embroidery can be shown to reflect some of those difficulties of nomenclature which pre-Linnaean natural history was having at this time, for Thevet describes this as a bird with hairy feet and legs that feeds on snakes, just as we see it doing in his woodcut and in Mary's embroidery. The bird, he explains, is called 'pa' in the native tongue, and 'en Persien, pié ou jambe' [foot or leg in Persian]. The comment is certainly puzzling, and the reference to Persian utterly confusing, most likely based on a bit of inventive comparative philology on Thevet's part, taking the native name as an echo of the French word for 'foot' (*pied*) and as referring to the bird's hairy legs. Mary, however, seems to have confounded this confusion by reading 'pié' as the unaccented 'pie', which means magpie in French. Hence this third bird of America appears in her embroidery as a Persian magpie, her 'Pye of Persia'. Once again, however, she copies Thevet's woodcut and follows his description of its plumage – silver with black on its head, and huge ear-like flaps hanging down to its neck – so closely as to leave no doubt as to the provenance or identity of this strangely named species.

Whatever their names, these are all real species of birds whose modern botanical identities we could surely discover if necessary. With the last of these American species, however, we encounter one of those creatures whose existence has never been verified. The bed valance preserved at Oxburgh includes a four-legged mammal carrying its young on its back whose label is now illegible, but which can now be shown to copy Thevet's woodcut of the animal known as a su. This fierce beast, according to Thevet, is hunted for its skin and it flees from its pursuers carrying its young on its back. Thevet's description supplied later writers, including Gessner, with all that has ever been known about this most fabulous of beasts. Although Gessner copies Thevet's picture for his discussion of the su in a supplementary note to his *Historia animalium*, the embroidery has the same orientation as Thevet's, which it almost certainly copies, whereas Gessner's image is reversed.

Mary did not find all her American creatures in Thevet, however, for the Cavendish Hanging shows a creature labelled 'A Tatou' which is evidently an armadillo. There is no armadillo illustrated in Thevet, but according to Gessner it was found by travellers in New Guinea and the New World; unknown to ancient writers (*cuius mentio nulla apud veteres*) it was called by the natives 'tatus' or 'tatu'. Gessner explains that he was sent the skin and tail of one of these by a pharmacist in Germany, and his picture is based on this specimen.

The circulation of such specimens of exotic beasts is confirmed by what Pierre Belon informs us about the beak of a toucan which he illustrates at the end of Book Three of his *Histoire de la nature des oyseaux* (1555) under the heading, 'Du bec d'un oyseau des terres neufves, incognu aux anciens' (p. 148). Travellers to new lands, says Belon, often bring back anything they can sell to merchants even though it may have no practical use; thus the beak of a strange bird, as big as a child's arm but as light and transparent as parchment, can now be seen in various people's cabinets of curiosities, 'les cabinets des hommes curieux de choses nouvelles'. Since all he has seen of this bird is its beak Belon illustrates only this, whereas both Thevet and Gessner show the whole toucan. As mentioned above, according to Gessner he was sent his toucan beak 'by the very learned man, Ferrerius of Piedmont'. Thevet was certainly one of the travellers who brought such specimens back from Brazil – indeed he presented them to King Henri II, for he mentions a headdress of bright yellow toucan feathers and also 'three beaks of these toucans' which were given to him by the natives with many other skins and feathers of different birds. He claims that the toucan's bright yellow breast feathers are used by the natives to decorate their swords, robes and headdress, and he states he presented such a headdress to the late King Henri II 'comme chose rare et singuliere, digne d'estre admirée, veu la gentilesse de l'oeuvre'. A fine yellow cape

Figure 4.21 This illegible label would undoubtedly have identified this animal on the Oxburgh Valance as the fabulous creature allegedly discovered in Brazil and known as a su. Oxburgh Hall, Norfolk.

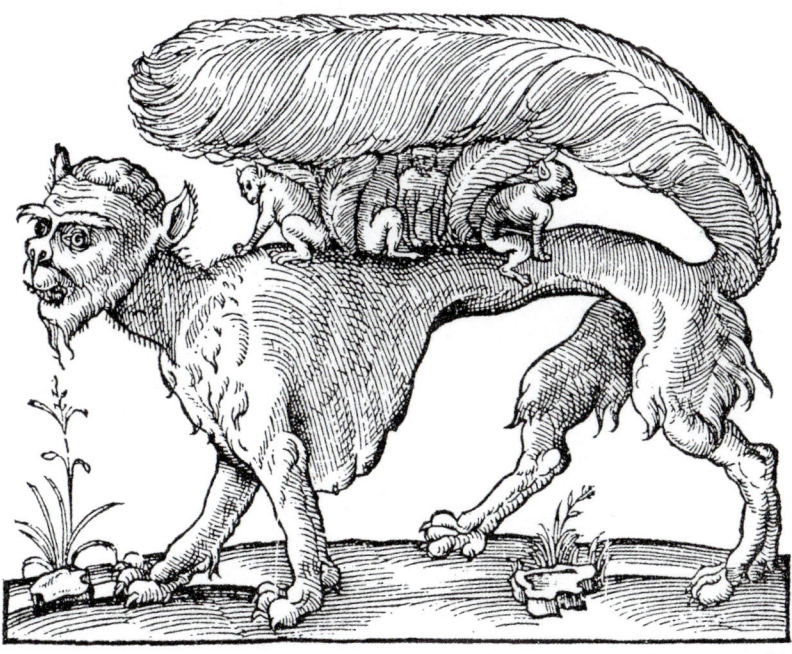

Figure 4.22 A Brazilian beast known as a su that carries its young away on its back when hunted by natives for its skin, woodcut (André Thevet, *Les singularitez de la France antarctique*, 1558, p. 109).

Figure 4.23 'A Tatou' or armadillo, Cavendish Hanging, panel 12. Oxburgh Hall, Norfolk.

Figure 4.24 'Tatus', woodcut (Conrad Gessner, *Icones animalium*, 1560, p. 103).

made wholly of such feathers survives in the Musée de l'Homme, Paris and has been identified from accession records as having indeed been one of these very specimens brought back to France by Thevet.[22]

If we are right about Mary's teenage fascination with the Villegagnon expedition to Brazil, then it seems most likely that she would have seen this same cape. Moreover, in 1578 an inventory of the possessions that Mary had left behind in Edinburgh when she fled into English exile ten years before, includes 'The beik of a foule of India or Brasile' together with 'Ane paper of fedderis of sindrie sortis'.[23] These are among a number of curiosities owned by Mary of the type described by Belon: they include a bezoar stone and a unicorn's horn.

Where might Mary have obtained this toucan beak and feathers, if not from the *singularitez* which Thevet had brought back to Paris and presented to her father-in-law three years before she left France? Mary may well have asked Henri II whether she could have one of the toucan beaks and a few of the feathers that had been brought back as curious rarities from Brazil by Admiral Villegagnon, and if that was indeed the case, then we should be entitled to conclude that, in sewing her 'Byrd of America' on the Marian Hanging, she was copying the picture of a bird illustrated by Thevet of which she herself owned the actual remains. Clearly by the time she came to sew her embroideries she must have owned copies of both Thevet's and Gessner's books in which these two 'Birds of America' are described or illustrated, but in the case of the toucan she would also have been representing in her embroidery something which had particular personal associations. If this hypothesis is correct, then Mary's embroidery could now be described as illustrating an object of which she not only knew the provenance, but had actually seen and touched.

Gessner's description of the toucan would also have informed her that he had obtained his toucan beak from an Italian Catholic, Giovanni Ferrerio, a person of whom she almost certainly would have heard. Ferrerio spent 13 years in Scotland, having been recruited by Robert Reid, Bishop of Orkney and Abbot of Kinloss, to establish a humanist academy at Kinloss, of which Ferrerio later wrote the history. On his arrival in Scotland he had spent four years at the Scottish court, where he wrote a book of advice on the foolishness of astrology for Mary's father, James V. In 1549 Ferrerio sought Reid's assistance in furnishing Gessner with information about animals, and in 1553 he approached Henry Sinclair, Dean of Glasgow, for help in what Ferrerio calls Gessner's 'herculean labour' (*herculeum vere laborem*) of writing the *Historia animalium*.[24] Gessner was particularly keen for local information on a breed of wild white Caledonian cattle and in *Historia animalium* he not only describes these but acknowledges his informant as 'a man of noble birth and more noble knowledge of letters, Henry Sinclair, dean of the metropolitan church of Glasgow in Scotland, through the most learned Giovanni Ferrerio of Piedmont'.[25] As John Durkan (1980) notes, Gessner's account of these white Scottish cattle also cites Hector Boece's description of Scotland to the effect that they were now only found at Cumbernauld, and his Scottish materials include descriptions of such Scottish species as blackcock, moorcock and capercaille.[26] It was Sinclair, as we have seen, who is also acknowledged by Gessner as his source for the picture of the gannet which Mary copied for her 'Solen Goose' on the Marian Hanging. In 1555, Ferrerio wrote to Reid that he was receiving almost daily reminders from Gessner about the pictures of rare species of fish that Reid had promised to supply Gessner with almost two years earlier, but which had failed to materialise.[27] Such species doubtless included some of those that Gessner had read about in the opening 'Description of Scotland' that prefaces Boece's *Scotorum historia*.

Gessner in Scotland

Although no copy of *Historia animalium* is recorded as belonging either to Mary or to Bess of Hardwick, a copy of the first volume (*De quadrupedibus viviparis*, 1551) that belonged to John Leslie, Bishop of Ross, has survived and is now in the library of St Andrews University.[28] Leslie was, of course, in regular contact with Mary during her years of exile and must have been familiar with her embroideries, since it was he who described the cushion cover with the *Virescit vulnere virtus* emblem cited in evidence at the trial of the Duke of Norfolk. The possibility that this was the actual copy used as their pattern book for these embroideries by Mary and Bess suggests its potential importance. The copy reached St Andrews in the late seventeenth century along with another book which, like this, carries both the *ex libris* inscription of John Leslie and also that of William Guild, Principal of Aberdeen University 1586–1657. Leslie's copy has numerous marginal notes in an early unidentified hand, which are mostly concerned to gloss Gessner's Latin name for a species with its Scots equivalent. Thus beside Gessner's *De Catus* header (p. 344) we find 'Catus vel felis. Ane catt', and *De Dama* (p. 334) is glossed 'Ane fallowe Deere. In Scotland', *De Ibice* is 'Ibex. non constat in Scotice' [Ibex does not exist in Scots], while *De Uro* (p. 157) carries the despairing note 'Urus I will nevir find the Scottish name of it'. It is just possible that these notes represent an attempt by Leslie, or some other helper, to provide Mary with the Scottish names for various animals that she wished to label in her embroideries, but if so it has to be said that the particular names seldom correspond to those actually found on the embroideries. Thus Bess labels her copy of Gessner's ibex '[Stei]nbock', borrow-

Figure 4.25 'A Stork of the Montaynes', Shrewsbury Hanging, panel 1. Oxburgh Hall, Norfolk.

Figure 4.26 Oripelargus or mountain stork, woodcut (Conrad Gessner, *Icones animalium*, 1560, p. 5).

ing Gessner's German name, and similarly Leslie's glossator calls Gessner's Lynx 'ane beast lyk ane wolff having spottes' whereas Mary has no hesitation in calling it by its variant English name of 'once', i.e. ounce. Although we should, therefore, dismiss the possibility that this was the actual copy used by Mary or Bess for their embroidery patterns, the survival of such a copy suggests how familiar those who moved in Mary's circle at this period would have been with Gessner's work.[29] Moreover the interest taken in the Scottish names (and habitats) of many of Gessner's animals by an early reader as evidenced by these margin notes is echoed by the interest which, as already noted, Mary seems to have taken in the Scottish connections and names of many of these creatures.

It can easily be shown that both Mary and Bess often took the sometimes curious names they included on the embroidery labels from Gessner's nomenclature; indeed sometimes the form of the name enables us to identify which source was used, as with the panel from the Shrewsbury Hanging which names 'A Stork of the Montaynes'. Gessner's name for this is Percnopterus, but it is only the *Icones avium* (1560, p. 5) that elaborates on this by informing the reader that it is also called 'Oripelargus, id est Ciconia montana' [Oripelargus, that is Mountain Stork]. The embroidery obviously took the hint for its label from this comment, which means that the *Icones avium* and not the longer *Historia*, which has the same illustration, must have been the source.

As for the *Icones*, Gessner, or his publisher Froschauer, seems to have realised early on that there was a wider market for the fascinating woodcut illustrations and so, even before the main edition was complete, he began to produce slimmed down editions containing just the illustrations with much briefer notes on each, identifying the species in different languages and recording a few of its characteristics. These abridged editions appealed to a growing market for the pictures, a market which may well have been influenced by the demand for pattern books in the applied arts, and they can be recognised by Froschauer's use of the word *Icones* in their titles. It would be interesting to know whether Mary or Bess used the complete and unabridged volumes, comprising more than 3,000 pages, which I shall refer to as *Historia animalium*, or whether they used the less informative but much handier *Icones*. Because of their more modest price, the abridged volumes might possibly have been owned by a craftsman *brodeur* or *maître tapissier*. Of these abridgements, the *Icones animalium quadrupedum viviparorum et oviparorum* first appeared in 1553, with a dedication to Henry Grey, Earl of Suffolk, and was reissued in 1560 with further illustrations. *Icones avium omnium*, which appeared in 1555 and, again, in 1560, includes all the birds the embroideries copy, and finally *Icones animalium aquatilium*, on fishes, appeared also in 1560. The 1560 second edition of the *Icones* on mammals was dedicated to Queen Elizabeth of England, most likely because the Earl of Suffolk, dedicatee of the 1553 edition, had died in 1545. There were further Latin editions from other publishers, and also German translations, before the end of the century. The English translation by Edward Topsell, whose *Historie of Foure-Footed Beastes* appeared in London in 1607, was illustrated with the same woodcuts used by Gessner, but though Topsell's version, which ran to a second edition in 1658, was an important resource for decorative artists in seventeenth-century Britain, its value for the understanding of the Marian embroideries is largely confined to providing a crib for those of us needing help with Gessner's Latin.

It is not known who designed or executed these woodcut illustrations, which are unsigned. Clearly they represent a major investment of time and money over many years of which some record ought to survive in Zürich archives. We do know, however, that Gessner was in the habit of making drawings of plants and other specimens that interested him, and he tells us from time to time in the *Historia* that he supervised the content of the illustrations and sometimes, as with the toucan beak, supplied specimens to be copied. The author portrait printed in *Historia*, Book III, and in *Icones avium* is signed with the initials of Jos Murer, who has been identified as 'one of the main illustrators of the *Historia animalium*', and a woodcut portrait of Gessner printed in Zürich in 1564 has been shown to copy a drawing by Johannes Thomann, who was a relative of Gessner's and who may also have engraved the *Historia* woodcuts.[30]

Sea monsters

The Marian Hanging includes several strangely named but evidently monstrous types of fish, mostly copied from illustrations which, according to Gessner, are based on various monsters depicted in the great history of Scandinavia written by Olaus Magnus, the Bishop of Uppsala. The *Historia de gentibus septentrionalibus* was first published in 1555 in Rome, where it attracted readers' attention to the fascinating, if outlandish, geography and customs of the northern nations of Europe. It is much less of a history, despite its title, than a description of the exploits, way of life and customs of the northern peoples, and successive books in the latter part are devoted to a description of the domestic and wild animals of the region, its birds, fishes and, in the penultimate chapter, its marine monsters: 'De Piscibus Monstrosis' as the title of Book XXI describes them. Olaus's history is illustrated throughout with vigorous if rather crudely executed woodcuts, of which those showing what he calls the 'horrible monsters on the shores of Norway' evidently excited the curiosity not only of Conrad Gessner, but also of other readers at this period. Gessner demonstrably takes Olaus's illustrations as his pattern for nearly all of the woodcuts which the Marian embroideries of sea monsters can be shown to copy, and in 1550 Olaus's monsters also found their way into another great topographical work, Sebastian Munster's *Cosmographiae universalis*, published in Basel, whose copiously illustrated description of the diverse nations, inhabitants, customs and creatures of the known world includes one illustration, filling two whole pages of a single opening, showing the 'Land and sea monsters which are to be found in the northern regions'.[31]

Mary's embroideries are not the only place where these monsters are depicted; the Hardwick portrait of Queen Elizabeth, which shows her dressed in a white satin petticoat painted with plants, birds and sea monsters, must also be indebted to one or other of these sources, all of which go back to Olaus Magnus. Once thought to be one of the dresses which Bess of Hardwick sent as a New Year's gift to Queen Elizabeth and for which she paid £50 to the queen's embroiderer, this has now been called into question since the dress is slightly

Figure 4.27 Sea monsters that haunt the northern oceans (as illustrated in Sebastian Munster's *Cosmographiae universalis*, 1575).

Figure 4.28 Studio of Nicholas Hilliard (attrib.), *Queen Elizabeth I*, c.1599. The dress is decorated with what are probably painted animals and flowers, including sea monsters similar to those copied from contemporary prints in Mary's needlework. The Devonshire Collection, Hardwick Hall, Derbyshire.

too late in style for this particular gift, recorded in 1591/92.³² The designs on the skirt are, moreover, almost certainly painted on the satin, not embroidered. That such designs appealed to Bess is however apparent from the Hardwick long cushion showing Europa and the bull, in which the designer has added three sea monsters and a mermaid to the woodcut by Virgil Solis after Bernard Salomon, which it copies for its main subject. At least one of these does indeed go back to the monsters illustrated in Sebastian Munster's northern oceans.

The sea monsters that the various Oxburgh embroideries copy from Gessner are those labelled 'A Scolopender', 'A Zyph Whale', 'A Thorne Back' and 'A Rhinocerote of the Sea'. The 'Scolopender', Gessner informs us, is a kind of marine centipede, so-called from the large number of appendages with which it propels itself like oars; Olaus Magnus depicts it as a monstrous whale. Mary's 'Zyphwhale' takes its name from a 'horrible marine monster', also depicted by Olaus, which Gessner suggests may be called *Zyffwal* or *Suffwal* in German from its habit of swallowing animals as big as seals, which is what we see it doing while being attacked by another sea monster in Gessner's woodcut. Mary refuses the challenge of depicting these secondary creatures in her embroidery panel, though she signs it with her monogram. The 'Thorne Back' takes its name from Gessner's commentary on a type of ray (it is not a hedgehog, as Zulueta supposes³³) which, he tells us, is called 'Ray' (*Raia*) in Latin, 'Roach' (*Roch*) in German and 'Thornback' in English because of its spiny back: Oliver Goldsmith still knew this as 'Thornback ray' in his *History of Animated Nature* (1774). Olaus Magnus illustrates one in the waters beyond Denmark, where it is protecting itself from a man swimming by a host of dog fish which attack the swimmer, and this is what his own picture shows. Also copied from Olaus Magnus, Gessner explains, is the 'Rhinocerus Whale' (*Rhinocerotis cetus*) because it has a humped back: it eats giant crabs, which is what both Olaus and Gessner, though not the embroidery, show it doing.

Another panel that copies an illustration in Gessner (which goes back to a woodcut in Olaus Magnus) is the Shrewsbury Hanging panel with Mary's initials showing a woman milking what is evidently a reindeer. Margaret Swain illustrates the woodcut from Gessner which this copies.³⁴ Gessner's image copies that in Olaus Magnus (1555, p. 596), which accounts for the somewhat unusual nature of the image in this embroidery, with its inclusion of both animal and human subjects, since the Swedish writer is concerned throughout to show how the inhabitants of northern countries make use of their natural environment and its creatures. Olaus's woodcuts are often closer to genre pictures and Mary's rather anomalous image of the milkmaid with her reindeer reflects this impulse in what can now be identified as the ultimate source of her picture.

Figure 4.29 Cushion cover embroidered with the myth of Europa and the bull, copying a woodcut by Virgil Solis after Bernard Salomon from a sixteenth-century edition of Ovid's *Metamorphoses*. The Devonshire Collection, Hardwick Hall, Derbyshire.

Figure 4.30 'A Scolopender', Marian Hanging, panel 21. Oxburgh Hall, Norfolk.

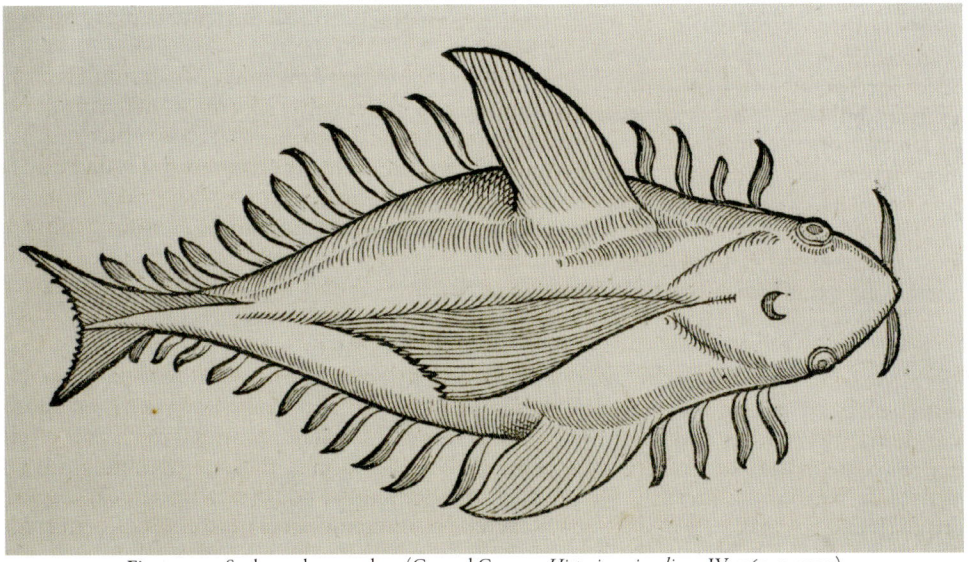

Figure 4.31 Scolopender, woodcut (Conrad Gessner, *Historia animalium*, IV, 1560, p. 1009).

Figure 4.32 'Zyphwhale', Marian Hanging, panel 14. Oxburgh Hall, Norfolk.

Figure 4.33 Zyphwhale, a formidable sea monster unlike any other (according to Conrad Gessner, *Icones animalium*, 1560, p. 249).

Figure 4.34 Xiphia, woodcut (Olaus Magnus, *Historia de gentibus septentrionalibus*, 1555, p. 743).

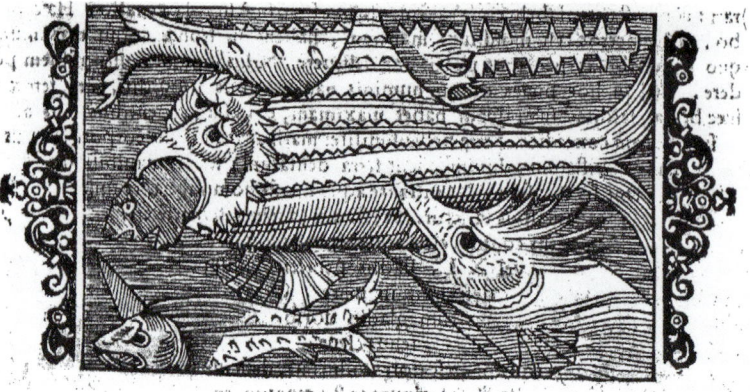

Figure 4.35 'Thorne Back', Marian Hanging, panel 25. Oxburgh Hall, Norfolk.

Figure 4.36 Fish which 'Spaniards and Latinists write and call a ray ... Germans and Flemish roach and English knows as a thornback', woodcut (Conrad Gessner, *Historia animalium*, IV, 1560, p. 941).

Figure 4.37 Man-eating ray, a Danish species that attacks swimmers with the help of a pack of 'dog' fish who do its hunting for it (Olaus Magnus, *Historia de gentibus septentrionalibus*, 1555, p. 764).

Figure 4.38 'A Rhinocerote of the Sea', Marian Hanging, panel 23. Oxburgh Hall, Norfolk.

Figure 4.39 Monster resembling a rhinoceros that eats giant lobsters, woodcut (Conrad Gessner, *Historia animalium*, IV, 1560, p. 348).

Figure 4.40 'Reindeer', Shrewsbury Hanging, panel 12. Oxburgh Hall, Norfolk.

Figure 4.41 Reindeer being milked, woodcut (Conrad Gessner, *Historia animalium*, I, 1551, p. 950).

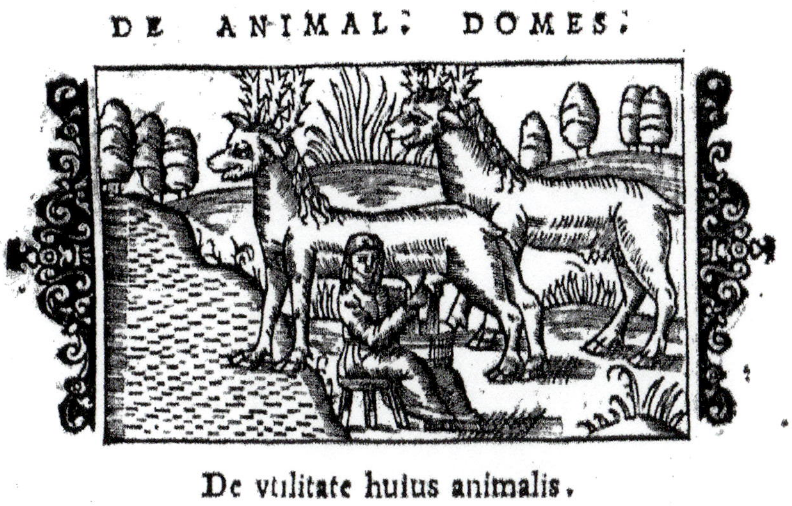

Figure 4.42 Reindeer milking, woodcut (Olaus Magnus, *Historia de gentibus septentrionalibus*, 1555, p. 596).

Animals as emblems

These strange sea monsters must have appealed to the embroiderers purely because of their striking appearance and their outlandish provenance. At least a few of the panels, however, show animals that have some emblematic potential. Gessner illustrates the bird he calls 'Pelecanus' as a spoonbill, but he also recognises that the 'philological' records identify the pelican as a quite different and doubtless fabulous bird that pecks its breast and feeds its nestlings with its lifeblood in ancient zoology and in Christian art: Gessner therefore also offers a woodcut of the conventional motif known to Christian iconography as the 'Pelican in her Piety'. Gessner's actual spoonbill supplies the pattern for the detached panel with the label 'A Shofler', but Mary signs with her own initials the 'Pellican' panel on the Marian Hanging, which copies Gessner's image of the pelican 'as it is commonly portrayed'. It is surely inconceivable, given her Catholicism, that Mary would have copied this image without wanting to retain its received symbolism, but in any case Gessner's readiness to illustrate not only accurate, scientific images of the creatures he is describing, but also their traditional, iconic, not to say fabulous, characteristics, is a useful reminder of the overlap between the purely natural and the potentially emblematic form of so many of these images. The bird we now call a pelican, with a large pouch below its beak, is illustrated by Gessner under the name of 'Onocrotalus' and is copied on the fragmentary embroidery in the Victoria and Albert Museum (T33: R) which carries the damaged label ' ... Byrd'. Gessner does not supply an English name for this species and nothing in his commentary offers any hint as to what its name might have been on the damaged label to the embroidery. He does tell us that, once again, his picture is based on that in Olaus Magnus's *Historia de gentibus septentrionalis*.[35]

Gessner's philological interests motivated the inclusion of proverbial, literary and emblematic sources

Figure 4.43 'A Pellican', Marian Hanging, panel 9. Oxburgh Hall, Norfolk.

Figure 4.44 Conrad Gessner's illustration of 'The Pelican as it is commonly represented by painters', i.e. the Christian 'Pelican in her Piety', shown pecking her breast to feed her young with her own lifeblood (*Historia animalium*, III, 1555, p. 639).

Figure 4.45 'A Shofler', or spoonbill, detached panel T33.X. London, Victoria and Albert Museum.

Figure 4.47 Damaged embroidery panel with an unidentified bird, but copying what Gessner describes as an Onocratalus, known in German as *Kropffvogel*. London, Victoria and Albert Museum, T33.R.

Figure 4.46 Pelecanus, German *Löffler* (as named and illustrated in Conrad Gessner, *Icones avium*, 1560, p. 92).

Figure 4.48 Onocratalus, or bird resembling the pelican with its large pouch, woodcut (Conrad Gessner, *Historia animalium*, III, 1555, p. 605).

in his description of these animals – indeed each of Gessner's chapters in the *Historia* volumes is divided into eight different parts with an alphabetical key identifying the various sections in which he deals successively with such things as the animal's name in different languages, its various habitats and subspecies, its behaviour, its medicinal and culinary uses, and finally any metaphorical or moral meanings it may have been assigned in pictures, among which he singles out specifically Alciato's emblems.[36] Accordingly Gessner regularly cites the emblems of Andrea Alciato, a number of which use animals, and it is that omnivorous determination to leave no classical stone unturned, no relevant Latin source uncited, which accounts for Gessner's inclusion of these highly regarded neo-Latin emblems in his book on natural history. It is by no means safe to assume that Mary or Bess would have noticed these references despite Mary's interest in emblems and a direct knowledge of several emblem books. But, given the tendency to use speaking pictures, which is evident in her other images, it is worth looking a little more closely at one or two of the animals in Gessner which are also the subject of emblems by Alciato.

A suitable candidate might be the unsigned panel on the Shrewsbury Hanging which shows a bird called 'A Porphyry'. This copies Gessner's picture for a bird called 'Porphyrion' (German *Pupuurvogel*), because of its purple beak and feet. Alciato has an emblem featuring this bird, under the motto *Pudicitia* [Chastity], which informs us that the porphyrio is a bird which dies of grief if its wife commits adultery. Gessner gives a very full account of classical authors' descriptions of this characteristic, citing Oppianus to the effect that the porphyrio is so wedded to the idea of chastity that if it sees its wife *in flagrante* it is so overcome with sorrow that it wastes away with grief; Aelianus confirms this opinion.

Figure 4.49 'A Porphyry', Shrewsbury Hanging, panel 15. Oxburgh Hall, Norfolk.

Figure 4.50 Porphyrion, woodcut (Conrad Gessner, *Icones avium*, 1560, p. 126).

Figure 4.51 'A Robin', Shrewsbury Hanging, panel 13. Oxburgh Hall, Norfolk.

Figure 4.52 Rubecula, robin redbreast, woodcut (Conrad Gessner, *Icones avium*, 1560, p. 48).

Figure 4.53 Trochilus, i.e. robin, woodcut (Pierre Belon, L'histoire de la nature des oyseaux, 1555, p. 343).

Although Gessner does not cite Alciato on this occasion, his commentary goes back to the same classical sources, and Mary had could hardly have embroidered such a panel without regard to her own marital circumstances and the accusations that had led to her present exile in England. The panel may not be hers, however, and there is no way of discerning whether the bird really has any symbolic function on the embroidery.

In at least one case the problem of naming is not simply a question of labelling: it raises more important issues in the panel showing 'A Robin' on the Shrewsbury Hanging since, despite the label, what this panel can now be shown to copy is not Gessner's picture *De Rubecula*, the redbreast, but rather Pierre Belon's woodcut of the bird he identifies as *Trochilus* in Greek, *Rex avium*, *Senator* and *Regulus* in Latin, and *Roytelet*, *Boeuf de Dieu* and *Berichot* in French. The wattle fence and tree stump on which the bird perches leave no doubt that it was Belon and not Gessner who supplied the pattern for this unsigned panel. Belon offers no English name for this bird, but he notes that its various names in Latin and French include references to kingship: *Rex avium*, he explains, means that it is 'king of birds', while *Roytelet* means 'little king'. Modern dictionaries translate this name as referring not to the robin but to the goldcrest, for which the English name 'kinglet' is also recorded from an early date.37 Aristotle, whom Belon quotes beneath the picture, authorises the Greek name, though the Greek *Basileus* [king] is also recorded for this bird, and the Latin *Rex avium* goes back to Pliny. Such royal naming of the smallest of European birds is what motivates Belon's commentary on it, a commentary which, I suggest, might well account for Mary's motives for including such a bird in her embroidery, if it is indeed her work and not Bess's. Belon accounts for the bird's Latin names as referring to the little bird's habit of fighting with mighty eagles, combat which is made inevitable by the royalty which they have in common, despite their differing powers ('non pas de force, mais de la dignité royale', p. 242). It is therefore no surprise to find hostility between individuals of dissimilar qualities, he moralises, seeing that the tiny kinglet can make trouble for the eagle which otherwise lords it over all the birds. It is very unlikely that Mary, in reading Belon's moralising of the name, would not have made the connection between her own feeble powers and those of Elizabeth, or with her remaining ability to make trouble ('faire nuisance à l'aigle' is Belon's phrase) for the mightier bird whose royalty she shared. Belon's comment turns ornithology into emblem, and his moralising is based on an Aesopic fable of the eagle and the wren which tells how, when the eagle boasted that it could fly higher than any other bird, the wren hitched a lift on its back and thus won the contest by flying even higher: the moral of the fable is that cunning may overcome naked power, and Mary (if the panel is indeed hers) could hardly not have referred such a moral to her own situation. It might reasonably be pointed out that the fact that the embroidery changes the bird's name invalidates my suggestion that this image has any emblematic significance, since it is only the name of the bird that makes it relevant to Mary's situation, but I would maintain that Mary might have good reason for sometimes obscuring the significance of such potentially incriminating emblems. Labelling the panel 'Kinglet' might well have been asking for trouble: much safer to call it a robin even though, as we have seen and as she must have known, this is not the species illustrated by her embroidery.

Speculative though all such interpretation must remain, we do need to recognise that the choice of which animals to include on her embroidered furnishings was not necessarily accidental. The readiness of 'scientific' writers such as Gessner and Belon to summarise the received meanings which many of these animals traditionally held in fable and emblem can only have narrowed any clear distinction between purely decorative and more significant or symbolic subjects in the decorative arts. As Alain de Lisle put it in the twelfth century, *Omnis mundi creatura/ Quasi liber et pictura/ Nobis est et speculum* [The whole world of created things is like a book and a mirror for us], and medieval habits of moralising the bestiary meant that the impulse to find emblematic meaning in the 'book of the creatures' would always be likely to assert itself when animals were concerned; such habits died out only very slowly, if at all, in the renaissance. That is not to say that every animal in these embroideries must have some 'deep' emblematic significance – the dangers of over-interpretation are real – it is merely to raise the possibility that the motives that determined Mary's (and Bess's) choice of subjects for the various types of embroidery which they created were always likely to have been mixed. So when we find references in Gessner's or Belon's commentary which evidently speak to her situation, or to things that we know she cared deeply about, we should be prepared to entertain at least the possibility that the significance of the image for her went some way beyond a dispassionate interest in natural history.

Margaret Swain (1973) comments, for instance, that those with a knowledge of French would have recognised that the dolphin label on a panel copied from Pierre Belon on the Marian Hanging implies a pun on the French *dauphin*. Mary had, after all, been married to a dauphin, or heir to the French throne, François II.[38] The heraldic arms of the dauphin show the three fleurs de lis of *France moderne* quartered with silver dolphins, and during the short period when Mary was Dauphinesse of France (April 1558 to July 1559), her coat of arms displayed these dolphins impaled with the arms of Scotland; indeed Mary herself used two badges at this period which also feature either one or two dolphins beneath a closed crown.[39] Perhaps most suggestive of all is the fact that another panel on the same Marian Hanging represents what the label calls 'A She Dolphin'. Damaged as the panel now is, it is quite impossible for the viewer to know what gender-specific features would justify the label, but once we discover Mary's source we are left in no doubt, for it copies Gessner's woodcut showing what he calls 'Delphinus foemina' [Female dolphin], which he illustrates in the very act of parturition with a newborn baby dolphin hanging from its umbilical cord. The fact that Gessner's caption identifies the suspended foetus specifically as male (*cum foetu masculo*) can only have confirmed its appropriateness as an emblem of a queen who had, after all, produced a male heir to the throne of Scotland. As mentioned in Chapter 3, Mary used a similar emblem of royal parturition – the fable of the lioness which gives birth to noble offspring – on her bed hangings. Although this 'She Dolphin' is one of the panels which has been brutally cut in half and joined to a quite different fragment on the Marian Hanging, it almost certainly originally showed the suspended foetus, and we might well see such excision as itself an ironic emblem of the exiled

Figure 4.54 'Delphin', Marian Hanging, panel 9. Mary's inclusion of her crowned initials undoubtedly signals the close identification she felt, as sometime Dauphinesse of France, with this creature. Oxburgh Hall, Norfolk.

Figure 4.55 A She Dolphin', Marian Hanging, half of composite panel 27 with an unidentified fish sewn onto it. Oxburgh Hall, Norfolk.

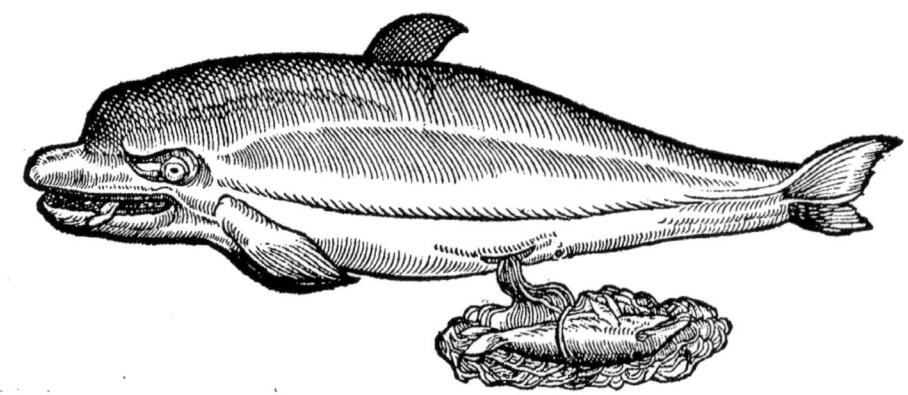

Figure 4.56 The female dolphin shown with attached foetus, woodcut (Conrad Gessner, *Historia animalium*, IV, 1560, p. 381).

queen's cruel separation from her own offspring, even if it was not her own scissors that cut the panel in half.

Another pattern book: Mattioli

The sources used as pattern books for embroidered panels of animals thus include Gessner, Thevet and Belon. To these must now be added the illustrated herbal of Pietro Andrea Mattioli, whose commentary on Dioscorides (*Commentarii in Dioscorides*), has long been recognised as the principal source for the plant-slip embroideries. However, it appears to have gone unnoticed that Mattioli's herbal has a whole section describing some of the animals commonly used in medicine, and these were the source for several of the cruciform animal panels. The Shrewsbury Hanging, for instance, includes a bird which it labels 'A Bon Brek', shown with half-spread wings and grasping a bone in its claws while another bone lies on the ground. These details might suggest that the bird is a vulture, but in Mattioli's herbal we find the source of this image of a bird that not only stands with the bones of the carcass on which it feeds but also with its Latin name declared in the caption as 'Ossifragus' [Bone breaker]. The bird illustrated is what we know as the German Lämmergeier or bearded vulture, the largest bird of prey inhabiting mountains from the Alps to the Himalayas where it is known to drop bones from a height so as to break them on rocks.

Figure 4.57 'A Bon Brek', Shrewsbury Hanging, panel 4. Oxburgh Hall, Norfolk.

Figure 4.58 'Ossifragus' or bone-breaker, i.e. Lämmergeier falcon, woodcut (Pietro Andrea Mattioli, *Commentarii in Dioscoridis*, 1558, p. 213).

Chapter 17 of Mattioli's section on animal-based medicines also describes the medical uses of snake skins, and illustrates them with a picture of two elegantly intertwined snakes. This is the pattern for the cruciform panel on the Cavendish Hanging with the label 'Knotted Serpentes'. As remarked in Chapter 2, the knotted serpent was one of the Cavendish devices, which is why that motif is found used not only on the Eglantine Table at Hardwick Hall but also in the square 'Extinctam Lacrimae ...' centrepiece to this hanging, along with those other devices – broken rings, stag and knotted girdle – which declare the emblematic intention of this strongly sententious panel. Clearly the 'Knotted Serpentes' panel, although it copies its

Figure 4.59 'Knotted Serpentes', Cavendish Hanging, panel 22. Oxburgh Hall, Norfolk.

Figure 4.60 'Senecta Anguium', woodcut (Pietro Andrea Mattioli, *Commentarii in Dioscoridis*, 1558, p. 193).

image from Mattioli's unmoralised herbal and carries no emblematic motto, can only have been chosen because of its conformity with these highly significant personal devices. It follows that this readiness to use images with emblematic meanings was not excluded from these cruciform panels of animals, nor was it confined to Mary alone.

Mattioli's herbal also supplied Bess or Mary with the picture of a basket filled with shells which is copied on the Oxburgh Valance in the cruciform panel labelled 'Sand Cockles'. Mattioli also has a woodcut showing a basket full of eggs, on which two birds are perched, illustrating (somewhat unnecessarily, one might think) 'Ovum' or the egg. The Oxburgh Valance has a panel

Figure 4.61 'Sand Cockles', Oxburgh Valance, panel 5, Oxburgh Hall, Norfolk.

Figure 4.62 'Chamae' woodcut (Pietro Andrea Mattioli, *Commentarii in Dioscoridis*, 1558, p. 180).

which has decided that these birds are not ordinary farmyard fowl but rather dottrel, or so its label would have us believe since it reads 'A Dotrel' despite the fact that there are two of them.

Mattioli's medicinal creatures include spiders, illustrated by a web spun between two branches, exactly as we find it shown and sewn on the Oxburgh Valance panel labelled 'A Spider'. The Cavendish Hanging

Figure 4.63 'A Dotrel', Oxburgh Valance, panel 6, Oxburgh Hall, Norfolk.

Figure 4.64 'Ovum' woodcut (Pietro Andrea Mattioli, *Commentarii in Dioscoridis*, 1558, p. 210).

includes a cruciform panel entitled 'Scorpions' that copies Mattioli's picture illustrating 'Scorpio Terrestris'. These cruciform panels are very similar to the animal embroideries copied from Conrad Gessner or Pierre Belon. Unlike the octagonal panels of plant slips copied also from Mattioli (see Chapter 5), however, they do not include a motto and they are not emblems.

Emblems and fables: the Hardwick cushion covers

The two types of subject, emblems and animals, that are found separately on the Oxburgh embroideries, each in a differently shaped frame, come together in fables, moralising tales about animals. The relevance of fables to

Figure 4.65 'A Spider', Oxburgh Valance, panel 3, Oxburgh Hall, Norfolk.

Figure 4.67 'Scorpions', Cavendish Hanging, panel 10. Oxburgh Hall, Norfolk.

Figure 4.66 'Araneus', woodcut (Pietro Andrea Mattioli, *Commentarii in Dioscoridis*, 1558, p. 222).

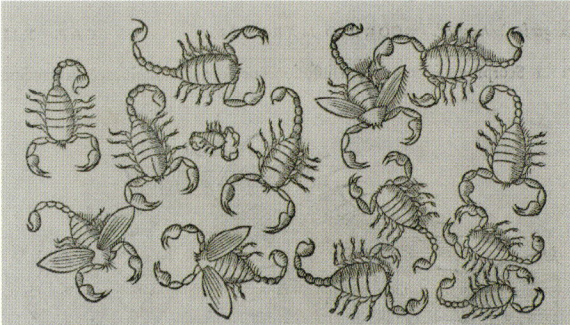

Figure 4.68 'Scorpio terrestris' woodcut (Pietro Andrea Mattioli, *Commentarii in Dioscoridis*, 1558, p. 165).

one or two of the topics identified on these embroideries has already been noted, for instance the bird known as 'kinglet' has a name which signals its rivalry with the imperial eagle in the fable cited by Pierre Belon, and the *Unum quidem sed leonum* motto on Mary's Bed of State echoes the fable of the lioness and the vixen, which authorised the hieroglyphic symbol for a woman who gives birth only once. There is, however, one surviving example of Mary's embroidery that makes more extensive use of fables, copying its images from the pictures to a well-known, sixteenth-century collection (first edition Rome, 1563), which had turned Aesop into Latin verse, by the Italian Gabriello Faerno, illustrating 100 fables with copperplate pictures that make it look very much like an emblem book, though these are more strictly classified as illustrated fables.

The two cushion covers at Hardwick Hall have a more complex design and use a greater variety of stitches than the embroideries from Oxburgh, with cross stitches worked both horizontally and vertically, running and speckled stitches, and the applied roundels in tent stitch.[40] In view of this we might wonder whether these were in fact Mary's work, rather than that of her professional embroiderer, but one of the covers has Mary's crowned monogram, sewn into the centre roundel showing two frogs sitting on a well, so we can be reasonably certain that she sewed at least these intricate roundels; both covers are also divided by interlocking plant stems into lozenge-shaped compartments containing one of three flowers: the lily (for France), thistle (Scotland) and rose (England) symbolising the three countries over which she had claims to sovereignty. It

Figure 4.69 Cushion cover with illustrated fables, The Devonshire Collection, Hardwick Hall, Derbyshire.

is the five inserted roundels at the centre and corners of each cover that copy illustrations from Faerno's *Fabulae centum*. One shows a crow trying to fly up from a snake that bites its leg, copying Faerno's fable of the crow that was caught by a snake which it tried to snatch, the moral being that anticipated gains may turn out to be a curse: *Infausta multis sunt sua ipsorum lucra* [Unlucky to many are their own profits]. The centre roundel of the same embroidery shows two frogs sitting on a wellhead, with Mary's cipher to its left. This echoes Faerno's fable of two thirsty frogs who find a well during a drought: one is keen to jump in but the other prudently hesitates in case it is dry and the moral is 'Look before you leap', or as Faerno puts it, *Negotiorum iubeo spectari exitum/ Iis, qui inchoare quid volunt* [I advise anyone thinking of getting into a business to know how they will get out of it].

It is not difficult to suggest reasons why Mary should have chosen these fables, or how she might have applied their morals to her own situation, just as we (and her contemporaries) have assumed she did with the emblems. Thus Nevinson (1939–40) comments on the crow-and-snake fable: 'The suggestion might be that Elizabeth will suffer for her theft.'[41] The essential conformity of these fables with emblems is, indeed, suggested by the fact that the three roundels on these cushions, which do not copy fables from Faerno, actually copy emblems from books by Hadrianus Junius, Gabriele Simeoni and (possibly) Claude Paradin, the three sources we have identified for nearly all of Mary's other 'emblematic' embroideries. The emblem copied from Junius's *Emblemata* (1565) would certainly seem to provide any justification that might be needed for

Figure 4.70 Cushion cover with illustrated fables, The Devonshire Collection, Hardwick Hall, Derbyshire.

Figure 4.71 The fable of the crow and the snake, copperplate (Gabriele Faerno, *Fabulae centum*, 1563, no. 24).

Figure 4.72 The fable of the two thirsting frogs at a well, copperplate (Gabriele Faerno, *Fabulae centum*, 1563, no. 37).

Figure 4.73 *Impunitas ferociae parens* [Licence is the parent of ferocity], the mice mock the cats caught in their trap, woodcut (Hadrianus Junius, *Emblemata*, 1565, no. 4).

Figure 4.74 The fable of the fox and the eaglet, copperplate (Gabriele Faerno, *Fabulae centum*, 1563, no. 60).

Figure 4.75 'A Catte', detached panel with Mary's monogram, copying Gessner's woodcut, to which the detail of the mouse is added. Margaret Swain suggests that Mary made this cat ginger so as to reflect Elizabeth I's famous red hair, though her claim that the embroidery shows the cat 'wearing a small gold crown' (1973, p. 78) is not accurate. Ginger cats are, in any case, invariably male. Royal Collection, by gracious permission of H.M. Queen Elizabeth II, Edinburgh, Palace of Holyroodhouse.

Figure 4.76 The fable of the cat and the cock, copperplate (Gabriele Faerno, *Fabulae centum*, 1563, no. 42).

applying these subjects, yet again, to Mary's own circumstances, dealing as it does with the idea of imprisonment: a cat, shut in a cage, is surrounded by mice, copying Junius's emblem *Impunitas ferociae parens* [Licence is the parent of ferocity].[42] Junius's epigram explains the moral – that the wicked will rejoice if just men are persecuted and confined. The application of such a moral to Mary's own imprisonment seems at least as likely in this case as in the various other emblems of imprisonment found elsewhere in her needlework.

A similar interpretation could be offered of the roundel showing a fox eating a young eaglet which has fallen to the ground out of the nest above, which copies Faerno's fable of the fox and the eagle who were friends before the eagle carried off the fox's cubs, after which the fox ate the eagle's young when they fell from the tree. Nevinson comments that the fable 'is hard to relate to [the] Mary Queen of Scots' story', yet Faerno's explication of the moral – that someone who damages even a weak friendship will attract divine punishment – surely reflects Mary's sense of her treatment by Elizabeth, whose friendship she had so mistakenly counted on when seeking asylum in England.[43] Whether or not the roundel that shows a cat devouring a cock is making a similar point might depend on whether we accept Margaret Swain's contention that Mary habitually thought of Elizabeth as 'A Catte', as in the embroidery with this label, now at the Palace of Holyroodhouse.[44] The roundel certainly copies Faerno (no. 42), with the moral that reason and justice will not deter those who are prepared to use force: *Vim qui inferre parat, cupidus, certusque nocendi,/ Frustra illum ratione premas, aut iure refellas*. 'This might imply,' suggests Nevinson, 'that no amount of just argument would make the wicked Elizabeth relax her hold.'[45] Mary's 'A Catte' certainly copies Gessner's illustration[46] to which she adds, significantly, a mouse. She would also surely have found Paradin's cat emblem suggestive in *Devises heroïques* (p. 62), for Paradin tells us that the cat was an emblem of liberty since it cannot stand being imprisoned, 'beste que lon connoit assez impaciente de prison', for which Paradin supplies the motto, *Arbitrii mihi iura mei* [My own judgement is my law]. Mary's readiness to combine fables of Faerno with images drawn from emblem books on these cushion covers reflects the connections that were often recognised at this period between fable and emblem in the way they moralise their images of animals.

5

The Language of Flowers

Plant slips

The fashion for embroidery decorated with short stems of plants or flowers became increasingly popular towards the end of the sixteenth century. These motifs are known as 'plant slips' or 'slip decoration' from the habit of taking cuttings – 'slip' was the word for a twig or shoot used in grafting or planting. In the embroideries of Mary Queen of Scots and of Bess of Hardwick, however, these plant slips take a form which is unique to the work of these two women. Invariably in the shape of octagonal panels, their borders are inscribed with a moralising Latin proverb or adage. There are a number of such panels among the Oxburgh embroideries, along with similar octagonal panels showing monograms rather than slip decoration. Those with plants include the evidently emblematic marigolds turning towards the sun, NON INFERIORA SECVTVS, which began our emblematic enquiries in Chapter 1, and the tortoise climbing a palm tree, DAT GLORIA VIRES, whose emblematic meanings were explored in Chapter 2. While these two panels carry Mary's initials, the majority of the octagons with slip decoration carry the 'ES' initials of Elizabeth of Shrewsbury. That Mary herself worked on embroideries using plant slips is, however, suggested by the Chartley inventory of her possessions in 1586, which records 52 'diverse flowers, in *petit point*, drawn from life, of which there are 32 not cut out, the rest cut each in its square'.[1] Those with Bess's monogram include the cherry branch on the Shrewsbury Hanging with its motto FVGACIA SIC SPECIOSA [As fleeting as it is beautiful] where it is difficult not to see the motto as making at least some kind of emblematic comment on the picture. Such Latin adages are, indeed, exactly the kind of thing that emblems used for their mottoes, and many of them can be found recorded in same source – Erasmus's *Adagia* – to which the emblem writers habitually resorted. Erasmus culled his great anthology of proverbial expressions from the works of ancient Greek and Latin authors, and such anthologies of cuttings from the poets were also known as 'florilegia' (bunches of flowers) – the so-called 'flowers' of rhetoric. Our task in this chapter will be to ask whether these embroidered flowers were devised as a rhetorical *florilegium*: what is the relationship between the posy and the poesie?

It has to be said that in most cases we should be hard pressed to find any meaningful link between the Latin motto which encircles these plant slips and the particular flower or plant that they portray. That is not to say that such plants did not, in many cases, come down to the sixteenth century linked with a host of associations in folklore, in medicine, or in herbals, which, rather like the similar associations that animals held in the fables and bestiaries, made them particularly suitable for emblematic treatment. The language of flowers 'devisefully being set' (as John Donne puts it in his 'Elegie VII') was a symbolic language whose received meanings were available to lovers and emblematists alike. But if we ask ourselves why the panel showing a large turnip on the Shrewsbury Hanging should have a motto which means 'The outcome stands in God's own hands' (EVENTVS

Figure 5.1 Cherry branch, Shrewsbury Hanging, octagon C, with the motto 'As fleeting as it is beautiful'. Oxburgh Hall, Norfolk.

Figure 5.2 'Cerasia', woodcut (Pietro Andrea Mattioli, *Commentarii in Dioscoridis*, 1558, p. 147).

REI IN MANV DEI), we should look in vain for any answer in the received lore of the turnip or in anything that the book this panel copies – Mattioli's *Commentarii in Dioscoridis* – says about turnips. Margaret Swain (1980) identifies and illustrates Mattioli's woodcut as the source, but fails to explain how the turnip 'had as much significance to Bess of Hardwick as the dolphin to Mary Queen of Scots' or what relevance it could possibly have to this particular motto.[2]

When we find the oak tree, however, on the Cavendish Hanging with the motto INTEGRITAS VI ROBORA PERENNIVS EST [Integrity is more lasting than oak] then we clearly have something like an emblem. Even more suggestive of an emblem is the apple tree on the Marian Hanging with its motto alluding to the Judgement of Paris. This is clearly a significant, that is to say emblematic, conjunction of word and image – indeed the allusion might well be more pointed in this case, as Paris awarded the apple of discord which sparked off the Trojan War to the fairest of three goddesses, Juno, Minerva and Venus. But Mary's motto to this plant-slip emblem, PVLCHRIORI DETVR, means 'Let it be given to the fairer'. The motto uses the comparative degree of the adjective and not the superlative: you can only be the 'fairer' of two things, whereas of three or more things you have to be the 'fairest'. So did the embroiderer really mean to write PVLCHERRIMI DETVR [Let it be given to the fairest]? Or might this grammatical faux pas be deliberate? And if the grammar of this motto is meant to allude to only two persons, rather than three, then could those be the two queens, Mary and Elizabeth? Elizabeth had certainly been portrayed, in 1569, as intervening in the Judgement of Paris: the painting by 'HE' shows the crowned queen holding her orb and sceptre and passing judgement on the three goddesses, who are overwhelmed by the superior beauty of their new judge. Could Mary possibly have seen or heard of this painting? It bears the date '1569', and the initials 'HE' ought to be those of Hans Eworth, though this has been questioned and the jury

Figure 5.3 Turnip, Shrewsbury Hanging, octagon B, with the motto 'The outcome stands in God's own hands'. Oxburgh Hall, Norfolk.

Figure 5.4 'Rapum', woodcut (Pietro Andrea Mattioli, *Commentarii in Dioscoridis*, 1558, p. 266).

is still out on the correct attribution.³ Eworth had been working in England since the 1540s, and had painted Henry Darnley's portrait in 1555 and again (with his brother) in 1562. Although Mary could not have seen this painting herself, she is very likely to have known the name of the artist who had painted portraits of her second husband, and might well have heard about the 1569 portrait of Elizabeth claiming (or awarding herself) the prize in this classical beauty contest, though I am not suggesting that the apple-tree octagon should necessarily be read as a direct allusion to the painting. However, I do think we have now discovered enough about the way the emblematic allusions work in these embroideries to support my suggestion that the PVLCHIORI DETVR motto on this octagon, if it is Mary's work, has to allude to the rivalry between herself and Elizabeth. She is unlikely to have made a grammatical mistake with her motto, and the use of the comparative adjective in place of the superlative is unlikely to have been unmotivated.

The cedar tree, copied from Mattioli's 'Cedrus', on the Cavendish Hanging has the motto VERA FELICITAS SEMPER ILLESA [True happiness is always unscathed]. The cedar is a biblical tree, where it is associated with stateliness and divine favour. This is not the only cedar tree recorded in the embroideries for, as noted in Chapter 2, her Bed of State apparently had an emblem showing two trees, one upright and one fallen, with the motto *Ploret picea quod cedrus cecidit* [The pitch pine weeps because the cedar has fallen]. These trees are certainly emblematic, and the emblem probably has a biblical basis since we find Ezekiel proclaiming that the Assyrian nation was a proud cedar of Lebanon which God cast down so that all of Lebanon mourned for it 'and all the trees of the field fainted for him' (Ezekiel 31: 15). The Bible, however, makes no mention of a weeping *picea*, which is the name for what we know as the spruce or, more literally, the pitch pine (the Latin name derives from *pix*, meaning pitch). We can at least begin to reconstruct the process of emblematic inven-

Figure 5.5 Apple tree, Marian Hanging, octagon B, with the motto that means 'Let it be given to the fairer', alluding to the classical Judgement of Paris. Oxburgh Hall, Norfolk.

Figure 5.6 Monogrammatist HE (?Hans Eworth), *Elizabeth I and the Three Goddesses*, 1569. Holding an orb, not an apple, Elizabeth overwhelms the three classical goddesses with her beauty in a replay of the Judgement of Paris. Royal Collection, by gracious permission of H.M. Queen Elizabeth II.

Figure 5.7 Cedar tree, Cavendish Hanging, octagon D, with the motto 'True happiness is always unscathed'. Oxburgh Hall, Norfolk.

Figure 5.8 'Cedrus Phoenicea', woodcut (Pietro Andrea Mattioli, *Commentarii in Dioscoridis*, 1558, p. 91).

tion that might associate the strongly resinous pitch pine with weeping, specifically its tendency to extrude a tear-like gum. William Fowler has a curious amplification of the motto on the Bed of State: he writes that it ended with the phrase *non pro meo captu* [not for my taking], which can only be read as applying this fallen but unlamented cedar to Mary's situation in England. The motto on the Cavendish Hanging must also allude to this biblical tendency of stately cedar trees to get felled, although we cannot read anything into its potential application to the embroiderer's situation, and it may well have been sewn by Bess. As we shall see, the conjunction of word and image on these octagonal panels of plant slips is sometimes emblematic, but sometimes wholly arbitrary.

The Oxburgh embroideries are not the only extant examples to use plant slips – 30 more such octagonal panels were discovered at Hardwick by the Duchess of Devonshire in the 1930s, packed away in cloths. She had them mounted on the present six-fold hinged wooden screen, each section holding five of the embroidered panels. Many of the panels carry the initials 'ES' and these, together with the inscriptions, were overpainted by the sixth duke to make them more legible. Most of these copy the illustrations to Pietro Andrea Mattioli's commentary on the *Materia medica* of Dioscorides (*Commentari in Dioscorides*). Mattioli's catalogue of medicinal plants (and some animals, as we have seen) was first published in 1554 in Venice with woodcut illustrations. As a standard work for physicians it appeared in numerous editions which often adapted and expanded the number of illustrations, making it difficult to discover precisely which edition might have supplied the pattern book for these plant-slip embroideries. In the 1550s several illustrated editions were published by Valgrisi in Venice, and a new improved set of larger, very handsome illustrations appeared in the 1560s which were used or copied in later editions published both in Venice and in Lyon up until the end of the sixteenth century (and later). I have not found any edition that includes every plant slip in the embroideries, although most of them appear to be copied from the set of illustrations found in editions produced in the 1560s and 1570s, probably in Venice.

Flowers of rhetoric? Adages from Erasmus

John Nevinson (1976) published a short article on the Hardwick octagons in which he identified sources both for the plant slips in Mattioli and for most of the Latin mottoes in Erasmus's great collection of classical commonplaces, the *Adagiorum chiliades* ('Thousands of Adages'– each successive edition added precisely a thousand new proverbial expressions to its predecessor). The relationship of the Latin adage to the plant-slip decoration on these panels shows the same kind of variation noticed on the Oxburgh panels of plants, for, as Nevinson notes, the choice of the laurel to accompany the motto referring to the conventional reward for virtue or bravery, VIRTUTIS PRAEMIVM, can hardly be accidental, whereas it may well be stretching credibility to suggest that the inclusion of two birds pecking up the grain from a bunch of rye grass (no. 11) 'is to be taken as a warning to them not to stray on to the high road' – PER PVBLICAM VIAM NE AMBVLES.[4] This adage is one of an evidently self-contradictory pair, since we find octagon no. 10 advising us to do quite the opposite: EXTRA PVBLICAM VIAM NE DEFLECTAS [Do not turn off the highway]. That kind of contradiction is, of course, characteristic of proverbial sayings and had long been accommodated to the rhetorical uses to which such commonplaces were put in the classroom, where rhetoric taught pupils to argue the case both pro and contra and encouraged them to compile handbooks of *loci communes*. Although we cannot be sure that the rye grass with its fowl has any connection with the advice not to walk in the highway, we should have less doubt about its argumentative partner, since the motto EXTRA PVBLICAM VIAM NE DEFLECTAS is illustrated by the plantain, which commonly grows on roads and pathways and whose medicinal properties reflect its resilience when trodden or crushed underfoot; its dialect names 'wayberry', 'waybread', 'waaverin-leaf' record its

Figure 5.9 Laurel branch, Hardwick Hall, octagon 9, mounted on a modern screen with the motto 'The reward of virtue'. Oxburgh Hall, Norfolk.

Figure 5.10 'Laurus', woodcut (Pietro Andrea Mattioli, *Commentarii in Dioscoridis*, 1558, p. 97).

Figure 5.11 Rye grass with two cocks eating seeds, Hardwick Hall, octagon 11, mounted on a modern screen with the motto 'Do not walk in the highway'.

Figure 5.12 'Lolium', woodcut (Pietro Andrea Mattioli, *Commentarii in Dioscoridis*, 1558, p. 253).

Figure 5.13 Plantain, Hardwick Hall, octagon 10, mounted on a modern screen with the motto 'Do not turn off the highway'.

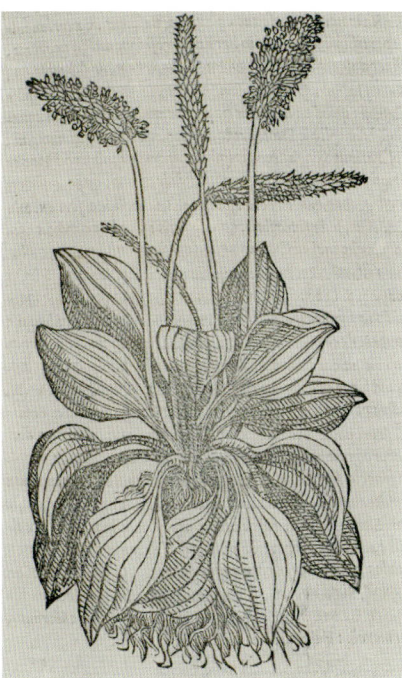

Figure 5.14 'Plantago Maior', woodcut (Pietro Andrea Mattioli, *Commentarii in Dioscoridis*, 1558, p. 281).

wayside characteristics, to which Bess's motto 'Do not turn off the highway' must surely refer.⁵

Erasmus compiled the fullest and most influential collection of such classical commonplaces, though his was by no means the only such printed *florilegium* at this period. The likelihood that the inscriptions derive at least indirectly from Erasmus is suggested by the fact that the adage to the effect that many talk though few are wise (no. 16) is quoted by Erasmus in his short commentary on *Extra publicam viam ne deflectas*, but not anywhere else in the *Adagia*. Six of these embroidery inscriptions are not recorded by Erasmus, suggesting that whoever chose the mottoes also had access to some other commonplace book. Three of the adages – including the two about walking, or not walking, on the highway – come from the list of 36 sententious commonplaces attributed to Pythagoras and known as the 'Pythagorean Symbols'. These are treated as a single group, which is why the reference for each is 1.1.2 (i.e. *Adagia*, no. 1,102), and those selected for embroidery also include the political *Coronam ne carpito* [Pluck not the crown]. Given the political background which we have been defining as a context for interpreting the emblematics of these embroideries so far, it is difficult to imagine that Bess of Hardwick could have selected or sewn such a motto without thinking of Mary Queen of Scots, but it is not clear what her motives would be for associating it with the plant known as gladdon, even though this is better known by the name stinking iris. And although I am convinced that the properties of the plantain must illustrate the 'Keep to the highway' adage on panel 10, I am mystified as to why the same motto should be associated with the lily of the valley in panel 21, and I can find nothing in the received lore of this plant, or in Mattioli's commentary, which would justify our reading of this as an emblem, even though this flower has a rich body of biblical and folkloric symbolism: the Song of Solomon's 'I am the Rose of Sharon, and the lily of the valley' made it a symbol of the Virgin, and German folktales explained it as springing from the tears of the Virgin at the foot of the cross. None of this seems relevant to a moral about keeping to the highway.⁶

Much the same is true of the teazle, which copies Mattioli's 'Dipsacus, sive Labrum Veneris'. Used in

Figure 5.15 Gladdon, or stinking iris, Hardwick Hall, octagon 3, mounted on a modern screen with the motto 'Pluck not the crown'.

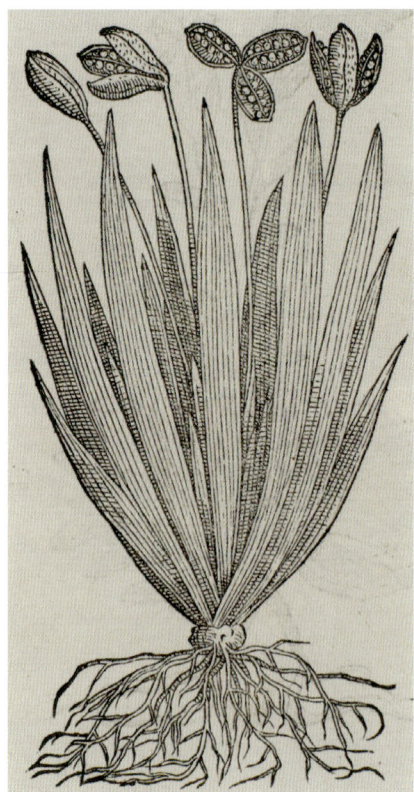

Figure 5.16 'Xyris', woodcut (Pietro Andrea Mattioli, *Commentarii in Dioscoridis*, 1558, p. 446).

the fulling of cloth, its alternative Latin name means 'Venus's basin' and is explained by William Coles in 1657: 'because whores are as ready to be kissed as those hollow leaves to receive the rain, and afterwards to card and teare the estates, if not the bodies of their followers',[7] none of which seems relevant to the motto from Erasmus, *Adagia* 1.3.14: FERAS NON CVLPES QVOD VITARI NON POTEST [Endure what cannot be avoided, rather than complaining at it], even if the idea of harsh treatment is appropriately associated with the uses to which the teazle was commonly put. Another of Bess's octagons on the Hardwick screen shows a hawthorn branch, whose Latin name Mattioli identifies as *Acuta spina* [sharp thorns], which is certainly relevant to the motto: AB OMNI PARTE EQVALITER PVNGO [I wound from all sides alike], an adage not found in Erasmus. Another octagon shows the orpine, a plant which carries a rich body of potentially emblematic significance, both in its alternative name of 'livelong' and in magic and medicine, where it was used in midsummer rites to divine sexual partnerships or fatalities,[8] but none of this accounts for the motto CVM MINERVA MANVM QVOQVE MOVE [Set about thy task with Minerva's aid]. Minerva is the goddess of wisdom, learning and handicrafts, not love matches. Bess also copies a rather striking illustration of two mandrake roots from Mattioli, but although the powerful symbolism of this root that was thought to resemble a naked man, so that it would shriek when pulled up, includes the idea that when eaten it would make you vain (if it did not poison you), none of this would seem to justify the motto advising us that hidden vices give less offence, VITIA OCCVLTA MINVS NOXIA.

This all suggests that we should keep an open mind about the possible emblematic functions of these plant-slip octagons in the way they associate word and image. In some, at least, of these embroidered octagons we can see a correspondence between received ideas concerning the plant and the moralising inscription, but more often there seems to be no very clear connection between image and adage.

Figure 5.17 Lily of the Valley, Hardwick Hall, octagon 21, mounted on a modern screen with the motto 'Do not walk in the highway'.

Figure 5.18 'Lilium Convallium', woodcut (Pietro Andrea Mattioli, *Commentarii in Dioscoridis*, not included in early editions – this illustration is taken from the 1598 edition, p. 631).

EMBLEMS FOR A QUEEN

Figure 5.19 Teazle, Hardwick Hall, octagon 14, mounted on a modern screen with the motto 'Endure what cannot be avoided, rather than complaining at it'.

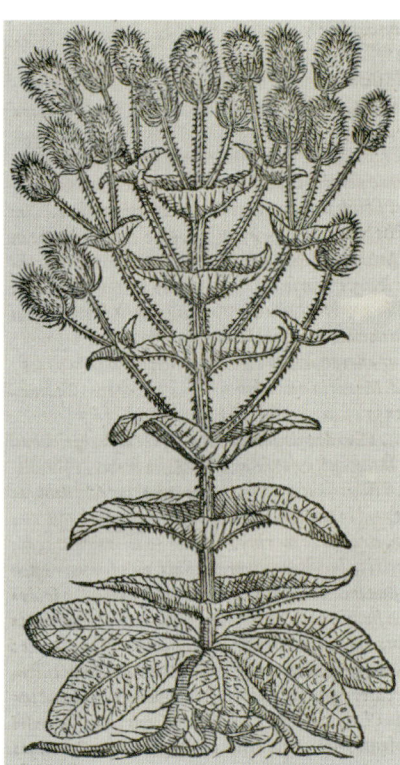

Figure 5.20 'Dipsacus', woodcut (Pietro Andrea Mattioli, *Commentarii in Dioscoridis*, 1558, p. 356).

Figure 5.21 Hawthorn, Hardwick Hall, octagon 29, mounted on a modern screen with the motto 'I wound from all sides alike'.

Figure 5.22 'Acuta Spina', woodcut (Pietro Andrea Mattioli, *Commentarii in Dioscoridis*, 1558, p. 100).

Figure 5.23 Orpine, Hardwick Hall, octagon 16, mounted on a modern screen with the motto 'Set about thy task with Minerva's aid'.

Figure 5.24 'Telephium', woodcut (Pietro Andrea Mattioli, *Commentarii in Dioscoridis*, 1558, p. 340).

Figure 5.25 Mandrake, Hardwick Hall, octagon 12, mounted on a modern screen with the motto 'Vices hidden give less offence'.

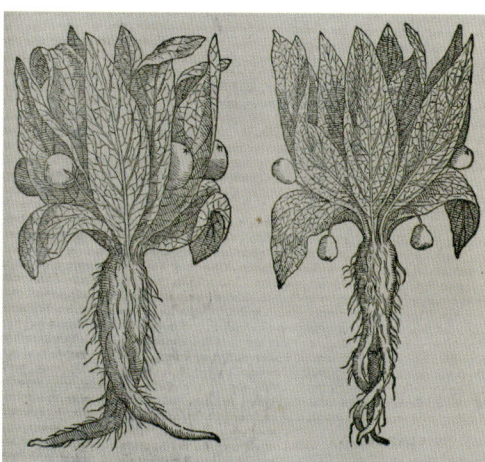

Figure 5.26 'Mandragora', woodcut (Pietro Andrea Mattioli, *Commentarii in Dioscoridis*, 1558, p. 535).

Conclusions

Although the different shapes of the panels suggest a clear coding for different types of motif and subject in these embroideries, we have often had to recognise that there is overlap both in the sources used and in the way the images are functioning. The large square centrepieces to the Oxburgh Hangings are the most clearly emblematic of these embroidered panels in the way they combine word and image to express Mary's (or Bess's) sense of her own situation through what appears to be a series of personal *imprese*. That this was exactly how these were read – as 'speaking pictures' – in their own day is evident from the way they were used as potentially incriminating evidence in the various legal and diplomatic manoeuvres examined in Chapter 1.

Unlike the Oxburgh Hangings, the panels on Mary's Bed of State were all evidently emblems or *imprese*, combining symbolic pictures with sentientious Latin mottoes, for many of which we can identify sources and analogues in particular emblem books. Mary's animal fables on the cushion covers at Hardwick express the same mentality in their relevance to her personal situation and their combination of illustrations taken from Faerno's *Fabulae centum* with pictures drawn from the emblem books of Hadrianus Junius and Claude Paradin. When it comes to the embroideries of named animals we need to be far more cautious in claiming any emblematic function, even though many of these creatures carried meanings and associations which might well have been suggestive, at least to Mary, if she had read what Belon, Gessner or Mattioli (though he is less expansive) said about them. Many of these animal embroideries reflect, rather, a less sophisticated taste for the varied creatures of the natural world for their own sakes, whether homely and familiar or more exotic and extraordinary, and may well have attracted Mary's interest because of Conrad Gessner's references to the Scottish provenance of quite a few of them in his *Historia animalium*. Whether Mary had any direct knowledge of the correspondence between Gessner and his Scottish informants, such as Henry Sinclair or Giovanni Ferrerio, is unclear, though it seems very likely that the toucan beak which the latter sent to Zürich to supply Gessner with a life model for his woodcut illustration was the same beak which, when it came back to Scotland, evidently found its way into Mary's personal possessions (and the Chartley inventory in 1586 records that her cabinet at that date also included such similar curiosities as a unicorn horn on a gold chain, and a bezoar stone mounted in gold).[9] Most of the octagonal embroideries of plants are the work of Bess, and may be no more significant than is usual with the plant slips, which became fashionable in amateur needlework at this period; however the tendency to associate such slip decoration with sentientious Latin mottoes is unconventional and sets these octagons apart from such similar work by her contemporaries. Although it is impossible to find any significant connection between the Erasmian adages and the particular plants in most cases, there are some clear exceptions and, as with the animal embroideries, we appear to have a type of motif which slides into and out of emblematic signification quite unpredictably.

The tendency of so many of these embroideries to exploit the symbolic associations traditionally ascribed to plants and animals should undoubtedly be seen, however, as an expression of the two women's instinctive acceptance of a traditional world-view which saw the whole created world as a collection of speaking pictures. The persistence of that mentality can easily be documented in a variety of media and artefacts of the early modern period. Characteristic of those assumptions is what we find in Edward Topsell's 'Epistle Dedicatory', which he wrote in 1607 for his English translation of Gessner's *History of Animals*. Writing as an Anglican priest – 'Chaplain in the Church of St Botolph Aldersgate' as he signs himself at the conclusion to his dedication – Topsell insists that the study of natural history is far from being disinterested science and that 'the knowledge of Beasts, like as the knowledge of other creatures and works of God, is Divine'. Holy scripture, he argues, shows that animals were created for man's use in three different ways, 'one for Sacrifice, another in Vision, and a third for Reproof and Instruction', and it is their usefulness for 'Reproof and Instruction' that leads him to single out the way various animals have been adapted to emblematic purposes: 'And for the knowledge of man, many and most excellent rules for private and public affaires, both for preserving a good conscience, and avoiding an evil danger, are gathered from Beasts.'

> Who is so unnatural and unthankful to his Parents, but by reading how the young Storkes and Wood-peckers do in their parents old age feed and nourish them, will not repent, amend his folly, and be more natural? What man is so void of compassion, that hearing the bounty of the Bone-

breaker Bird to the young Eagles, will not become more liberal? Where is there such a sluggard and drone, that considereth the labours, pains and travels of the Emmet, little Bee, Field-mouse, Squirrel, and such other that will not learn for shame to be more industrious, and set his fingers to work? Why should any man living fall to evil against his Conscience, or at the temptation of the Devill, seeing a Lion will never yield? *Mori scit, vinci nescit*; and seeing the little wren doth fight with an eagle, contending for Soveraignty? .... And what King is not invited to clemency, and dehorted from tyranny, seeing the King of Bees hath a sting, but never useth the same?

(fol. 5^r, unpaginated)

We could hardly wish for a clearer statement of the readiness of readers only 30 years after the embroideries were executed to read Gessner's animals – including several of those we have encountered in particular pieces of needlework – as moral emblems. Gessner's *Historia animalium* 'sheweth,' writes Topsell, 'that Chronicle which was made by God himself, every living Beast being a word, every Kind being a sentence, and all of them together a large History, containing admirable knowledge and learning'. And although this lore is moralised not only in such biblical writers as Job and Solomon but also in the pagan writers who, as we have seen, Gessner so frequently cites, 'I will be bold to aver that for truth in the Book of Creatures (although first observed by Heathen men) which is not contrary to the book of Scriptures.'

We would not have to look far at this period to find evidence of belief in the appropriateness of using images offering such moral instruction in personal furnishings, and although the application of many of these images to Mary's or Bess's own situation in much of this embroidery brings such morals closer to a personal *impresa* than to the more general moral counselling characteristic of emblems, the relationship of *impresa* to emblem at this period was particularly close. That Mary and Bess were prone to read the images they used in their embroideries in much the same spirit that Edward Topsell is claiming as the essential *raison d'être* for his translation of Gessner in 1607 is surely not unlikely.

We might conclude that this was a decorative art which, at this period, utilised a number of different vocabularies and styles, and as an amateur pastime it was relatively unregulated by strict rules or clearly deliberated conventions. Concentrating on the emblematic function or potential of these embroideries, as I have done in this study, admittedly lays me open to the accusation of undervaluing some of its other attractions; however if this was, as recent research has suggested, a period which has some claim to be characterised as *aetas emblematica* – 'l'âge de l'emblême'[10] – then we should not be surprised to find these embroideries using emblematic motifs or combining word and image in ways that continually move into emblematic forms, however erratically. Whatever its diversity of form and function, a fair case can be made for characterising this extraordinary and distinctive body of needlework as 'emblems for a queen'.

APPENDIX 1

The Oxburgh Hangings

On display at Oxburgh Hall, Norfolk (a National Trust property). The property of the Bedingfeld family since 1761, the hangings were bought in 1953 by the National Art Collections Fund and gifted to the Victoria and Albert Museum, on the understanding that, after due conservation work and a temporary exhibition in London, they should be returned on permanent loan to Oxburgh.

The Marian Hanging (Fig. 1.8)

Square centrepiece (Fig. 3.11)
Disembodied hand reaches down from the sky to prune the unfruitful branches of a vine which is growing between two fruit trees. Motto in a scroll: VIRESCIT VVLNERE VIRTVS [Virtue flourishes from its wounds]. Mary's distinctive cipher/monogram beside tree on the left side, royal arms of Scotland on the right.

Octagonal panels
- A Crowned monogram spelling MARIA STVART flanked by two thistles, with Mary's cipher above each of the top two corners; octagonal frame carries the inscription SA VERTV MATIRE [Its strength attracts me] (Fig. 1.5).
- B Apple tree; octagonal frame carries the inscription PVLCHRIORI DETVR [Let it be given to the fairer], alluding to the Judgement of Paris, who awarded the golden apple to the fairest of the three goddesses, Juno, Minerva and Venus (Fig. 5.5).
- C Crowned monogram spelling ELIZABETH MARY flanked by a lily and a rose, and a thistle bent or crushed beneath; octagonal frame carries the inscription ARCTIORA SVNT VIRTVTIS VINCVLA QVAM SANGVINIS [The bonds of virtue are tighter than those of blood] (Fig. 2.27).
- D Monogram spelling GEORGE ELIZABETH below a coronet, with smaller monograms each side; octagonal frame has inscription GEORGE ELIZABETH SHREWSBURY.
- E Three marigolds turning towards the sun, with Mary's cipher; octagonal frame carries inscription NON INFERIORA SECVTVS [Not having followed lower things], the *impresa* of Marguerite de Navarre, sister of François I (Fig. 1.4).
- F Tortoise climbing a crowned palm tree; octagonal frame carries inscription DAT GLORIA VIRES [Glory gives strength]; this emblem with the same motto had been used in 1565 on a coin known as the Mary *ryal* (Fig. 2.28).
- G Plant with conventionalised foliage and snake coiled out from its stem; octagonal frame has motto SVB HERBA LATET ANGVIS [A snake lurks under the grass]; emblem based on Paradin's *Latet anguis in herba* device, 1557, p. 70, though the picture does not copy Paradin's engraving (Fig. 2.26).
- H Plant with elaborate and symmetrical foliage and flowers; octagonal frame with inscription

NE NIMIVM CREDE COLORI [Do not place too much trust in appearances]. Motto quotes Virgil, *Eclogues* II, 17, 'O lovely boy, do not place too much trust in appearances, The white privets fall, the dark hyacinths are culled'.

Cruciform panels

1. SOLEN GOOSE, i.e. gannet, standing on rocks, copying the *Anser Bassanus* from Gessner, *Historia*, p. 158, *Icones*, p. 83. Gessner's description of this as a bird found in Scotland is likely to be what recommended it to Mary: 'Anser Bassanus vel Scoticus, avis marina. SCOTICE vulgo a Solendguse. GERMAN. dici potest Solendganz/ oder Schottengans' [The Bass Rock goose, or Scottish goose, a sea bird; in Scots a Solendgoose; in German can be called Solend goose or Scottish goose] (Fig. 4.12).
2. A JAY, standing on cut log with leaf twig. Gessner illustrates 'Pica Glandaria ... Anglis a jay', *Historia*, p. 672, *Icones*, p. 26, with an image resembling the embroidery but reversed.
3. PHENIX, shown rising from its flaming nest, with Mary's cipher and letter R top left and right. The phoenix is not illustrated in Belon or Gessner, although Gessner has a chapter on the phoenix, *De avium natura* (1555), pp. 663–6. Though the resemblance is not close enough to be certain, it may be copied from the phoenix in Paradin, p. 89, with the motto *Unica semper avis* [Always a unique bird], identified by Paradin as the *impresa* of Eleanor of Austria, widow of François I.
4. A TVRTEL DOVE, standing on a cut branch, with Mary's cipher top left, copied from Gessner, *Historia*, p. 769, *Icones*, p. 66 'Turtur'.
5. DRAGON, with MR monogram, not copied from Gessner.
6. A BYRD OF AMERICA, a toucan, with MR monogram below. Gessner does not illustrate this in *Historia*, but in *Icones*, p. 130, he describes and illustrates 'PICA Bressillica, cuius rostro Io Ferrerius Pedemontanus summae eruditionis vir me donavit, quod hic expressi, reliquum corpus ex Galliae Antarcticae descriptione Andreae Theveti Gallice adieci' [Brazilian woodpecker, of which I was given the beak by the very learned Giovanni Ferrerio of Piedmont, which I show here, to which I have added the remainder of the body from the French description in French Antarctica of André Thevet]. Gessner's acknowledgement of André Thevet as his source for information about the toucan takes us to Mary's actual pattern for the embroidery, which was not Gessner's illustration in the *Icones* but rather the woodcut illustration that Thevet himself had included in his *Singularitez de la France antarctique* (1558) (Fig. 4.14).
7. Eagle standing on a dead hare with marigold and rose, and MR monogram, unlabelled, but copied from Gessner, *Historia*, p. 169, *Icones*, p. 4.
8. AN VNICORNE with Mary's cipher at left; though the image is reversed, and the head turned back, this is undoubtedly based on Gessner, *Historia*, p. 781, *Icones*, p. 28, 'Monoceros'.
9. A PELLICAN feeding young with its blood, with MR monogram. Copies Gessner, *Historia*, p. 639, *Icones*, p. 91 'Pelecanus ut vulgo ... effingitur' [as commonly portrayed], the conventional icon or emblem of Christian sacrifice known to art historians as the 'Pelican in her Piety' (Fig. 4.43).
10. A COCKATRICE, with Mary's cipher; not copied from Gessner.
11. A LYONE, with Mary's cipher, copied from Gessner, *Historia*, p. 642, *Icones*, p. 36.
12. A PHESANT, its long tail feathers cut off for lack of space and inserted above it, with MR monogram to the left, copied from Gessner, *Historia*, p. 658, *Icones*, p. 62.
13. AN ONCE, i.e. ounce or lynx, with Mary's cipher, copies Gessner's, 'Lynx', from *Historia*, p. 769, *Icones*, p. 32.
14. ZYPHWHALE, i.e. swordfish, with MR monogram, copies Gessner's 'Rana', from *Historia*, p. 119. Takes its name from Gessner's commentary, which explains, 'Zifius or Ziphius ... is a most formidable sea-whale ... In German it can be called a Zyffwal or Suffwal from its swallowing, because it devours even great creatures such as seals', which is what we see it doing both in Gessner's illustration and in the woodcut from Olaus Magnus, p. 743, which Gessner's copies (Fig. 4.32).
15. BEES shown flying around a hive. Not copied from Gessner.
16. A HARTE with two flowering plants, and MR monogram, copies Gessner's 'Tragelaphus', *Historia*, p. 1101, *Icones*, p. 24. The name of this species of deer goes back to Greek authors Xenophon and Plutarch, though Gessner explains that he was sent his picture of it by a correspondent and suggests

that this Eastern variety differs very little from ordinary deer and may not be a separate species; Mary evidently thought the similarity close enough to illustrate her panel of the hart, or stag.

17 Two SNEILES on plant stems, with Mary's cipher, copied from Gessner, *Historia*, p. 349.
18 A TIGER, copied from Gessner, *Historia*, p. 1060, *Icones*, p. 35, adding a chequered floor, with Mary's cipher.
19 DELPHIN, above crowned MR monogram, copied from Belon's *Nature et diversité des poissons*, 1555, p. 8 (Fig. 4.54).
20 SEA MOONKE, or monkfish, copied from Belon, *Nature*, p. 33, 'Le monstre marin ayant facon d'un moyne', although Gessner (*Historia*, p. 174) has a very similar engraving (Fig. 4.5).
21 A SCOLOPENDER fish. Copies Gessner, *Historia*, p. 1009, 'Scolopendra' (Fig. 4.30).
22 A HORSSE. Does not copy Gessner's illustration.
23 A RHINOCEROTE OF THE SEA, copies Gessner, *Historia*, p. 248, 'De Rhinocerote Ceto' whose picture copies Olaus Magnus's and shows this monster devouring a giant lobster. Cardanus is cited to the effect that it has a pointed back and a disappearing nose ending in a horn; the embroidery omits the lobster (Fig. 4.38).
24 Three BUTTERFLIES on stems of a plant below MR monogram. These do not appear to be copied from Gessner.
25 A THORNE BACK, copies Gessner, *Historia*, p. 941, whose commentary supplies the label, 'Hispani ut Latini et scribunt et pronunciant Raia ... Germani et Flandri *Roch* ... Raiam Angli vocitant a *Thornebacke*: a tergo spinosa nam *Back* tergum est, *thorn*, spina' [Spaniards like Latinists both write and call it 'Ray' ... Germans and Flemish 'Roach' ... The English call the ray 'a Thornback' from its spiny back, since 'back' is Latin *tergum*, and 'thorn' means a spine] (Fig. 4.35).
26 TROUTE, showing a bridge with fish passing under it. Not copied from Gessner.
27 A SHE DOLPHIN, two panels have been cut in half and joined awkwardly so that the dolphin is joined vertically onto another unidentified fish. The dolphin portion copies Gessner, *Historia*, p. 381, 'Delphinus foemina' [Female dolphin] (Fig. 4.55).
28 THE CANKER, caterpillars with a cabbage-like plant and Mary's cipher, cf. Mattioli, *Commentarii in Dioscorides*, 1558, p. 220, 'Cantharides', showing beetles with a number of caterpillars that were thought to attack vines and other plants; the embroidery may copy these caterpillars though it shows no beetles and adds the plant.

The Shrewsbury Hanging (Fig. 1.9)

Square centrepiece (Fig. 2.18)
Executed by the Countess of Shrewsbury, with monograms GS and ES for George and Elizabeth Shrewsbury on either side of the central motif, an emblem illustrating the fable of the thirsty crow or raven which, unable to drink from a deep vase, raised the water level by filling the vase with stones. The fable was turned into an emblem by Paradin, with the motto *Ingenii largitor* [Bestower of wit], and Bess's picture copies Paradin's with the same motto in a scroll beneath the vase, adding background details such as birds in the sky, two butterflies on the extended handles of the vase and a grotesque claw-footed winged head as the foot of the vase. Similar grotesque detail fills the decorative border surrounding the emblem, which has been shown to copy, among other things, two caryatid designs from Vredeman de Vries's *Caryatidum* (*c*.1565) while the two bottom corners – showing a nude male figure retreating out of the picture from a stepped plinth upon which stands a male nude with crown and sceptre in front of a man saying his prayers – copy a detail from another decorative print by Vredeman de Vries from his *Grottesco* series (*c*.1565–71) (see Wells-Cole, *Art and Decoration*, 1997, p. 256, fig. 433). This same detail was copied, along with further details from the *Grottesco* series and two of Vredeman's caryatids (human busts or term figures emerging from an architectural plinth), in Mark Kerr's extraordinary grotesque painted ceiling at Prestongrange, Lothian, in 1581 (see Bath, *Renaissance Decorative Painting in Scotland*, 2003, p. 114).

Octagonal panels
A Above centrepiece, monogram spelling ELIZABETH TALBOT surmounted by coronet; octagonal frame carries the inscription ELIZABETH SHREWESBVRY.
B Left of centrepiece, turnip with flowering stems, copied from woodcut in Mattioli (*Commentarii*, 1558, p. 266, 'Rapum'); inscription in frame

EVENTVS REI IN MANV DEI [The outcome stands in God's own hands] (Fig. 5.3).

C Right of centrepiece, cherry branch with monogram ES, copies Mattioli (*Commentarii*, 1558, p. 147, 'Cerasia'); inscription in frame FVGACIA SIC SPECIOSA [As fleeting as it is beautiful] (Fig. 5.1).

D Below centrepiece, spray of flowers; inscription in frame FECEM BIBAT QVI VINUM BIBIT [Let him drink the dregs that drinks the wine', Erasmus, *Adagia* 1.6.73].

Cruciform panels

1 A STORK OF THE MONTAYNES, copies Gessner's mountain stork [Lat. 'Percnopterus'], *Historia*, p. 193, *Icones*, p. 5. The embroidery takes the hint for its name-label from Gessner's comment in *Icones*, 'Vocatur et Oripelargus, id est Ciconia montana' [Also called Oripelargus, that is to say Mountain Stork]; Gessner had not noted this version of the name in *Historia*, although it includes the same woodcut, which means that *Icones* must have been the embroidery source (Fig. 4.25).

2 COCKE, copies Gessner, *Historia*, p. 414, *Icones*, p. 52.

3 A PYE OF PERSIA, copies woodcut to Thevet's *Singularitez de la France antarctique* (1558), fol. 45r, illustrating the bird known in Brazil as 'Pa, en Persien, pié ou iambe', which eats worms in trees and has enormous pendent earflaps, a raised cap on its head and hairy legs, from which Thevet derives its name (Fig. 4.19).

4 A BON BREK, i.e. 'bone breaker'. Copies Mattioli (*Commentarii*, 1558, p. 213, 'Ossifragus') showing a bird with raised wings, open beak and bones at its feet. The Latin *ossifragus* is identified as a type of sea eagle by Pliny, but the bird illustrated corresponds to the German Lämmergeier or bearded vulture which drops bones from a height so as to break them on rocks (Fig. 4.57).

5 A CRANE, copies Gessner, *Historia*, p. 510, *Icones*, p. 19.

6 A COCK OF MAVRTAIN, copies Gessner's guinea fowl, 'Gallus Numidicus vel Mauretanus [A cock of Numidia or Mauretania], *Historia*, p. 772, *Icones*, p. 61.

7 A [ ] SWAL[ ], copies Gessner, *Historia*, p. 160, *Icones*, p. 51, 'Apodes', English swift or martlet.

8 A man hiding behind a tree spears a passing wild ox, unlabelled. Copies Gessner's 'Urus', *Historia*, p. 157.

9 A CHAMEL OF INDYE, copies Gessner's 'Camelopardus', *Historia*, p. 160, *Icones*, p. 28.

10 AN ASSE, picture shows a laden ass with its nose to a thistle, and another thistle below it, possibly copying part of the illustration to Mattioli (*Commentarii*, 1558, p. 208) on the medicinal use of asses' hoofs, which shows a man driving a laden ass into a doorway; the 1558 woodcut shows a similar pack saddle to that in the embroidery and also the bell suspended from its neck, but only the illustrations to some later editions of Mattioli show a thistle.

11 DRAGON, not copied from Gessner, whose Book V, on serpents, was only published posthumously in 1587, cf. Marian Hanging, no. 10.

12 [REINDEE]R. Reindeer being milked by a milkmaid, with MR monogram; copies Gessner, *Historia*, p. 950, *Icones*, p. 26, whose picture is based on that in Olaus Magnus's *Historia de gentibus septentrionalibus*, p. 796 (Fig. 4.40).

13 A ROBIN, copies Pierre Belon's woodcut of the bird he identifies as *Roytelet*, *Boeuf de Dieu* and *Berichot* in French. *Roitelet* remains the modern French name for the bird known as a gold-crested wren, also known in English as 'kinglet', modern goldcrest. The embroidery changes the appearance of the bird only slightly, cf. the three redbreasts on the Cavendish Hanging no.17 (Fig. 4.51).

14 A FYRETE, i.e. ferret, copies Gessner, *Historia*, p. 862, *Icones*, p. 44.

15 A PORPHYRY, copies Gessner, *Historia*, p. 776, *Icones*, p. 126, 'Porphyrion' (Fig. 4.49).

16 CROCODIL, copies Gessner's 'Crocodilo terrestri', *Historia*, p. 25.

17 Dog chewing bone, label illegible, no source identified.

18 BOARE, copies Gessner, *Historia*, p. 1040, *Icones*, p. 35.

19 A STERLIN, copies Gessner, *Historia*, p. 715, 'De Sturno' shown perched on a wooden branch, to which the embroidery adds leaves and bunches of grapes.

20 THE BYRDE OF PARADYSE, copies Gessner, *Historia*, p. 612, 'Paradys vogel', *Icones*, p. 20.

The Cavendish Hanging (Fig. 1.10)

Centrepiece (Fig. 2.23)

Tears fall from the sky upon a heap of quicklime; in a scroll the motto EXTINCTAM LACHRIMAE TESTANTVR VIVERE FLAMMAM [Tears witness that the quenched flame lives]. This was the device of Catherine de Medici, queen of Henri II and (at various times) Regent of France, adopted by her after the death of Henri in the fatal tournament of 1559 to express her enduring love for her late husband, whose death in the tilting accident made Mary Stuart Queen of France. The border is filled with monograms of Elizabeth Shrewsbury and William Cavendish, with emblematic and heraldic motifs, and the date 1570, top left. Top border has WC monogram flanked by a broken fetter to the left and a broken mirror to the right, and the Cavendish arms in either corner. Right border has three rings, interlaced and broken; ES monogram below a coronet; a knotted and broken girdle; ES monogram; a stag. Bottom border has a similar knotted, broken girdle; EC monogram; a torn gauntlet. Left border has (from the top down) a broken mirror; monogram ES below coronet; fan with falling feathers; the Cavendish motto CAVENDO TVTVS [By guarding safe]; a knotted serpent.

Octagonal panels

A Above centrepiece, monogram spelling GEORGE SHREWSBURY surmounted by coronet, with the name spelled out in the octagonal frame.

B Left of centrepiece, oak tree showing leaves and acorns, copies Mattioli (*Commentarii*, 1558, p. 138, 'Quercus'); inscription in octagonal frame INTEGRITAS VI ROBORA PERENNIVS EST [Integrity is more lasting than oak].

C Right of centrepiece, three differently flowering stems springing from a single leaf base, copied from Mattioli (*Commentarii*, 1558, p. 261, 'Faba Aegyptica'); inscription in octagonal frame, VERA VIRTVS PERICVLVM AFFECTAT [True courage seeks out danger] with ES initials.

D Below centrepiece, cedar tree, copies Mattioli (*Commentarii*, 1558, p. 83, 'Cedrus'); inscription in octagonal frame, VERA FELICITAS SEMPER ILLESA [True happiness is always unscathed] (Fig. 5.7).

Cruciform panels

1 [CER]SEREL, shows a kestrel perched, a smaller bird beside it; copies Gessner *Historia*, p. 53, *Icones*, p. 8, for which Gessner supplies the French name 'Quercerelle'.

2 FAVCONET, cf. Belon, *L'histoire de la nature des oyseaux*, 1555, p. 377, 'Grande Hirondelle'.

3 A GLEADE, copies Gessner *Historia*, p. 586, *Icones*, p. 8, Lat. 'miluus', which Lewis and Short's Latin dictionary translates as 'kite, glede'. Shown standing on stony ground pecking a frog, with a smaller bird below it.

4 QUAIL, copied from *Historia*, p. 338, *Icones*, p. 71.

5 THE ESTRICHE, copies Gessner, *Historia*, p. 708, *Icones*, p. 69. Embroidery adds a horseshoe in the bird's beak.

6 A SWALLOE, shows two swallows facing different ways; both copied from Gessner's single 'Hirundo', repeating and reversing the image, *Historia*, p. 528, *Icones*, p. 51. It might be significant that, as Palliser notes, 'The swallow, *hirondelle*, is the punning cognisance for Arundel … By the marriage of Mary, heiress of the Fitzalans, to Thomas Howard, the ill-fated Duke of Norfolk, the Fitzalan badges passed into the house of Norfolk' (*Historic Devices, Badges and War-cries*, 1870, p. 271).

7 A TVRKIE COCKE, copies Gessner, *Historia*, p. 464, *Icones*, p. 56.

8 A LEPARDE, copies Gessner, *Historia*, p. 935, *Icones*, p. 32.

9 A CIVET CATTE, copies Gessner, 'Catus aut Feles Zibethi', *Historia*, p. 948, *Icones*, p. 33.

10 SCORPIONS, copied from Mattioli, *Commentarii*, 1558, p. 187, 'Scorpio terrestris' (Fig. 4.67).

11 A [SATYR]; damaged panel, only half remaining, but this clearly shows a horned and goat-legged man blowing a trumpet, hence a satyr. Not found in Gessner.

12 A TATOU, i.e. armadillo, copies Gessner's 'Tatus' (*Icones*, p. 103); his description states that it represents a creature which Pierre Belon found in 'Turchia' among the mountebanks and apothecaries, commonly known as a tatu, which had been brought from Guinea and the New World. Gessner's picture was copied from Belon, *Observations de plusieurs singularitez*, 1555, and Gessner uses Belon's description (Fig. 4.23).

13   A MULE, copies Gessner, *Historia*, p. 793, *Icones*, p. 16.

14   A MOLE WORTE, i.e. mole, copies Gessner, *Historia*, p. 1055, *Icones*, p. 52.

15   A BYRDE OF AMERICA, same label but not the same bird as the toucan in the Marian Hanging (panel 6), this copies the woodcut from fol. 115r of André Thevet's *Les singularitéz de la France antarctique*, 1558, showing an unnamed bird which Thevet describes as having a large crest 'yellow like fine gold', a black tail, and the rest of its plumage sprinkled with black and yellow and waved with various colours' (Fig. 4.17).

16   A BVKE, i.e. buck, copies Gessner, *Historia*, p. 1100, *Icones*, p. 25.

17   [LABEL ILLEGIBLE] three redbreasts, copying Gessner's illustration 'de Rubecula', *Historia*, 1555, p. 698, *Icones avium*, p. 48.

18   [LABEL ILLEGIBLE] copies Gessner, *Icones*, p. 147, 'Porcus Marinus', Italian 'Porco Marino', German 'Sawhund, Hundfisch, Thornhund'.

19   CORDILE, copies an illustration which reappears in several places in Gessner, who appears to have copied the 'Crocodyle d'Arabie' illustration from Pierre Belon's *Nature et diversité des poissons*, 1555, p. 39. The name on the embroidery was evidently suggested by Gessner's entry in *Historia*, p. 357, 'De Cordylo', describing a type of crocodile identified by Aristotle.

20   CAMEL, copies Gessner's dromedary, *Historia*, p. 172 , *Icones*, p. 18.

21   A BVLL BAYTED, bull set upon by dogs, ES monogram, not copied from Gessner.

22   KNOTTED SERPENTES, copies woodcut showing shed snake skins from Mattioli (*Commentarii*, 1558, p. 193, 'Senecta Anguium') (Fig. 4.59).

APPENDIX 2

The Oxburgh Valance

Bought with other Oxburgh embroideries by the National Art Collections Fund from the Earl of Bedingfeld, and gifted to the Victoria and Albert Museum in 1955, a condition of the sale was that the mounted hangings and the similarly mounted valance should be on permanent loan to Oxburgh Hall, where it is now held in store. Consisting of four detached sections, each with three, or in one case four, cruciform embroidered panels of the same size as those on the Oxburgh Hangings (29 × 29 cm), the panels are embroidered with animals and mounted on the same green velvet decorated with loops of sewn red cord that is used for the hangings.

Section A

1. A CAPON, copies Gessner, 'Capo', English 'capon', a castrated cock, *Historia*, p. 411, *Icones*, p. 54.
2. A DAKER HEN, copies Gessner, 'Trochilus Terrestris', identified by the English name only in *Historia*, p. 490, '*Angli vocant* a dakerhen, *Germani* ein Schryck'. The *OED* records 'dakerhen' as dialect, 1552, for the corncrake or land-rail. Also illustrated in *Icones*, p. 68, where the English name is not recorded, suggesting that the longer *Historia* was the embroidery source.
3. A SPIDER, shown in the centre of a web between two plant stems, with five more spiders on the further side of the plant stems, copied from Mattioli (*Commentarii in Dioscorides*, 1558, p. 222, 'Araneus') (Fig. 4.65).

Section B

1. A BLAK BYRDE, copies Gessner, 'Merula', the English name recorded in *Historia*, p. 580: '*Anglis* a blak osel, a blak byrd', *Historia*, p. 579, *Icones*, p. 33.
2. SAND COCKLES, shows seashells in a rectangular basket, copied from Mattioli (*Commentarii*, 1558, p. 180, 'Chamae') (Fig. 4.61).
3. A DOTREL, shown as three birds standing on a rectangular basket with handles, containing eggs, copies Mattioli (*Commentarii*, 1558, p. 210, 'Ovum'); Mattioli does not identify these birds as dottrel (Fig. 4.63).

Section C

1. A CLIFFE [FISH], copies Gessner, 'Anarrhichas', thus named by Gessner for a large fish found in the German ocean, the picture drawn from a specimen sent to him by George Fabricius with a description; called *Klipfisch* [Cliff Fish] in German from its alleged habit of climbing cliffs, *Icones*, p. 116.
2. Label no longer legible, but picture shows a deep-chested, ape-like creature carrying its young on its back beneath its long, bushy tail. This is a reverse copy of the quadruped Gessner' identifies as a creature from the New World known as a su. 'When the hunters that desire her skin set upon her, she flyeth very swift, carrying her young ones upon her back, and covering them with her broad tail' (trans. Topsell 1605, p. 511). Gessner

(*Icones*, 'Additiones', p. 127) cites his source for all this information as André Thevet in his *Les singularitéz de la France antarctique* (1558), fol. 109r, where it is illustrated; Gessner's woodcut is a reverse copy of Thevet's. The orientation of the embroidery follows Thevet's woodcut rather than Gessner's (Fig. 4.21).

3 Two panels joined, the larger part entitled SERPENT OF THE SEA copies Gessner, *Historia*, p. 1038, *Icones*, p. 90, 'Serpens Marinus'. The smaller portion, of which little remains, and with no label, shows creatures very similar to the damaged SCORPIONS panel on the Cavendish Hanging.

Section D

1 A GENETTE (illust. Swain, 1973, pl. 70), copies Gessner, *Historia*, 'Appendix', p. 21, 'Genetha'.
2 A FROGGE, shows two frogs copied from separate illustrations on the same page of Gessner, *Historia*, pp. 58–9, *Icones*, p. 58, which Gessner labels 'Rana, vel Rubeta gibbosa' [hump-backed frog] and 'Rana' [frog].
3 A LION OF THE SEA, copies Gessner, *Icones*, p. 173, 'Monstrum Leoninum' (Fig. 4.8).

APPENDIX 3

Two Hardwick Cushion Covers

Both square cushion covers (Figs 4.69 and 4.70) are divided by interlocking plant stems into lozenge-shaped compartments containing one of three flowers: the lily (France), thistle (Scotland) and rose (England). This alternating pattern is varied in the five compartments, one at the centre and one in each corner, of each cover, which contain inserted roundels illustrating particular animal fables copied from the illustrations to Gabriello Faerno's *Fabulae centum* (1st edn, 1563), together with one from the *Emblemata* of Hadrianus Junius (1565), and another almost certainly copied from the *Imprese heroiche et morali* of Gabriel Simeoni (*Le sentenziose imprese*, 1559, and many later editions). The two corner roundels on one edge of both covers have been badly cut, so that only fragments remain; however the top right roundel in cushion cover (b) still shows the rear part of a bird of which enough is still visible to leave no doubt that it copied Faerno no. 13, illustrating the fable of the crow and its mother. See Nevinson, 'English domestic embroidery patterns', 1939–40, p. 6 (n. 2) for comment on the possible significance of the emblems.

Cushion cover (a)
1 Centre roundel. Fable of the fox and the eagle, showing a fox eating a young eaglet which has fallen to the ground out of the nest above with the eagle flying away; three further eaglets are falling to the ground. Copies Faerno, no. 60, the fable of the fox and the eagle who were friends before the eagle carried off the fox's cubs, after which the fox ate the eagle's young when they fell from the tree. Faerno's moral is: *Qui tenuem amicum laedit, huic, si humanitus/ Impune fuerit, imminet vindex Deus* [S/he who damages a weak friendship, even if s/he has suffered no human punishment, will call down the vengeful God].
2 Top left roundel. Damaged, unidentifiable subject.
3 Top right roundel. A cat shut in a cage, surrounded by mice. Copies emblem *Impunitas ferociæ parens* [Licence the parent of cruelty], Junius, *Emblemata*,1565, no. 4. Junius's epigram explains the moral, that the wicked will rejoice if just men are persecuted and confined.
4 Bottom left roundel. Damaged, unidentifiable subject.
5 Bottom right roundel. A leaping horse, almost certainly copying a detail from Simeoni's *Solus promeritus* [Only one deserves the praise]. Simeoni's picture shows two riders brandishing whips as they chase a third, riderless horse towards a standard on a pole; the commentary explains that this *impresa* illustrates a horse race, of which only one can be the winner.

Cushion cover (b)
1 Central roundel. Two frogs sitting on a wellhead, with Mary's cipher to the left of the wellhead. Copies Faerno, no. 37, the fable of the frog which fears to jump into a well in case it is dry, the moral being that this shows the danger of embarking on affairs too precipitately: *Negotiorum iubeo*

spectari exitum/ Iis, qui inchoare quid volunt [I advise anyone thinking of getting into a business to know how they will get out of it,' or simply 'Look before you leap!'].

2. Top left roundel. A cat devours a cock. Copies Faerno, no. 42, with the moral that reason and justice will not deter those who are prepared to use force.
3. Top right roundel. Damaged, but still shows the tail of a bird, of which enough is visible to leave no doubt that it copied Faerno, no. 13, the fable of the crow which, when in mortal danger, asks its mother to seek prayers for its deliverance, only to be told that one who has never prayed for others can hardly expect their intercession in return.
4. Bottom left roundel. A crow tries to fly up from a snake which bites its leg. Copies Faerno, no. 24, the fable of the crow which was caught by the snake which it tried to snatch. The moral is that anticipated gains may turn to our own disadvantage: *Infausta multis sunt sua ipsorum lucra* [Unlucky to many are their own profits].
5. Bottom right roundel. Damaged, though it appears to show the rear legs of an animal, cf. Paradin, *Horrent commota moveri* [Disturbed things hate being aroused], an angry bear breathing smoke is a warning that we should not provoke those who are already angry; but the legs are repositioned, and this may not be the same image.

APPENDIX 4

The Hardwick Octagons

Thirty octagons conforming to the similar ones showing plant slips and Latin mottoes on the Oxburgh Hangings were discovered at Hardwick Hall packed away in cloths by the sixth Duke of Devonshire in the late nineteenth century, when one was loaned to an exhibition; in 1933, Duchess Evelyn noted correspondence relating to this loan and ordered a search which led to the discovery of 30 panels, which she had mounted on the present wooden screen at Hardwick consisting of hinged panels each holding five of the embroidered octagons. A further octagon showing an arum lily with the inscription OMNIVM EX DISPONENTIS ARBITRIO [I judge all things as they are disposed] was separately mounted on a frame with other embroidery fragments, possibly for the earlier exhibition. The octagons measure 34 × 34 cm and are worked in silk and wool cross and tent stitch, c.400 stitches to the square inch, on linen canvas. Many carry the initials ES and these, together with the inscriptions, were overpainted by the sixth duke to make them more legible. The panels are otherwise indistinguishable from the octagonal plant slips among the Oxburgh embroideries. Most copy the illustrations to Mattioli's commentary on the *Materia medica* of Dioscorides, and my references are to the expanded edition, *Commentarii in Dioscorides*, which appeared in Venice published by Vincent Valgrisi in 1558. References to Erasmus's *Adagia* below are to the standard edition in the *Opera omnia* printed in Leiden, 1703, though the numbering remains the same in most editions from the early sixteenth century onwards. Richard Taverner translated the *Adagia* into English in 1539 and I cite his translation of the motto where it seems appropriate.

1. Onion, copies Mattioli (*Commentarii*, 1558, p. 308, 'Ceparum'). Motto: VT PLVRES SAPIENDVM VT PAVCI LOQUENDVM [As many may be wise, so few should speak], not found in this form in *Adagia*, although Erasmus uses a variant: *loquendum ut plures, sapiendum ut pauci* in his essay on the proverb *Extra publicam viam ne deflectas* which is copied for the inscription to no. 10.
2. Field garlic, copies Mattioli (*Commentarii*, 1558, p. 307, 'Ampelo prasum'). Motto: MINVTVLA PLVVIA IMBREM PARIT [Little drops make up the shower, or 'A misseling rayn gendreth great wet] (*Adagia* 1.3.2, trans. Taverner).
3. Gladdon, aka stinking iris, copies Mattioli (*Commentarii*, 1558, p. 499, 'Xyris'). Motto: CORONAM NE CARPITO [Pluck not the crown] (*Adagia* 1.1.2) (Fig. 5.15).
4. Iris, copies Mattioli (*Commentarii*, 1558, p. 17, 'Iris Sylvestris'). Motto: FRATRVM INTER SE IRE SVNT ACERBISSIME [Most bitter are the quarrels of brothers] (*Adagia* 1.2.50).
5. Elm branch, copies Mattioli (*Commentarii*, 1558, p. 104, 'Ulmus'), though Nevinson ('An Elizabethan herbarium', 1976, identifies this as mulberry (Mattioli, *Commentarii*, 1568, 'Morus'). Motto: NEQUICQVAM SAPIT QVI SIBI NON SAPIT [He knows naught who knows not himself] (*Adagia* 1.6.20).

6   Lungwort, copies Mattioli (*Commentarii*, 1558, p. 1094, 'Hepatica'). Motto: SEMENTEM ALII FACIVNT ALII METENT [Some sow, others reap] (*Adagia* 1.5.32). Same adage used for no. 27.

7   Gourd, copies Mattioli (*Commentarii*, 1558, p. 293, 'Melones'). Motto: NVLLVM SPECIOSVM NON CADVCVM [Naught that glitters will fail to fall], not found in *Adagia*.

8   Poppy, copies Mattioli (*Commentarii*, 1558, p. 525, 'Papaverus'). Motto: QVOD CARET ALTERNA REQVIE DVRABILE NON EST [That which hath not its turn of rest will not endure], not found in *Adagia*.

9   Laurel, copies Mattioli (*Commentarii*, 1558, p. 97, 'Laurus'). Motto: VIRTVTIS PRAEMIVM [The reward of virtue] (commonplace phrase not listed as an adage in its own right by Erasmus though used at 1.8.92, for instance) (Fig. 5.9).

10 Plantain, copies Mattioli (*Commentarii*, 1558, p. 281, 'Plantago maior'. Motto: EXTRA PVBLICAM VIAM NE DEFLECTAS [Do not turn off the highway] (*Adagia* 1.1.2) (Fig. 5.13).

11 Rye grass, with two cocks eating seeds, copies Mattioli (*Commentarii*, 1558, p. 257, 'Lolium'). Motto: PER PVBLICAM VIAM NE AMBVLES [Do not walk in the highway] (*Adagia* 1.1.2) (Fig. 5.11).

12 Mandrake, copies Mattioli (*Commentarii*, 1558, p. 535, 'Mandragora'). Motto: VITIA OCCVLTA MINVS NOXIA [Vices hidden give less offence], not found in *Adagia* (Fig. 5.25).

13 Palm branch with fruit, copies Mattioli (*Commentarii*, 1558, p. 141, 'Palma'). Motto: MALVM CONSILIVM CONSVLTORI PESSIMVM [He who gives bad advice, suffers most by it, or: Evil counsel is worst to the counsellor] (*Adagia* 1.2.14, trans. Taverner). This maxim is apparently quoted in a letter written to Shrewsbury in 1590 from Overton, Bishop of Lichfield and Coventry (see unpublished Hardwick typescript inventory, p. 14).

14 Teazle, copies Mattioli (*Commentarii*, 1558, p. 356, 'Dipsacus, sive Labrum Veneris'). Motto: FERAS NON CVLPES QVOD VITARI NON POTEST [Endure what cannot be avoided, rather than complaining at it] (*Adagia* 1.3.14) (Fig. 5.19).

15 Dittander, aka pepperwort, copies Mattioli (*Commentarii*, 1558, p. 329, 'Lepidium'). Motto: SATIVS EST INITIIS MEDERI QVAM FINE [Early remedies are better than late] (*Adagia* 1.2.40).

16 Orpine, copies Mattioli (*Commentarii*, 1558, p. 340, 'Telephium'). Motto: CVM MINERVA MANVM QVOQVE MOVE [Set about thy task with Minerva's aid] (*Adagia* 1.6.18) (Fig. 5.23).

17 Red clover, copies Mattioli (*Commentarii*, 1558, p. 440, 'Trifolium Pretense'). Motto: OMNIVM RERVM VICISSITVDO EST [Change is in all things] (*Adagia* 1.7.64).

18 Beech branch, copies Mattioli (*Commentarii*, 1558, p. 135, 'Fagus'). Motto: OCVLIS MAGIS HABENDA FIDES QVAM AVRIBVS [Trust more to the eyes than to the ears] (*Adagia* 1.1.100).

19 Ivy, copies Mattioli (*Commentarii*, 1558, p. 335, 'Hedera'). Motto: CAECA FORTVNA EST ET SVOS EFFICIT CAECOS [Fortune is blind and makes her victims blind], not found in *Adagia*.

20 Houndstongue, copies Mattioli (*Commentarii*, 1558, p. 578, 'Cynoglossum'). Motto: NATVRA EA QVE NOCENT ABSCONDIT [Nature hides harmful things], not found in *Adagia*.

21 Lily of the valley, copies Mattioli (*Commentarii*, 1558, p. 454, 'Lilium convallium'). Motto: PER PVBLICAM VIAM NE AMBVLES [Do not walk in the highway] (*Adagia* 1.1.2) (Fig. 5.17).

22 Male fern, copies Mattioli (*Commentarii*, 1558, p. 624, 'Polypodium'). Motto: ARTEM QVAEVIS ALIT TERRA [Each land nurtures its own art] (*Adagia* 1.7.33).

23 Moon wort, copies Mattioli (*Commentarii*, 1558, p.465, 'Lunaria minor'). Motto: PECVNIAE OBEDIVNT OMNIA [Unto money be all things obedient] (*Adagia* 1.7.87, trans. Taverner).

24 Hartstongue fern, copies Mattioli (*Commentarii*, 1558, p. 438, 'Phyllitis'). Motto: LEONEM NE STIMVLES [Rouse not the fury of the lion], not found in *Adagia*.

25 Mushrooms, copies Mattioli (*Commentarii*, 1558, p. 545, 'Fungi'). Motto: OMNES SIBI ESSE MELIVS VOLVNT QVAM ALTERI [Every man loveth himself better than he loveth another] (*Adagia* 1.3.91, trans. Taverner).

26 Citron branch, copies Mattioli (*Commentarii*, 1558, p. 150, 'Medica Malus'). Motto: FELICITAS VERA NVNQVAM CADVCA [True happiness faileth never], not found in *Adagia*.

27 Campion, copies Mattioli (*Commentarii*, 1558 p. 433, 'Lychnis'). Motto: SEMENTEM ALII

FACIVNT ALII METENT [Some do the sowing, others reap it] (*Adagia* 1.5.32). Same adage used for no. 6.

28 Hazel branch with filberts, copies Mattioli (*Commentarii*, 1558, p. 166, 'Nuces Avellanae'). Motto: NEMO BENE IMPERAT NISI QVI PARVERIT IMPERIO [No man can be a good ruler unless he hath been first ruled] (*Adagia* 1.1.3, trans. Taverner).

29 Hawthorn, copies Mattioli (*Commentarii*, 1558, p. 113, 'Acuta Spina'). Motto: AB OMNI PARTE EQVALITER PVNGO [I wound from all sides alike], not found in *Adagia* (Fig. 5.21).

30 Primula (cowslip), copies Mattioli (*Commentarii*, 1558, p. 491, 'Sanicula overa Orecchia di Orso'). Motto: VT SEMENTEM FECERIS ITA ET METES [As you sow so also shall you reap] (*Adagia* 1.8.78).

31 Detached panel, separately mounted. Cuckoo-pint, copies Mattioli (*Commentarii*, 1558, p. 324, 'Arum'). Motto: OMNIA EX DISPONENTIS ARBITRIO [I judge all things as they are disposed], not found in *Adagia*.

Note: For further examples of plant slips with Latin mottoes see: Marian Hanging, panels B, G, H; Shrewsbury Hanging, panels B, C, D; Cavendish Hanging, panels B, C, D; Detached panels, B, E, F.

APPENDIX 5

Detached Panels

Thirty-eight separate panels, nearly all of which conform in style, size and subject matter to the panels on the three great Oxburgh Hangings and on the Oxburgh Valance, were purchased, along with the other Oxburgh embroideries, by the National Art Collections Fund in 1953 and gifted to the Victoria and Albert Museum where they are now conserved; these are listed below using the museum accession numbers. Two detached cruciform panels (HW1-2) showing animals (a 'Falcon' and 'A Cockle Crab') were preserved not at Oxburgh but at Hardwick Hall where they are now displayed. Three further detached panels from Oxburgh (HR1-3) were bought at Sothebys in 1957 by the Friends of the Palace of Holyroodhouse, Edinburgh, where they are now displayed. One further panel (X) was recorded by Zulueta at Hardwick in 1923 but is now unlocated and has not been seen.

V&A T.33 detached square centrepiece: *Las pennas passan* panel

Square panel consisting of an emblematic device and motto within a double border (Fig. 2.9). Centre panel shows, at the top, an armillary sphere from which feathers are falling, with the Spanish motto in a scroll LAS PENNAS PASSAN Y QUEDA LA SPERANZA [Sorrows pass but hope survives], punning on 'pennas' as both 'sorrows' and 'feathers'. The background shows stylised waves in which float various boats, birds and sea monsters: top left, a sail boat with two passengers; top right, a duck catching a fish; bottom left, a gondola-shaped boat with one oar and above it a monstrous fish, other sea creatures including a seahorse and tusked monster; bottom right, a galleon with three masts. The sea monsters go back to illustrations based on Olaus Magnus's *Historia* as copied in Sebastian Munster's *Cosmographiae universalis* (1550, pp. 852–3). The outer border is red and gold brocade, 63 mm wide with a single carnation at the centre of each side; the original round corner bosses have been removed. The inner border is filled with four heraldic shields at the corners and eight emblematic devices, two on each side, all but one copied from the emblem books of Claude Paradin (1557) and Gabriel Simeoni (1560).

Heraldic shields (inner border)

I Top left: royal arms of France with cockleshell collar of the Order of St Michel.
II Top right: royal arms of Spain with collar of the Order of the Golden Fleece.
III Bottom right: royal arms of Scotland with what may be a collar of the Order of the Thistle.
IV Bottom left: royal arms of England with collar and motto of the Order of the Garter.

Emblematic devices (inner border)

(a) Top left: *impresa* showing a crowned five-pointed star, with motto on a scroll: MONSTRANT REGIBVS ASTRA VIAM [The star shows the way to kings]. Copies Paradin, p. 18, who identifies this as the device of the Knights of the Star founded by Jean

II of France in 1351. Two dogs running behind the scroll are decorative and not part of the *impresa*.

(b) Top right: *impresa* showing an eagle perched on the antlered skull of a stag, with motto on a scroll: ARDVA DETVRBANS VIS ANIMOSA QVATIT [The strength of courage bearing down on lofty things, breaks them]. Copies Paradin, p. 87, who does not identify any bearer of this *impresa* but explains that it is based on a description in Pliny's *Natural History* of the way an eagle will land on a stag's head and scatter dust in its eyes until the stag hurls itself blindly from a cliff.

(c) Upper right: disembodied hand holds a scimitar with which it cuts a knotted rope that hangs from a cloud, with motto on a scroll: NODOS VIRTVTE RESOLVO [I untie the knots through my virtue/power]. Copies Paradin, p. 214, who identifies it as the *impresa* of Jacques d'Albon, Mareschal de St André, who died in 1561, and explains that it represents the Gordian knot which Alexander the Great cut in fulfilment of the prophecy that whosoever untied the knot would rule over Asia.

(d) Lower right: a marigold, or marguerite, shown turning towards the sun in splendour, with motto on a scroll: NON INFERIORA SECVTVS [Not having followed lower things]. Copied from Paradin, p. 41, who identifies it as the *impresa* of Marguerite de Valois, Queen of Navarre and sister of François I. This *impresa* is also used on the octagonal panel, Marian Hanging E, with the same motto.

(e) Bottom right: disembodied hand holds a snake over a fire of sticks, with motto on a scroll: QVIS CONTRA NOS [Who is against us?]. Copied from Paradin, p. 187, who does not ascribe it to any bearer but explains its basis in Acts 28, where St Paul suffers no harm from a viper that bites his finger as he is laying sticks on a fire, but shakes it into the flames thus demonstrating to the unbelievers surrounding him that God is on his side. Behind the scroll is a black and white dog with a curly tail, apparently in pursuit of the running stag in the opposite corner. Zulueta (1923, p. 13) notes that this is very similar to the dog labelled 'Jupiter' on panel T.33P

(f) Bottom left: two disembodied hands are clasped around a cornucopia full of plants, with motto on a scroll: DITAT SERVATA FIDES [Keeping one's faith makes one rich], copied from Simeoni (p. 31); to the left of this *impresa* is a tiny bird on a tree stump, and the stag fleeing from the dog in the opposite corner.

(g) Lower left: a five-pointed star shown with arrows shooting out from it, motto in an encircling banderole, the upper loop of which is damaged but almost certainly containing the first two words of the motto: VIAS TVAS DOMINE DEMONSTRA [Show me your ways, O Lord]. Copied from Paradin, p. 88, where it is the *impresa* displayed on a ship belonging to Emperor Charles V as a reminder of the need to pray for divine directions; the motto quotes Psalms 25.4.

(h) Upper left: two intertwined columns surmounted by a crown with enfolded scroll on which is inscribed the motto: PIETATE ET JVSTICIA. Not copied from Paradin or Simeoni, this was the device of Charles IX, adapted from that of his godfather, Charles V, who famously adopted the columns of Hercules with the motto *Plus Ultra* [More beyond]. The twin columns of Piety and Justice had long featured in French royal iconography. Charles IX was Mary's brother-in-law, succeeding François II to the throne of France in 1560.

Detached octagonal panels

T33A Damaged half panel showing fragmentary monogram, with border inscription: GRA[CE CAVEN]DISSHE.

T33B Unlabelled plant, a houseleek, copied from Mattioli (1558, p. 550), 'Sedum Maius', 'Sempervivum', also known as 'Sempervivum Tectorum', its name reflects an ancient and widespread custom of growing it on the roofs of houses, and its evergreen habit inspired belief in its protective powers against thunder. Motto: HOSTIVM MVNE[RA NON MVNE]RA [The gifts of enemies are no gifts] (Erasmus, *Adagia* 1.3.35).

T33C Damaged half panel showing fragmentary monogram, with border inscription GRA[CE CAVEN]DISSHE.

T33D Damaged half panel showing fragmentary monogram, with border inscription '[HEN]RY CAVEN[DISSHE].

T33E Octagon showing a cactus with motto HABEAS EXTRA LVTVM PEDES [Keep your feet out of the mud]. The cactus plant does not seem to copy any illustration in Mattioli, although the motto corresponds to Erasmus, *Adagia* 1.2.81: *Extra lutum pedes habes*. Zulueta comments: 'The cactus is said to clear muddy water' (1923, p. 12), but offers no evidence for this received idea.

T33F/I Plant slip, cut into two parts, both mounted separately on green velvet, of which the lower portion T33I also has the cruciform panel labelled 'A SEELE', upper portion T33F also has cruciform panel labelled LOCVSTE OF THE SEA. The plant is coltsfoot, and copies Mattioli, 1558, p. 444, 'Tussilago'. Motto: INTRA TVAM PELLICVLVM TE CONTINE [Keep within your own skin], Erasmus, *Adagia* 1.6.92. Signed ES.

HR1 Octagon with crowned monogram showing letters ??S, flanked by a lily (France) and thistle (Scotland) below smaller monograms for ΦR (François Rex) above the lily, and Mary's cipher above the thistle; border inscription: NON HORA SOMNIAMVS QUOD AMAMVS NVLLA [We do not sleep for an hour because we love no woman]. Panel originally at Oxburgh, but acquired for the Palace of Holyroodhouse, Edinburgh, in 1957, where it is now displayed.

HR2 Octagon with monogram showing GEORGE ELIZABETH between two floral plant slips and beneath coronet, with border inscription GEORGE ELIZABETH SHREWSBURY. Panel originally at Oxburgh, but acquired by the Palace of Holyroodhouse, Edinburgh, in 1957, where it is now displayed; this panel is very similar to Marian Hanging D.

X1 Octagonal panel with monogram showing ELIZABETH beneath coronet, flanked by two flowers, inscription in octagonal border reads: ELIZABETH SHREWSBERY [sic]. Recorded at Oxburgh by Zulueta in 1923, now unlocated and not seen.

Detached cruciform panels of animals

T33F A LOCVSTE OF THE SEA, signed ES, showing a seahorse, copied from Mattioli (1558, 'Hippocampus'), who says it is a type of locust corresponding to the species identified by Pliny, *Natural History*, 32, 2. Gessner has a very similar picture (*Historia*, p. 267), but does not give any variant of the name that includes the word 'locust'. Panel mounted on green velvet together with portion of octagonal CONTINO INTRA TUAM PEL panel.

T33G A DOG FISH, with Mary's crowned cipher, mounted on green velvet. Copies Gessner, *Icones*, p. 152.

T33H A COCK OF TH'ALPES, signed ES, copies Gessner, *Icones*, p. 59.

T33I A SEELE, signed ES, mounted on green satin on which is also portion of the octagon showing coltsfoot plant. Copies Gessner, *Historia*, p. 366, *Icones*, p. 164, 'Phoca'.

T33J AN EAPE, copies Gessner, *Historia*, p. 957, *Icones*, p. 40. 'Simius'.

T33K A PEACOCKE, signed EB, mounted on green velvet. Gessner, *Historia*, p. 631, *Icones*, p. 55, 'Pavo'.

T33L A PIE, bird standing beside four-branched plant, signed MR. Copies Gessner *Icones*. p. 28, 'Pica'.

T33M AN ... OF IND, damaged panel with right-hand side cut off, but showing quadruped with scaly bracts, not corresponding to any creature in Gessner.

T33N A GOR GLUT [...], damaged panel with right-hand side cut off, remainder showing rear half of an unidentified quadruped standing behind a tree with objects, possible food remains, on the ground beneath it. Neither the animal nor the remaining letters of the name on the damaged label appear to correspond to any illustration in Gessner.

T33O [STEIN] BOCK, signed ES, panel damaged with left half cut off, but enough remains to leave no doubt that this copies Gessner's picture of the ibex (*Icones*, p. 39) for which he supplies the German name *Steinbock* which Bess evidently took as her label for the embroidery.

T33P JUPITER, signed MR; shows a black and white dog with a curled-back tail, not copied from any of the various types of dog illustrated by Gessner. Zulueta (1923, p. 13) notes its resemblance to the small dog that is shown running at the bottom corner of the *Las pennas passan* panel, and the likelihood is that it represents an actual pet belonging to Elizabeth Shrewsbury.

T33Q AN EWTE, shows two newts, one side view and another seen from above, facing in opposite directions, and based on Gessner, *Historia*, p. 27, *Icones*, p. 31, 'Lacertus aquaticus'.

T33R [...] BYRD, damaged panel, left-hand side cut off. Copies Gessner, *Historia*, p. 605, *Icones*, p. 94, 'Onocrotalus', i.e. pelican; Gessner does not give an English name, although he identifies the German name as *Kropffvogel* [crop bird], referring to the prominent goitre beneath its neck (Fig. 4.47).

T33S A NAUTILUS, damaged, only top left-hand portion remaining showing part of a shell, freely copying Gessner, *Historia*, p. 192, 'Nautilus'.

T33T SEA HORS, damaged panel with bottom portion cut off, but showing a fabulous hybrid creature with the front half of a horse joined to a serpentine fish tail, copied from Gessner, *Historia*, p. 182, 'Equus fabulosus Neptuni'.

T33U A [...], damaged panel with the bottom portion, bearing the lower label, cut off; remainder shows a fish with a large head, copied from Mattioli's picture of a species of gudgeon, 'Gobii aliud genus' (1558, p. 203).

T33V A WATER [...], damaged panel with bottom portion cut off, but clearly showing the species of flying fish which Gessner identifies as 'Hirundo marinis' [sea swallow], *Historia*, pp. 514–15, *Icones*, pp. 36–7.

T33W A HEARON, damaged panel with bottom portion cut off, but copies Gessner, *Historia*, p. 206, *Icones*, p. 117, 'Ardea'.

T33X A SHOFLER, i.e. spoonbill, copies Gessner, 'Pelecanus', *Historia*, p. 640, *Icones*, p. 92; embroidery shows bird with two small fish. Swain (1973, pp. 66–7) comments, 'The spoonbill, erroneously labelled '*pelecanus*' by Gessner, but given the correct German name of '*Loeffler*', has been drawn out and identified with its common name '*a shofler*', still called a 'shovelar' in parts of northern England.' Corners have plant slips (Fig. 4.45).

T33Y A DOWKER, copies Gessner, *Icones*, p. 88, 'Columbus maior'; corners have plant slips.

T33Z A QUAYLE, standing amidst long-stalked grasses, with plant slips in corners, possibly based on Gessner, *Icones* p. 71, 'Coturnix', 'Qualea', but cf. Cavendish Hanging no. 4.

T33AA THE OSPRAY, shown standing on its nest with head turned down to place an object in the nest. Not copied from Gessner, who illustrates the osprey in *Icones*, p. 129. Corners with plant slips.

T33BB THE HOBREAU, i.e. hobby, copies Belon, *L'histoire de la nature des oyseaux*, 1555, p. 119.

T33CC A POOLE SNYTE, i.e. great snipe (*OED* gives 'snite' as an early spelling of snipe), copies Gessner, *Historia*, p. 500, *Icones*, p. 114, German *Meerhun*, Latin *Limosa*; the Latin name means 'a muddy place' and the English label reflects both the Latin and German names for this species. Top corners have butterflies, bottom corners have snails.

T33DD AN APE OF TURKY, shows frontal view of ape-like creature with large ears, female breasts and a long, limp male member, not corresponding to any illustration in Gessner. Top corners with sky pattern, bottom with plant slips (Fig. 4.1).

T33EE A GREAT MUNKEY, signed ES, copies Gessner, *Historia*, p. 970, *Icones*, p. 95, 'Cercopithecus'. Top corners decorated with brick pattern, bottom with plant slips.

T33FF A GENE SKYN, copies Gessner's woodcut 'Genethae pellis' [The skin of a genette], *Historia*, p. 1102 (Fig. 4.3).

T33GG ELEPHANT, copies Gessner, *Historia*, p. 410, *Icones*, p. 29, 'Elephantus'. Top corners each have a bird flying up, bottom corners have a plant slip.

T33HH A WATER OWLE, fish with divided tail and human face. Copies Gessner, *Icones*, p. 296, 'Cyprinus', a species of monstrous carp found in Lake Constance; none of Gessner's names for the fish corresponds to that on the embroidery. Corners with brick pattern.

T33II A ZYDRACH, signed ES, showing hammerhead shark, copies Gessner, *Icones*, p. 150, 'Zygaena'. Fleur de lis in each corner.

T33JJ A MONSTER OF THE SEA, copies Gessner, *Icones*, p. 175, 'Monstrum marinum ... Pan vel Satyrus marinus, aut Ichthyocentaurus, aut Daemon marinus appelatur' [Sea monster ... called a sea Pan or satyr, or an Ichthyocentaur, or a sea-demon]; top corners show flying insects, possibly butterflies, bottom corners have plant slips.

T33KK A BOATE FISHE, copies Gessner, *Historia*, p. 257, 'Echinus' or sea urchin. Four corners have fish heads.

T33LL Unlabelled fragmentary panel of white satin with strapwork design in applied green velvet; interstices of the strapwork painted with a design of flowers and birds in black, green, pink and fawn. Detached from the back of T33J.

HR3 A CATTE, copies Gessner, *Historia*, p. 345, *Icones*, p. 19, with Mary's cipher, and shown facing a mouse, which is added. Formerly at Oxburgh Hall, but acquired for the Palace of Holyroodhouse, Edinburgh, in 1957, where it is now displayed (Fig. 4.75).

HW1 A COCKLE CRAB, hermit crab in cockleshell, copies Mattioli (1558, p. 186, 'Cancelli'). No border or corners. On display in needlework gallery at Hardwick Hall.

HW2 FALCON, copies Gessner, 'Falco', *Historia*, p. 58, *Icones*, p. 10. On display in needlework gallery at Hardwick Hall.

X2 THE HULLOT, recorded at Oxburgh in 1923 by Zulueta, p. 12 ('Fragments' no. 17), but now unlocated and unseen.

APPENDIX 6

Mary's Bed of State: Collated Entries from Four Early Descriptions of Embroidered Bed Hangings no Longer Extant

- National Archives (Kew) SP 53/21, fols 108r–v, 109v (109r is blank), French inventory listing 49 devices. Fol. 109v, a separate sheet comprising the last 11 devices, nos. 39–49 below, is in a different hand and with the date '9 Sept 1586'; the right-hand margin has the title *Devises le lict de la Reyne* written down the side. A translation is printed in *Calendar of State Papers (Scotland) 1547–1603*, vol. IX, Glasgow 1915, pp. 502–4, where it is treated as a single document headed 'Devices on the Queen of Scots' Bed' and dated Oct 1587 [*hereinafter referred to as* NAK *in the listing below*].
- National Library of Scotland, Hawthornden MSS, vol. XII, Fowler's Papers and Scrolls, ff. 50–52, undated inventory of 43 'Devyces' preserved among the papers of William Fowler, but unsigned and not in Fowler's hand, hence referred to in the present book as Hawthornden Anonymous [*hereinafter referred to as* NLS50–52 *in the listing below*].
- National Library of Scotland, Hawthornden MSS, vol. XII, Fowler's Papers and Scrolls, f. 21, numbered list of 31 devices, headed: '5 April 1603 after the King's departure I did observe these devyses vpon the queens his mother's bed', and the following note after the last entry at the foot of the page, where it is taken up into the left-hand margin: 'This wants the wurmanship [sic] of this more well done and more gloriuslyie then the inventory. W. Fowler' [*hereinafter referred to as* NLS21 *in the listing below*].

- Letter, dated 1 July 1619, from William Drummond of Hawthornden to Ben Jonson listing 30 devices, first printed in Drummond, *History of Scotland* (1655), pp. 263–5, then in *Works* (1711), p. 137; repr. Jonson, *Works*, ed. Herford and Simpson, vol. I, 208–10 [*hereinafter referred to as* Let. *in the listing below*].

1 Un sep de vigne et une main celeste tenant un pot plain de vin qu'elle respend sur ledit sep et y a escript *Mea sic mihi prosunt* [A stock of a vine and a heavenly hand holding a vessel full of wine which it is sprinkling over the said stock, and there is written, *Thus are mine profitable to me.*]
NAK

(25) Another devayce for hir Maj^{tie} a vayne growing is watred with wayne and by this watryng instead to make it florish it maketh it die the word is *Mea sic mihi prosunt*.
NLS50–52

(25) A Vine tree watred with Wine, which instead to make it spring and grow, maketh it fade, the Word, *Mea sic mihi prosunt*.
Let.

The same device and motto are used on a jetton of Mary Stuart dated 1579 (Fig. 3.22): de Bie, 1636, p. 62; Cochran-Patrick, 1884, no. 13, pl. I, fig. 9; Burns, 1887, no. 920.

2 Un lion pris et renverse dans des lacs et cinq ou six tant lievres que lappins dessus a y escript pour mot *Et lepores devicto insultant leoni.* [A lion taken and overthrown in some nets, and five or six hares and rabbits: above is written as a motto, *Even hares trample on the conquered lion.*] NAK

(9) Another devayce of her maje^ties a Layen taken in a net and the hares romb and sitt apon him who are the most cowardly beasts in the w[orld] the word is *Et lepores devicto insultant lionem.* NLS50–52

(13) a Lyon catched in a nett and hares wantonlye passing over him. *Et lepores* (which is naught) *insultant devicto leoni.* NLS21

(13) An emblem of a Lyon taken in a Net, and Hares wantonly passing over him, the Word, *Et lepores devicto insultant Leoni.* Let.

Cf. Alciato, *Cum larvis non luctandum* (*Emblemata*, 1551, p. 166), (Fig. 2.7). The emblem goes back to a Greek epigram (*Anthology* 16.4, *Planudean* 1.5) 'strike my body now after my death, for the very hares insult the body of a dead lion' from which Erasmus derives the adage, *Mortuo leoni et lepores insultant* (*Adagia* 4.7.82) which supplies the motto as recorded on the embroidery.

3 Une lionne et son petit Lionceau pres d'elle y a pour mot *Unum quidem sed leonem.* [A lioness, and her little cub near to her: there is as motto, *One only, but that one a lion.*] NAK

(8) Another devayce of her maje^ties a she layon and her young layon besyd her the word is *Vnum quidem sed Lionem.* NLS50–52

(14) A big lyon and a littill young one at his feete *Unum quidem sed leonem.* NLS21

(12) This for her self and her Son, a big Lyon and a young Whelp beside her, the Word *Unum quidem sed leonum.* Let.

Based on an Aesopic fable that was interpreted as a heiroglyphical sign by Horapollo Nilus and illustrated in printed editions of his *Hieroglyphica* (see Fig. 3.10). The same device was identified as one of the incriminating *imprese* cited as evidence in the trial of Philip Howard, Earl of Arundel, in 1589: 'Then was produced an emblematical piece found in the earl's cabinet ... a Lion Rampant, with his chops all bloody with this poesie, *Tamen Leo*' (Hargrave, *Complete Collection of State Trials*, I, 1776, col. 166).

4 Un Leopart tenant dans sa gueule un herisson lequel il ne peut avaller ny cracher y a pour mot *Premit et hæret.* [A leopard holding in its mouth a hedgehog which it can neither swallow nor cast out, and for the motto, *It presses on it and it sticks.*] NAK

(26) Another devayce for hir Maj^tie a Leperd haulding a hourchen in his mouth the word is *premit est* [sic] *haeret.* NLS50–52

OED identifies 'hurcheon' as a variant spelling for 'urchin' and as the northern dialect word for hedgehog. This curious device moralising the harmful properties of a spined animal was probably suggested by Louis XII's celebrated device of the *porc epic*, indeed both Fowler and Drummond call the sea urchin in no. 9 below a 'porcupine'.

5 Deux spheres et une espee droicte au mylieu, a la poincte de laquelle y a une couronne. Le mot *Unus non sufficit orbis.* [Two spheres, and an upright sword in the midst, at the point of which is a crown; the motto, *One world is not enough.*] NAK

(5) A devayce of king francis' the quines first husband tow pillars haynging in the ayre in the midest betwixt them is a sword and on the poynt thereof is a crowne the word is *Vnus non sufficitt* [sic] *orbis.* NLS50–52

(22) Two globs and a sword vpon the point of a crowne. *Unus non sufficit orbis.* NLS21

The same device and motto are on a jetton illustrated by de Bie (1636, pl. 61), who says it must go back to the time of Mary's marriage in 1558 to François when these would probably have been distributed as *pièces de largesse* (p. 184). Cochran-Patrick (1884, p. 9) records a similar jetton dated 1559 with the same motto, but showing only the sword with the crown on its point, but not the two spheres. The same motto with a similar device – an armillary sphere suspended from the heavens – is on the decorated binding of the book of hours, printed in Paris in 1549, which Mary received as a gift from her husband François, now preserved in the Bibliothèque de Reims (see Fig. 2.35).

6 Une pyramide haulte ellevee autour de laquelle y a une branche de liebvre le mot *Te stante virebo*. [A high, raised pyramid, around which is a bough of ivy; the motto, *Whilst you stand, I shall flourish*.]   NAK

(2) A devayes of the last cardenall of Loran the quienes onkell a pieram[ed] of marber woumpled about with aywie and on the top of the pieremied a cressant and aboufe it a cardinals hatt the word is mienyng by the king his master so long as ye lived he stood. *Testante verbo* [sic.]   NLS50–52

(10) The Impressa of the Cardinal of Lorrain her Uncle, a Pyramide overgrown with Ivy, the vulgar Word, *Te stante virebo*.   Let.

Cf. Paradin, 1557, p. 87 (see Fig. 2.3).

7 Un croissant au bout de l'espee, y a *Donec totum impleat orbem*. [A crescent at the end of the sword; there is, *Until it fills the whole world*.]   NAK

(5) The impresa of Henry II the French King, a Cressant, the Word, *Donec totum impleat orbem*.   Let.

Cf. Giovio, 1556, p 24; Paradin, 1557, p. 20, neither of which shows the sword.

8 Un port de mer et une main celeste jettans une pierre dedans et *Donec emerserit undis*. [A haven of the sea, and a heavenly hand throwing a stone into it, and *Until it is sunk beneath the waves*.]   NAK

(24) Another devayce of a fische swimyng for glaydnes half aboufe the walter and a hayvenly hand wavering aboufe it the word is *donec dimerserit Vndis*.   NLS50–52

9 Un herrison en mer a demy tempestueuse cet herrison quasi couvert de pierres y a pour mot *Ne voluetur*. [A hedgehog in a somewhat tempestuous sea, the said hedgehog almost covered with stones; and for a motto, *Lest it be rolled about*.]   NAK

(30) Another for hir Maj^tie a hourchen laying upon a hiepe of stone, *ne Voluteture*.   NLS50–52

(26) a porcupine amongst sea craggs *ne volutetur*.   NLS21

(18) A Porcupine amongst Sea Rocks, the Word, *Ne volutetur*.   Let.

This 'hedgehog' or 'porcupine' (cf. no. 4 above) was certainly what we would call a sea urchin.

10 Un navire tout droict, en mer tempestueuse les voiles mats et cordages rompus preste [a s]'inforcer *Numquam nisi rectam*. [A ship upright in a tempestuous sea, sails torn and ropes rent, ready to sink, *Never unless upright*.]   NAK

(7) Another devayce of hir majtes' Broken Shroud and the mast far to the waffes of the side the Word is *nunquam nisi rectam*.   NLS50–52

(15) a Schip with her masts brokken, *nunquam nisi rectam*.   NLS21

(11) A Ship with her Mast broken and fallen in the Sea, the Word, *Numquam nisi rectam*.   Let.

The same device and motto are used on a jetton of Mary Queen of Scots dated 1579 (see Fig. 2.17): de Bie, 1636, p. 62; Cochran-Patrick, 1884, no. 14, p. 13, pl. I, fig. 10; Burns, 1887, no. 921A.

11 Une roue de moulin dans l'eaue courante; ceste devise Espagnolle *Llena di dolore vada desperanza*. [A mill-wheel in running water; this Spanish device, *Full of griefs, empty of hope*.]   NAK

(33) Another devayce a while receving walter of the rocke the word is *Pliena di dolor Voyde dy sperance*.   NLS50–52

(31) a wheele rolled from a mountaine in the sea. *Plena di dolor voda di speranza*. This appears to be her own but not well expressed as it is conceaved so I would have sayd in italian.   NLS21

(26) A wheel rolled from a Mountain in the Sea, *Piena di dolor voda de Speranza*. Which appeareth to be her own, and it should be *Precipitio senza speranza*' [Downfall without hope].   Let.

See Figure 2.8. Despite Drummond's correction, the emblem is not Mary's own, but copies the *impresa* described and illustrated in Paolo Giovio's *Dialogo dell'imprese* (Lyon 1559, and numerous further editions) showing a wheel with buckets used for irrigation and the motto: *Los lienos de dolor y los vazios de speranza* [The full ones are full of grief; the empty are empty of hope] which, Giovio explains, is an emblem of frustrated love. The motto appears to have been Spanish, as in Giovio's original and the 1586 transcription, but Fowler and Drummond evidently assumed that it was Italian, though Fowler, who spoke good Italian having stayed in Italy, recognises that if so it is defective. The motto could well have been difficult to read on the embroidery.

12 Une colombe en une cage et une aigle au dessus preste de la devorer ou elle en sera sortie, ceste devise en Italien *Je suis ung mal mais je crains pis*. [A dove in a cage, and an eagle above ready to devour her when she shall come forth; this device in Italian, *I am in evil plight, but I fear worse*.] NAK

This device is recorded twice, cf. no. 37 below.

13 Les neuf cielx et l'estoille de mercure suivante le soleille *Comite mercurio*. [The nine heavens and the star of Mercury following the sun, *With Mercury as his companion*.] NAK
(29) Another devayce of the viii heavens the word is *Comite mercurio*. NLS50–52

14 Un bouclier comme suspendu dans l'air dessus une couronne *aut hanc aut super hoc*. [A buckler, as it were suspended in the air, above a crown, *Either this or above that*.] NAK
(28) A devayce of the kings Maj^tie a Bouckler efter the Latedemonian facon in the midest thereof the word is *aut hanc aut super hoc*. NLS50–52
(27) a schielde and a crowne above. *Aut hanc aut super hoc*. NLS21

15 Un arbre nomme picea et un cedre tombe a cette figure [*Sketch of two trees, one upright, one fallen] y a pour mot *Ploret picea quod cedrus cecidit*. [A tree called pitch pine and a fallen cedar as in this sketch; and for a motto, *The pitch pine weeps because the cedar has fallen*.] NAK

(31) A devayce for the kings Maj^tie and his mother a ceder trie fallen to the ground another a apell trie growing upright therby *ploret picea quod cedrus cecidit*. NLS50–52
(25) a trie of oak standing besyde another brokken and thwartlye traversed. *Quod cedo* [sic.] *cecidit ploret picea non pro meo captu*. [Because the cedar has fallen, the pitch pine tree weeps, not for my taking.] NLS21

Hawthornden Anonymous's mistaken identification of the second tree as an apple suggests that he did not understand the Latin, a suggestion strengthened by further mistakes elsewhere in his Latin transcriptions. Fowler's oak tree is more surprising, and his amplification of the motto on the embroidery is not supported by the other records.

16 Une aile d'Aigle entre plus[ieurs] petites plumes a demy rouges et consommees y a *Magnatum vicinitas*. [An eagle's wing among many little feathers partially reddened and consumed; there is, *The neighbourhood of great ones*.] NAK
(27) Another devayce a grayt hepe of wings and fedders, the word is *magnatum vicinitas*. NLS50–52
(28) wings and feathars dispersed. *Magnatum vicinitas*. NLS21
(27) A Heap of Wings and Feathers dispersed; the Word *Magnatum vicinitas*. Let.

17 Un sep de vigne et une main avec une serpe coupant ledit sep y a *Virescit vulnere virtus*. [A vine stock and a hand with a pruning knife cutting the said stock; there is, *Virtue flourishes from its wounds*.] NAK
(19) A devayce for the queen's majesty a hand from heavin haulding a scythe and cutting the vayne the word is *Virescit vulnere virtus*. NLS50–52
(17b) [continuous with Fowler's 17a, no. 50 below, and not separately numbered] a[n] aix upon a vyne trie *Virescit Vulnere Virtus*. NLS21

See Figure 3.11, Marian Hanging centrepiece. The same device and motto are also used both on undated jettons and on the silver hand bell owned by Lord Balfour of Burleigh (Fig. 3.12).

18 Un gros chesne au fond d'une vallee rompu et brisé par la force du vent, et un arbrisseau y a pour mot *Ut superis visum*. [A large oak at the bottom of a valley torn and broken by the force of the wind, and a bending shrub; there is for motto, *As it seemed good to those above*.] NAK

(6) a devayce of the quines and of the king hir sonnes a stock of a trie and on the on syd therof is a branch springing fourth out of the ground the other hath no other hould but of the stock either of them as well the stock as the branch and a scythe that seemeth to mow all the grass from about them that may have done them any harvest the word is *Vt superis visum*. NLS50–52

(21) two sythes falles cutting a great tree. *Ut superis visum*. NLS21

Also recorded on Mary's engraved watch in 1575 (see Fig. 3.1).

19 Une colonne d'or demie ouverte q'un homme fend a force de coigns et de marteaux y a *idem intus et extra*. [A pillar of gold, partially gaping, which a man is cleaving by dint of wedges and hammers; there is, *The same inside and out*.] NAK

20 Deux courones en terre et une au ciel compose d'estoiles les flambes de feu y deroulant *Manet ultima celo*. [Two crowns in earth and one in heaven composed of stars with flames of fire issuing from them, *The last one awaits in heaven*.] NAK

Adrien d'Amboise illustrates this device (see Fig. 2.33) in his *Devises royales* (1621) in which he explains that Mary Stuart used it with the motto *Aliamque moratur* (no. 21 below) to express her claim to the English crown, and that a Scotsman named Gordon bestowed Mary's device on Henri III of France with the motto *Manet ultima coelo* to refer to his title to the two thrones of France and Poland, and a heavenly crown which he would only attain after his death. Giordano Bruno makes much of Henri's use of this device in his *Spaccio della bestia trionfante*, published in 1584 and dedicated to Sir Philip Sidney, only slightly modifying the motto to *Tertio caelo manet* [The third awaits in heaven].

21 Une aultre quasi pareille horsmis icelle d'en hault semblable a celles qui sont en terre y a *Aliamque moratur*. [Another almost like it, except that the one above is like those that are in the earth; there is, *And awaits another*.] NAK

(4) A devayse for hir maj^tie thrie crounes and a scepter the thrie crounes standing abufe the other tow, the word is *Aliamque moratur*. NLS50–52

(23) Thrie crownes two opposite and another above in the the sky. *Aliamque moratur*. [The comment *fatidicum*, i.e. 'prophetic', is inserted above, and again following the motto.] NLS21

(29) Three Crowns, two opposite, and another above in the Sky, the Word, *Aliamque moratur*. Let.

The device is used with this motto on a jetton of 1560 showing two crowns, not three, between the earth and a clouded sky with a burst of stars shining through (see Fig. 2.32); Cochran-Patrick, 1884, p. 10, no. 10.

22 Une R[eine] au fond d'une croix son sceptre et Corone bas et sur un champ d'amaille fort doubles RR y a escript *undique Ra Ra*. [A queen at the foot of a cross, her sceptre and crown beneath, and on a field of deep enamel double RR there is written, *everywhere R[egin]a R[egin]a*.] NAK

(37) The first device that is in the rufe of the bed is the quines ma^tie pertrayd knieling before the cros and hir crowne and hire scepture laying at hir fite and haulding hir hands to heaven the word is *Vndique*. NLS50–52

(2) Her self upon her knees afore the crucifix. *Vndique*. NLS21

(2) This hath reference to a Crucifix, before which with all her Royal Ornaments she is humbled on her knees most lively, with the word *undique*. Let.

23 Trois oyseaulx en l'aire percez d'une flesche *Dederit Fortuna Deusve*. [Three birds in the air pierced by an arrow: *Either chance or God will show the way*.] NAK

(15) A devayce of Godfrey de Bouyllion a narrow [sic] shot through three Swallows *dederitne viam casus ve deus ve*. NLS50–52

(8) a long dart passing though three birds (vulgar) *dederit viam casusve deusve.* NLS21

(7) The Impresa of Godfrey of Bullogne an Arrow passing throw Three Birds, the Word, *Dederitne viam casusve Deusve.* Let.

Cf. Paradin, 1557, p. 38. The three birds pierced by a single arrow was the heraldic badge of the dukes of Lorraine, from a legend that their supposed ancestor, Godfrey of Bouillon (one of the famous Nine Worthies) had thus killed three birds with one shot while crusading in the Holy Land. These birds, known as 'alerions' therefore featured in the coat of arms of Mary's mother, Mary of Guise/Lorraine.

24 Un arbre charge de sceptres de Corones de mittres de crosiers de chappeaux rouges, de chesnes et pierres précieuses et cordes de besasses et bulles et pain, une femme au pied ayant les yeux bandez une verge en sa main dont elle bat ledit arbre le mot *Ut casus dederit.* [A tree laden with sceptres, crowns, mitres, crosiers, red hats, chains, precious stones, cords, wallets, papal bulls, bread: a woman at the foot with her eyes bandaged, and a rod in her hand wherewith she strikes the said tree; the motto, *As chance will have given.*] NAK

(38) Another devayce a trie of fourtune whereon ther is hanging all kaynd of troubles and a man that hath his aies bound with a cloth hath a staffe in his hand asayeth to strike doune his fortune the word is *Vt casus dederit.* NLS50–52

(5) a Trophee upon a trie with myters crounes hattes vi souns maskes flagons and a woman with a vayle about her eyes poynting to some of these with her stick. *Vt casus dederit.* NLS21

(28) A Trophie upon a Tree, with mytres, Crowns, Hats, Masks, Swords and Books, and a Woman with a Vail, pointing to some about her, with this Word, *Ut casus dederit.* Let.

25 L'ordre de L'annonciation avec les quartres lettres majuscules F E R T. [The order of the Annunciation, with the four capital letters F.E.R.T.] NAK

(13) Devayce of the last Deuck of Savoye the annunciation of Virgen maria the word is mienyng that so God wan roddes. *Fortitudo eius rhodum tennoyt* [His strength held Rhodes]. NLS50–52

(10) The annunciation of Savoy *fortitudo eius rodum tenuit.* NLS21

(20) The impresa of the Duke of Savoy. The Annunciation of the Virgin Mary, the Word, *Fortitudo eius Rhodum tenuit*, He had kept the Isle of Rhodes. Let.

Cf. Paradin, 1557, p. 39, whose image and commentary show us the collar of the order of chivalry instituted by the Duke of Savoy which had the letters FERT threaded on it and a pendant with the image of the Annunciation.

26 Le soleil levant pour mot *Quae cecidere resurgunt.* [The rising sun; for motto, *Those that fall rise again.*] NAK

(35) A devayce for the quines maj^{tie} wherin there is the sonne and the moun the word is *que ceder resurgunt.* NLS50–52

Also recorded on Mary's watch in 1575 (see Fig. 3.3).

27 Un rond et un triangle dedans. Le mot *Trino non convenit orbis.* [A circle, and a triangle within it; the motto, *The three do not fit the circle.*] NAK

(32) Another devayce a trieangell of gowld within a circle of silver and a s with in the triangell of gould the word is *trino non convenit orbis.* NLS50–52

(19) A triangle with a sunn in the midle of a circle. *Trino non convenit orbis.* faticidum. [i.e. 'prophetic'] NLS21

(17) A Triangle with a Sun in the Middle of a Circle, the Word, *Trino non convenit orbis* []. Let.

This device is described and illustrated, though with a different motto and with no reference to Mary Stuart, in Giovanni Ferro's *Teatro d'imprese* (1623), quoting Bartolomeo de' Rossi's *Hieroglyphica* (Verona, 1612), who explains the device as signalling that even though a man possessed the whole world (the circle) he would desire more (the triangle, symbol of man).

28 Un gros chesne et tous les vents soufflans dessus. Autour d'ung Chesne *Basta ch'io vivi* . [A great oak, and all the winds blowing above it: around the said oak, *Enough that I have lived.*] NAK
(34) Another devayce a hoke trie half weddred half griene and four wynds blowing att the tow sayds therof the word is *b'assta chio Vivi*. NLS50–52
(30) wynds blowing vpon a tre. *Basta ch'io vivo*. Vulgar. NLS21

29 L'estoile du pole et le quadran de marinier avec la calamite tournee droict vers le pole. autour d'ung Quadran *Sa vertu mattire* y a pour devise. [The pole-star and the mariner's compass, with the loadstone turned straight towards the pole: around the said compass is, *Its virtue draws me* for a device.] NAK
(12) Another devayce for the quienes' maj^{tie} a nadamite [sic] stone drawing starres called the poall the word is her maj^{ties} name turned *Maria Stewartt sa vertu matire*. NLS50–52
(11) a lodstone Magnetes with the pole vpon a pillar with her anagrame. *Sa vertu m'attire Marie Stuart*. NLS21
(1) The First is the Loadstone turning towards the Pole; the Word her Majesty's Name turned into an Anagram *Maria Stuart, sa vertu m'attire*, which is not much inferiour to *Veritas armata*. Let.

Also recorded on Mary watch in 1575 (see Fig. 3.2). Drummond's preferred anagram, which is not on the bed hangings, shows his knowledge of those 'designes for her delivery' which were cited in 1584 as evidence for removing Mary from the Earl of Shrewsbury's custody: 'Annagramma etiam VERITAS ARMATA literis transpositus, in peiorum partem acceptum' [That anagram also gave much distaste; Armata Veritas/ Maria Stvarta] (Camden, *Annales*, 1615–17, vol. 2, p. 363).

30 Un salamandre dans le feu y a *Nutrisco et extingor* [sic]. [A salamander in the fire; there is, *I both feed it and put it out.*] NAK
(11) A devayce of king Francois the fyrst a salamander crowned the mydest of the flambes of fayre the word is *Nutrisco est* [sic] *extingo*. NLS50–52
(29) Salamandra. *Nutrisco et extinguo*. Vulgar. NLS21

(6) The Impresa of King Francis I. A Salamander crowned in the Midst of Flames, the Word *Nutrisco et extinguo*. Let.

Cf. Paradin, 1557, p. 16 (see Fig. 2.1).

31 Une eclipse de la lune y a pour devise *Ipsa sibi lumen quod invidet aufert*. [An eclipse of the moon; there is for device, *She deprives herself of the light which she envies.*] NAK
(39) Another devayce wherin is the ecleps of the sonne and the moune the word is *Ipse sibi Lumen quod invidet aufert*. NLS50–52
(3) Luna super umbram columnarem terra marique circumscripta cum hoc titulo. *Ipsa sibi lumen, quod invidet aufert*. Glancing as I think at Queene Elizabeth. NLS21
(23) Eclipses of the Sun and the Moon, the Word, *Ipsa sibi lumen quod invidet aufert* , glancing, as may appear at Queen Elizabeth. Let.

Also recorded on Mary's watch in 1575 (see Figs 3.5 and 3.6). Cf. nos. 35 and 43 in which an eclipse also features; the eclipse was better known as the device of François II because of the fact that his birth occurred in 1544, a few days after a solar eclipse and shortly before a partial eclipse of the moon. This symbolism is recorded as the device of Dauphin François by Paradin (1557, p. 74), *Inter Eclipses Exorior* [I come forth between eclipses] showing a covered cup referring to the 'cup' constellation, thought to be visible at times that coincided with eclipses. The motto Paradin records is also recorded by de Bie (1636, p. 61) on a medal of François as dauphin showing lilies blooming beneath a sun and moon.

32 Quelques plantes de saffran sa assez haultes y a *Fructus calcata dat amplos*. [Some plants of saffron, and that fairly high; there is, *It is more fruitful when trampled on.*] NAK
(16) Another devayse a branche of saffron the word is *fructus calcata dat amplos*. NLS50–52
(7) papavera in a parked Gardin (in my opinion Improper) *fructus calcata dat amplos*. NLS21
(14) Cammomel in a garden, the Word *Fructus calcata dat amplos*. Let.

Also recorded on Mary's watch in 1575 (see Fig. 3.1).

33 Une fournaise dans laquelle y a de l'or et du mercuor ellognant l'un de l'autre *In fide societas*. [*A furnace in which are gold and mercury separating from one another, Fellowship in faith*.] NAK

34 Une Roue de moulin tournans dans l'eau. Le mot *moveor nec rapior*. [*A mill-wheel turning in the water; the motto, I am moved lest I should break.*] NAK

35 La lune fort claire du coste elle regard le soleil obscure du coste elle a la terre oppose la devise *Terrena obcecant*. [*The moon, very bright on the side which looks toward the sun; dark on the side which has the earth opposite; the device, They blot out earthly things.*] NAK

Cf. nos. 31 and 35, where the eclipse also features. Mary might well have been drawn to this motif because François II had been born during an eclipse, as Claude Paradin notes in his commentary on the *Inter eclipses exorior* device (1557, p. 74).

36 Plusieurs sources d'eau doulce faillans tomber dans la mer le mot *Sic dulcia in amarum*. [*Many springs of sweet water about to fall into the sea; the motto, Thus sweet things turn bitter.*] NAK

37 Un petit oiseau en cage et au dessus une aigle preste de l'engloutir en cas il sortira le mot est *Il mal mi preme, my spauenta il peggio*. [*A little bird in a cage, and above an eagle ready to devour it in case it should come forth; the motto is, I am crushed by wrongs, and I fear worse.*] NAK

(21) Another device for her maj^tie a peggion in a kayge and a falcon and hevoring aboufe the kayge the word is *Il mal me preme est mi speventa Il peggio*. NLS50–52

(16) a bird in a cage and a halk flying above. *Il mal mi preme et me spaventa il peggio*. Vulgar. NLS21

(16) A Bird in a Cage and a Hawk flying above, with the Word *il mal me preme et me spaventa Peggio*. Let.

Source: Hadrianus Junius, *Emblemata* (1565), p. 45, no. 39: *Malo oppressus, deterius formidat* [One who is badly oppressed, fears worse] (see Fig. 2. 6); Junius's picture shows the cage that holds the bird encircled by a scroll carrying the Italian inscription which supplies Mary's motto. This device repeats no. 12.

38 Une lieue laboure produisant au lieu d'espiz de blé [erased] des poinctes d'espees et quelques casques le mot est *Dabit Deus his quoque finem* [*A tilled field, producing instead of ears of corn points of spears and some helmets; the motto is, God will bring an end to these things also.*] NAK

(17) A device for the king's maj^tie all sortes of harness and wepons comming out of the ground, the word is *dabit deus his quoque finem*. NLS50–52

(20) hilts plumes speres helmets halbards Lires *dabit deus his quoque finem*. NLS21

This device is recorded and sketched in John Dunstall's 'Certaine Emblemes upon a clock of the Q. of Scotts', British Library MS Cotton Caligula C5, fol. 73 (see Fig. 3.7).

39 *Ambo utroque tenent* une vache tenue par deux mains. [*They hold either or both, a cow held by two hands.*] NAK

(10) Another device two hands haulding the tow horns of a broune cow the word is *Ambo vtreque tene*. NLS50–52

(12) a bull holden with tuo hands by the hornes. *Ambo utraque tene*. NLS21

40 *Pietas revocabit ab orco,* une montaigne au milieu de laquelle semble estre une caverne vectant du feu. [*Piety will recall them from the underworld, a mountain in the midst of which there seems to be a cavern spouting fire.*] NAK

(3) A devayse for the quines maj^tie and the king maj^tie hir sone fire comes a dray woded trie casting fourth att the top a branch of gould with a died man's head att fout thereof and abouf the died man's body a flambing fayre the word is *pietas vocabit ab orco*. NLS50–52

(24) a trie planted in a church yard surrounded with deade bones. *pietas revocabit ab orco*. NLS21

(21) A Tree planted in a Church-yard environed with dead Men's Bones, the Word *Pietas revocabit ab Orco*. Let.

Also recorded on Mary's watch in 1575 (see Fig. 3.2).

41 [Device not described] *Quid nisi victis dolor* [Nothing for the vanquished but grief.] NAK

(23) Another devayce a payre of Balances hanging on the point of a sword that was wayd att Rome by the hostages waying their gowld the word is *quid nisi victis dolor*. NLS50–52

(32) Brennus's ballances, a Sword cast in to weigh Gold, the Word, *Quis nisi victis dolor?* Let.

Brennus was leader of the Gauls who captured Rome in 390 BC; when the defeated Romans complained of false weights being used to calculate the ransom for the city, Brennus threw his sword into the scales, exclaiming 'Vae victis' [Woe to the defeated], or as we might say, 'Winner takes all'.

42 [No device described] *Pervigiles virtus excubias superat* [Courage overcomes vigilant sentinels.] NAK

(18) Another device for his Maj^tie the Branch of palme that was Harculesses and the two pellers. The word is *Pervigiles virtus excubeas supart* [sic]. NLS50–52

(18) 2 pillars or wache towers with a palme trie. *Per vigiles virtus excubias superat*. NLS21

This device is recorded and sketched in John Dunstall's 'Certaine Emblemes upon a clock of the Q. of Scotts', British Library MS Cotton Caligula C5, fol. 73.

43 *Un soleil demi eclipse, Medio occidit die* [A sun half eclipsed, *It grows dark at noon.*] NAK

(22) Another devayce of hir maj^tie a sunne all blacke with the eclipse the word is *medio occidit die*. NLS50–52

(31) The Sun in an Eclipse, the Word, *Medio occidit die*. Let.

Cf. nos. 31 and 35 which also feature an eclipse.

44 *Le palmier chargé Ponderibus virtus innata resistet*. [The palm-tree laden, *Innate virtue resists oppression.*] NAK

(14) A devayce for her maj^tie a palm tree laden with lead *ponderibus virtus inata resistit*. NLS50–52

(9) a palme trie. *ponderibus virtus innata resistit* (vulgar). NLS21

(15) A palm tree, the Word, *Ponderibus virtus innata resistit*. Let.

Also recorded on Mary's watch in 1575 (see Fig. 3.1). Camden, *Annales*, 1615–17, vol. 2, p. 363 describes this emblem: 'Palma oppressa sed resurgens cum PONDERIBUS VIRTUS INNATA RESISTIT' [A Palme depressed, yet rising againe with these words: Ponderibus virtus resistit].

45 *Non quae super terram un ciel fort tempestueux deux mains en l'air ne se tenants*. [*Not those things above the earth*, a very tempestuous sky, two hands in the air not holding one another.] NAK

46 *Le chardon coroné asperitate securus*. [The thistle crowned, *Made safe by its roughness*.] NAK

47 *Un palmier au pied une tortue essayant de monter amont dat gloria vires* [A palm tree, at the foot a tortoise trying to climb upwards, *Fame brings strength*.] NAK

Marian Hanging, octagon F (see Fig. 2.28), also used on coin known as Mary *ryal* first minted in 1565 (Fig. 2.29).

48 *Un soleil et lestoile de mercure Tantus mihi fulgor ab illo*. [A sun and the star Mercury, *So much brightness comes to me from him*.] NAK

49 *Per vincula crescit le pin*. [*Through chains it grows*, the pine tree.] NAK

(4) An apple tree growing in a thorn, the Word: *Per vincula crescit*. Let.

Also recorded on Mary's watch in 1575 (see Fig. 3.1). Camden, *Annales* (1615–17, vol. 2, p. 363) describes the same emblem: 'Surculus trunco insitus ligaminibusque caput obtruncans, tamen efflorescens, et circumscriptus PER VINCULA CRESCO' [A shoot grafted into a stock and bound with cords, yet budding forth, and written round it 'Through bonds I grow'].

50   (20) A devayce for the king's maj^tie mercures staf lapt about with swordes and aboufe it two winges and att the on sayde a pecokkes tayle and the other sayd tow flutes the word is *Eloquium tot lumina clausit* [Eloquence has closed many eyes].
                                                                                 NLS50–52

(17) Caduceus Mercurij pavonis cauda sua cum oculis ac duae fistulae *eloquium tot lumina clausit*. This is the best in my judgement of all because she was deceived. [The caduceus of Mercury, tail of a peacock with its eyes, and two flutes: Eloquence has closed many eyes.]   NLS21

(8) That of Mercurius charming Argos with his Hundred Eyes expressed by his caduceus, Two Flutes and a Peacock, the Word *Eloquium tot lumina clausit*.   Let.

This device is recorded and sketched in John Dunstall's 'Certaine Emblemes upon a clock of the Q. of Scotts', British Library MS Cotton Caligula C5, fol. 73 (see Fig. 3.4). This is the same emblem which Camden describes in *Annales*: 'Argus with his many eyes cast into a sleepe by Mercury, sweetly playing upon his Flute, with this Motto. Eloquium tot lumina clausit' (1625, vol. 3, p. 72).

51   (40) Another devayce of fourtune where ther is two women going on a whiell the word is *fortuna* [sic.] *comites* [Fortuna's companions].
                                                                                 NLS50–52

(4) two women upon the wheeles of fortoun. *Fortunae comites*. The one with a lance and the other cornucopia with a sheafe of corne and (?)thay burnes (papavera).   NLS21

My reading of Fowler's concluding phrase is uncertain, though the word 'papavera' (bracketed in the MS) is not in doubt; Fowler uses this Italian word (based on the Latin *papaver*) for poppy again in no. 32 when describing the plant which the other descriptions identify as saffron or camomile.

52   (41) Another devayce wher there is mercur's staf and tow horns of aboundance with a thesell on the on sayd of the staf and a wiayt rose on the other.   NLS50–52

(6) Caduceus Mercurij with the flouer de luce vpon the heade of it *arrest heureux es stable d'amitie* [A happy and firm announcement concerning friendship].   NLS21

It is not clear whether Fowler's French expression is quoting the motto to this emblem, though *arrest* means 'decree' or 'announcement' and would apply to Mercury as classical messenger of the gods, while the floral devices would apply to the two nations thus firmly linked in friendship, which must be Scotland and France, always assuming that Hawthornden Anonymous's white rose was a misidentification of Fowler's 'flower de luce', i.e. fleur de lis. Fowler's handwriting is difficult at this point, and my reading of the two words 'et stable' is tentative.

53   (1) A devayce of the quine mother's of france, timblyng tieres that falleth in quick layme the word is *ardorem extincta testantur flamma* [The extinguished flame shows passion].   NLS50–52

Hawthornden Anonymous is the only witness to this device on the Bed of State, whose bearer, as he recognises, was Catherine de Medici (see Figs 2.24 and 2.25). Bess uses the same device, with a similar motto, on the centrepiece to the Cavendish Hanging (see Fig. 2.23).

54   (42) A devayce in the sete of the chayer the Bayrer of the heavens with vii starres aboufe the word is *divinae Vindicta* [Divine punishments].   NLS50–52

This is the only record of this device, evidently noted when the Bed of State was still assembled and an embroidered side chair was in use.

55 (36) The Rufe of the bed att the four noukes hath the four armories half payrted the armories of Scotland and france att the one end of the rufe half payrted at another nouke Scotland and England half payrted att the thrid nouke Scotland and Lorrayn half payrted and at the fourth nouke Lorayne and Bourbon half payrted. NLS50–52

(1) Quatuor insignia Scotiae et angliae simul scotia et gallia niger leo et lilia cum obue[rse] ryssan larene. [Four devices of Scotland and England a black lion and a lily with opposite it ... Lorraine.]
NLS21

It is uncertain whether these are descriptions of the same details, though both are evidently identifying four impaled ('half parted') coats of royal arms. Given that they were on the 'roof' of the bed, it is uncertain whether they were embroidered rather than carved or painted: 'nouke' means corner. It is particularly difficult to read or make sense of Fowler's concluding phrase.

56 (3) An Impresa of Mary of Lorrain her mother, a Phoenix in Flames, the Word *en ma fin git mon commencement* [In my end is my beginning].
Let.

Cf. Oxburgh, Marian Hanging panel 3 showing the 'Phenix' device but no motto. Drummond's motto is the same as that recorded by Nicholas White on Mary's cloth of estate when he visited Tutbury in 1569.

57 (19) The Impresa of King Henry VIII. A Portcullis, the Word, *altera securitas* [Another safeguard].
Let.

Cf. Paradin, 1557, p. 36 (see Fig. 2.2).

Notes

Chapter 1: The Embroideries

1. Fleming, *Mary Queen of Scots*, 1897, p. 273.
2. Cited in Strickland, *Lives of the Queens of Scotland*, vol. 1, 1850, p. 224.
3. Wingfield Digby, *Elizabethan Embroidery*, 1963, p. 56, citing Maitland Club, *Illustrations*, 1837, p. 156.
4. *Calendar of the Manuscripts of the Marquis of Salisbury at Hatfield House*. Historical Manuscripts Commission, 1883, p. 400, cited Strickland, *Letters of Mary Queen of Scots*, vol. 2, 1842, p. 308.
5. *Calendar of State Papers Relating to Scotland and Mary Queen of Scots*, vol. 2: 1563–1569, 1900, p. 632.
6. The inventories are printed in Labanoff, *Lettres, instructions et mémoires de Marie Stuart*, vol. 7, 1844, pp. 231–73.
7. Renée de Beauregard is mentioned several times as one of Mary's servants in Amyas Paulet's letters where she is identified as French. Mary seems to have entrusted her more than once with passing valuables to their recipients when settling her affairs at Chartley in 1686; it was Beauregard whom she asked to convey money to her secretary Claud Nau, which Mary suspected Paulet of obstructing. Paulet's list of the 'goods found in the custody of the severall servants' after Mary's execution at Fotheringhay in 1587 identifies 'Renee Rallay alias Beauregard' but does not include any of the Chartley inventory's list of embroideries and other pieces of work in the goods Paulet found in her custody (Labanoff, *Lettres*, vol. 7, 1844, p. 259). If she did assume responsibility for their safekeeping then her role in their survival, and in establishing the exact provenance of the Oxburgh embroideries, could be crucial; however nothing seems to be known about her subsequent movements or connections.
8. Labanoff, *Lettres*, vol. 7, 1844, p. 240, 'Un petit quarré, faict à point tressé, ouvré par la vieille comtesse de Lenox, elle estant en la Tour'. Margaret, Countess of Lennox, was granddaughter of England's Henry VII and mother of Lord Darnley, hence Mary's mother-in-law; she had been committed to the Tower of London in 1565 as punishment for promoting her son's Scottish marriage, of which Elizabeth professed to disapprove.
9. 'dont y a trente-deux de non coupées, le reste coupé chascune en son quarré', Labanoff, *Lettres*, vol. 7, 1844, p. 240.
10. The list of Mary's servants compiled in August 1586 at Chartley includes not only grooms of the bedchamber, cooks, turncocks and pantrymen, grooms of the stable, laundresses and maidservants, but also an embroiderer named Charles Plouvart, identified as 'Frenche': Labanoff, *Lettres*, vol. 7, 1844, p. 254.
11. For more general histories of needlework see Hackenbroch, *English and Other Needlework*, 1960; Wingfield Digby, *Elizabethan Embroidery*, 1963; Swain 1970, 1986; Levey, *An Elizabethan Inheritance*, 1998.
12. Wardle, 'The embroideries of Mary, Queen of Scots: notes on the French connection', *Bulletin of the Needle and Bobbin Club (New York)*, vol. 64, 1981, pp. 3–14.
13. For the Burrell embroideries, see Arthur, *Embroidery 1600–1700 at the Burrell Collection*, 1995, plate 17, which illustrates an embroidered bed valance of unknown date or provenance using two emblems: *Mutuum auxilium* and *Semper praesto esse infortunia*, copying the woodcuts that appeared in Plantin editions of Alciato and, later, in Geffrey Whitney's *Choice of Emblemes* (1586). Neither emblem includes the Latin motto and they may not have any emblematic function on this embroidery. Five pieces of embroidery bought by Sir William Burrell in 1937 do, however, include symbolic devices with mottoes and, although not apparently copied from any printed emblem book, three of the five do correspond to particular emblems that are among the 61 devices in stucco on the caisson ceiling of the gallery in the Château de Dampierre-sur-Boutonne, Charente Inférieure. See Bath, 'Emblems from Whitney on an embroidered valance in the Burrell Collection', *Society for Emblem Studies Newsletter*, no. 41, July 2007, pp. 7–8, and Bath, 'An emblematic embroidery in the Burrell Collection', *Emblematica*, vol. 16, 2008 (in press).
14. Other embroidered hangings have sometimes been attributed to Mary Queen of Scots, though Margaret Swain showed that

five embroidered panels on red woollen cloth known as the Lochleven Hangings in the National Galleries of Scotland were probably wall hangings and are the work of a professional embroiderer, probably made in Edinburgh in the early seventeenth century: see Swain, 'The Lochleven and Linlithgow Hangings', *Proceedings of the Society of Antiquaries of Scotland*, vol. 124, 1994, pp. 455–66.

15. The list was submitted to the commissioners appointed by Queen Elizabeth to try to settle the marital dispute and is quoted and discussed by Kirke, 'An aristocratic squabble', *Derbyshire Archaeological Journal*, vol. 32, 1911, pp. 19–38 (see p. 36).

16. Cited by Kirke, 'An aristocratic squabble', p. 36; the original is *Historical Monuments Commission, Salisbury Papers*, vol. 3, pp. 158–61.

17. Swain, *Needlework of Mary Queen of Scots*, 1973, p. 103.

18. Ibid.

19. For Arbella Stuart see Gristwood, *Arbella: England's Lost Queen*, 2003. The letter of 25 May 1611, in which Arbella reports her sale of the embroideries to her aunt, Mary Talbot, is noted in Lefuse, *The Life and Times of Arabella Stuart*, 1911, pp. 268–9.

20. Labanoff, *Lettres*, vol. 7, 1844, p. 240. I have ignored Labanoff's punctuation, which is lacking in the original: his comma placement mislocates the national arms.

21. Although the February 1587 Fotheringhay inventory of goods 'in the custody' of Mary's servants makes no mention of the pieces of embroidery that Mary's own Chartley inventory of June 1586 states she had entrusted to Renée de Beauregard, it does mention 'Sowing silk and rawe silk of all colours' as being in Renée's possession (Labanoff, *Lettres*, vol. 7, 1844, p. 274), suggesting that Mary passed to her chambermaid not only the pieces of unmounted embroidery, but also the sewing silks used to create them. It is possible that Renée had already disposed of the actual embroideries, including the *Las pennas passan* panel, to the Countess of Shrewsbury, which is why there was no mention of them. There is nothing clearly corresponding to these, however, in the 1601 inventories of furnishings at Chatsworth and Hardwick that were compiled following Bess's death in 1601; these have been usefully edited by Levey and Thornton, *Of Household Stuff*, 2001.

22. Jonson, *Works*, vol. 1, 1925, p. 207. Exactly what type of book this was to be is unclear, though in his 'Conversations with Drummond' we are told that 'he heth intention to writt a fisher or Pastorall play & sett the stage of it in the Lowmond Lake' (p. 143, and cf. Herford and Simpson's note on this, pp. 168–9). Jonson's proposed book about Scotland was almost certainly lost in the fire of November 1623 which destroyed his library along with many of his unpublished writings, for in his poem *An Execration on Vulcan* listing his losses in the fire he mentions 'my journey into Scotland sung,/ With all the adventures'.

23. Bath, *Renaissance Decorative Painting in Scotland*, 2003, ch. 4; also Bath, 'Ben Jonson, William Fowler and the Pinkie ceiling', *Architectural Heritage: Journal of the Architectural Heritage Society of Scotland*, vol. 18, 2007, pp. 73–86.

24. Drummond printed the letter in his *History of Scotland*, 1655, 1681, and it was reprinted in the folio edition of his *Works*, 1711. It is reprinted in Jonson, *Works*, vol. I, 1925, pp. 208–10, and in Green, *Shakespeare and the Emblem Writers*, 1870, pp. 123–4.

25. As Jonson's editors, Herford and Simpson, note in *Works*, vol. I, 1925, p. 210.

26. Labanoff, *Lettres*, vol. 7, 1844, p. 254.

27. Masson, *Register of the Privy Council of Scotland*, vol. 10: 1613–1616, 1891, pp. 624–5.

28. For the Dean House painted ceilings, see Bath, *Renaissance Decorative Painting in Scotland*, 2003, pp. 201–9 and 241–2. Sir William Nisbet, who ordered the paintings, bought the estate in 1609 and is one of the Edinburgh worthies to whom Jonson asks to be remembered in his letter of 10 May 1619; Nisbet was Lord Provost in 1618 and had been instrumental in the town council's vote to make Jonson an honorary burgess of the city.

Chapter 2: Emblems

1. See Bath, 'Alciato and the Earl of Arran', *Emblematica*, vol. 13, 2003, pp. 39–52.

2. For the 'Shepherd's Buss' embroidery see Nevinson, 'English domestic embroidery patterns', *Walpole Society*, vol. 28: 1939–40, pp. 6–7, pl. 3; for Paradin on Scottish painted ceilings see Bath, *Renaissance Decorative Painting in Scotland*, 2003, pp. 34–45, 50–52, 239–40 and 247. Nevinson's identification of four emblems on the 'Shepherd's Buss' needs to be amplified by a further ten motifs in the outer border which can also be shown to copy the following devices from Paradin: *Turpibus exitium* (p. 274), *Spes altera vitae* (p. 258), *Fata obstant* (p. 161), *Heu cadit in tantum scelus* (p. 99), *Spe illectat inani* (p. 153), *In sibile aurae tenuis* (p. 96), *Inter eclipses exorior* (p. 74), *Pignora cara sui* (p. 13), *Monstrant regibus astra viam* (p. 18), *Hae conscia numinis aetas* (p. 155). For the Guise Palace, see Bath, 'Was there a Guise Palace in Edinburgh?', in Gowing and Pender (eds), *All Manner of Murals*, 2007, pp. 11–21.

3. Paradin, *Devises heroïques*, 1557, p. 16.

4. For details of the various editions see the 'Bibliography of emblem-books' in Praz, *Studies in Seventeenth-century Imagery*, 1975; Mary's books were listed in the 1569 'Inventaires off the buikis, ornamenis and maskyn cleis [clothes]' received by John Wood and James Murray from Servais de Condé, printed in Robertson, *Inventaires*, 1863, pp. cxliv–cxlvii and 179–87.

5. Camden in *Remaines, Concerning Britaine* (1615 repr. 1970, p. 372), identifies the portcullis as the badge of Henry VII.

6. Young, *Tudor and Jacobean Tournaments*, 1987, fig. 64. What appears to be a version of the same image of the entwined obelisk features on the dress of an unknown lady, c.1600, in a portrait at Cowdray Park, illustrated in Janet Arnold's *Queen Elizabeth's Wardrobe Unlock'd*, 1988, fig. 150, though the resemblance to the obelisk in Geffrey Whitney's emblem seems to me to be not close enough to justify Arnold's confidence that this was its inspiration, and it may not in my view be emblematic.

7. Young, *Tudor and Jacobean Tournaments*, 1987, p. 127.

8. I am indebted for most of this source identification to Robert Cummings, who discusses this adage in his 'Alciato's illustrated epigrams', *Emblematica*, 15, 2007, p. 211. The sources are *Iliad* 22: 369–75 and *Adagia* 4.7.82. It is only a Greek epigram

(*Anthology* 16.4, *Planudean* 1.5) which illustrates the adage about hares insulting dead lions from the Greeks' abuse of the dead Hector's body. Palliser (*Historic Devices, Badges and Warcries*, 1870, p. 236) compares Shakespeare, *King John*, 6.1, 'You are the hare of whom the proverb goes,/ Whose valour plucks dead lions by the beard.' The proverbial *topos* was evidently widely current, which means that direct source attribution to Alciato for the embroidery motif is unsafe.

9. Giovio, *The Worthy Tract of Paulus Iovius*, 1585, fol. C4ʳ.
10. Shakespeare has what must be a version of this emblem when Richard II offers to resign his crown to Bolingbroke: 'Now is this golden crown like to a deep well/ That owes two buckets, filling one another;/ The emptier ever dancing in the air,/ The other down, unseen and full of water./ That bucket down and full of tears am I,/ Drinking my griefs, whilst you mount up on high.' (*Richard II*, IV.2, 184–89)
11. See Rosenthal, 'The invention of the columnar device of Emperor Charles V at the court of Burgundy in Flanders in 1516', *Journal of the Warburg and Courtauld Institutes*, vol. 36, 1973, pp. 198–230.
12. See Höltgen, 'The ruler between two columns: imperial aspiration and political iconography from Emperor Charles V to William of Orange', in Bath *et al.* (eds), *Emblem Studies in Honor of Peter M. Daly*, 2002, pp. 143–68.
13. See Berger, *Public Access to Art in Paris*, 1999, pp. 44–50.
14. Southwell, *Collected Poems*, 2007, p. 118.
15. See Bath, *Renaissance Decorative Painting in Scotland*, 2003, pp. 114–15.
16. Russell, 'The ornamental image', in Bath *et al.* (eds), *Emblem Studies in Honor of Peter M. Daly*, 2002, pp. 207–8.
17. Stewart, 'Coinage and propaganda: an interpretation of the coin-types of James VI', in O'Connor and Clarke (eds), *From the Stone Age to the Forty-five*, 1993, pp. 450–62, discusses the early coinage of James VI, which is similarly exceptional and allusive in its designs, with inscriptions apparently supplied by the poet George Buchanan. In an earlier review article, Stewart (*Numistatic Circular*, 96, no. 2, March 1988, p. 48) notes that the varied and adventurous designs of Scottish coinage at this period are anticipated by the tortoise-and-palm-tree coin, though he rejects the idea that this alludes to Darnley, arguing instead that it might refer to events outside Scotland such as the raising of the Muslim siege of Malta in 1565; however he offers no evidence for this allusion to an event which does not appear to have caused much excitement in Scotland at the time, and although it makes good sense of the coin's inscription about God scattering his enemies (the Knights of St John successfully defended the island by destroying the Turkish fleet), this inscription had already been used, as he acknowledges, on Scottish coinage of the preceding reigns and for that reason, I suggest, is unlikely to have assumed any specific historical reference in 1565, having surely become formulaic.
18. Alciato, *Emblemata*, 1551, p. 210.
19. 'Cette couronne estoit la derniere des trois qu'il avoit prises avec le mot: *Manet ultima caelo*. Car les deux estoient celles de France, et de Pologne: et fut ce me semble un Gentil-homme Escossois nommé Gordon qui la lui donna, et l'avoit empruntée d'une que portoit la Royne de France Marie Stuart douayraire de France, la plus belle et parfaite de son siecle qui estoient deux couronnes seulement avec ce mot, *Aliamque moratur*. Voulant dire que celle d'Angleterre la regardoit, comme de faict elle en estoit la plus proche, et le Roy son fils admirable en vertus la possede paysiblement': Amboise, *Devises royales*, 1621, pp. 45–6.
20. Bruno, *The Expulsion of the Triumphant Beast*, 1964, pp. 270–71.
21. Ordine, *Giordano Bruno, Ronsard et la religion*, 1999, p. 198, citing Virgil, *Ecl.*, 1.66.
22. Ordine, *Giordano Bruno*, 1999, p. 199, citing Catullus, 2, 11–12, Horace, *Od.*, 35, 29–30.
23. Fowler, *Works*, vol. 3, 1940, p. xix, n. 4.
24. See Yates, *The Art of Memory*, 1966, p. 266.
25. On Dickson, Bruno and Fowler, see Stevenson, *The Origin of Freemasonry: Scotland's Century 1590–1710*, 1988.

Chapter 3: Incriminating Emblems

1. Young, *Tudor and Jacobean Tournaments*, 1987, p. 135.
2. Camden, *History of the Most Renowned and Victorious Princess Elizabeth*, 1688, repr. 1970, p. 183, the 1688 translator is unnamed; Camden's 1615 Latin reads: 'suspiciones quasi consilium eum liberandi iam initum esset arreptae sunt, ex quibusdam emblematibus ad eam transmissis. Haec erant: Argus multoculos, omnibus oculis conspitus Mercurio tibias modulante inflante, cum hac sententiola, ELOQUIUM TOT LUMINA CLAUSIT; Mercurius Argo Io custodienti caput obtruncans. Surculus trunco insitus ligaminibusque constrictis, tamen efflorescens, et circumscriptus PER VINCULA CRESCO. Palma oppressa sed resurgens cum PONDERIBUS VIRTUS INNATA RESISTIT. Anagramma etiam VERITAS ARMATA ex eius nomine MARIA STEUARTA, literis transpositis, in peiorem partem acceptum.'
3. London, National Archives, SP53/10, no. 76.
4. The best known example is Alciato's *Obdurandum adversus urgentia* emblem, with further examples in La Perrière, *Morosophie*, and Rollenhagen, *Nucleus emblematum*; see Henkel and Schöne, *Handbuch zur Sinnbildkunst*, 1967, pp. 192–3. The topos goes back to classical writers such as Plutarch, Strabo and Pliny, and was easily moralised.
5. This is the spelling used in Camden's Latin text: neither the French nor the Latin spelling of Mary's name contains all the letters required in the anagram, however, which thus remains inexact and faulty, although Scots MARIE STEVVART contains all the letters required if we accept the bad French spelling, *m'atire*, as recorded on the watch case.
6. British Library MS Cotton Caligula C.V., no. 40, fols 73–5; for a fuller account see Bath, 'John Dunstall's emblems of Mary Queen of Scots', *Review of Scottish Culture*, vol. 9, 2007, pp. 1–9.
7. For example, Leisher, *Geoffrey Whitney's Choice of Emblemes and its Relation to the Emblematic Vogue in Tudor England*, 1987, p. 279.
8. Emblems featuring lunar or solar eclipses are not as uncommon as might be thought; for a fascinating exploration of the way they were represented and moralised in the emblem books see Kemp, 'Lumine carens: zur Sonnenfinsternis in der Emblematik', in Harms and Peil (eds), *Polyvalenz und Multifunktionalität*

der Emblematik, vol. 1, 2002, pp. 303–18. I was privileged to hear this paper during the Fifth International Conference of the Society for Emblem Studies, which aptly coincided with a total eclipse of the sun that occurred on 11 August 1999 in Munich.

9. 'Une lieue laboure produisant au lieu d'espiz de blé des poinctes d'espees et quelques casques le mot est *Dabit Deus his quoque finem*.'

10. It is possible that the other two emblems that Dunstall records on this page are also mythical. *Ingenium insomnes sopivit ocellos* [Its nature has dulled sleepless eyes] shows what appears to be dead sheep hung on a pole projecting from a tower castle; *Pervigiles virtus excubias superat* [Courage overcomes an ever watchful guard] depicts two columns on either side of a water channel with a blossoming fruit tree. I do not understand either of these emblems, neither of which is recorded elsewhere.

11. The inventory is printed in Labanoff, *Lettres*, vol. 7, 1844, pp. 254–74.

12. *Calendar of State Papers Relating to Scotland and Mary, Queen of Scots, vol. 5 (1574–1581)*, pp. 341, item 414.

13. The letter is quoted in Tytler, *History of Scotland*, vol. 1, 1892, p. 181.

14. *Calendar of State Papers (Scottish)*, Glasgow 1915, p. 225, citing MS Cotton Galba C.V. fol. 263.

15. For instance, Thomas Palmer's *Two Hundred Poosies*, British Library Sloane MS 3794, presented to Robert Dudley, future Earl of Leicester, in 1565 consists of strict, tripartite emblems, including pictures, and has been justly described by its editor, John Manning, as 'England's earliest known emblem book', *The Emblems of Thomas Palmer: Two Hundred Poosies*, 1988.

16. Howard, Duke of Norfolk, *Lives of Philip Howard ... and of Anne Dacres*, 1857, pp. 173–4.

17. *Ibid.*, p. 13.

18. Hargrave, *Complete Collection of State Trials*, vol. 1, 1776, col. 166.

19. The medal is illustrated by Strong, *Portraits of Queen Elizabeth I*, 1963, no. 10, and by Pollard, 'England and the Italian medal', in Chancy and Mack (eds), *England and the Continental Renaissance*, 1990, fig. 6. Strong dates the medal to *c*.1600, though a date of 1572 has been argued to celebrate the queen's recovery from smallpox in that year. Primavera also designed a uniface medal of Mary Queen of Scots, undated but *c*.1578, see Scher, *The Currency of Fame: Portrait Medals of the Renaissance*, 1994, pp. 191–2. Primavera seems to have been active chiefly between 1569 and 1585.

20. Horapollo, *Hieroglyphics*, 1950, p. 103.

21. Murdin, *State Papers*, 1759, pp. 46–51.

22. *Ibid.*, p. 57

23. Watkins and Fiennes, *Mary Queen of Scots*, 2001, p. 187.

24. Labanoff, *Lettres*, vol. 7, 1844, p. 247. In the inventory taken 20 February 1587, possessions in the safekeeping of Elizabeth Curle include 'a little silver bell' (*ibid.*, p. 362).

25. *Catalogue of the Tercentenary Exhibition of Mary Queen of Scots*, 1887, p. 17. The hand bell was also exhibited in Edinburgh 1856, Glasgow 1888 and London 1889.

26. Way, 'The signet-ring and silver bell of Mary Queen of Scots', *Archaeological Journal*, vol. 15, 1858, pp. 253–66; Gibb, *Royal House of Stuart*, 1890, pl. 13.

27. The hand bell is one of several objects reputedly acquired by Sir James Balfour from Mary that have survived, including an agate tankard, the Kennet ciborium, a bloodstone cameo of the Crucifixion, all of which are illustrated in Gibb, *Royal House of Stuart*, 1890.

28. Jacques de Bie, *La France metallique*, 1636, p.187, illust. p. 62.

29. Labanoff, *Lettres*, vol. 7, 1844, p. 246.

30. *Noctes Atticae* 18.xi.

31. Scottish familiarity with this motto is further evidenced by the use William Fowler makes of it in the prefatory remarks to his *Answer to the Calumious Letter of ... Io. Hammiltoun* (1581, repr. Meikle *et al.* (eds), *Works*, vol. 3, 1914–40, p. 15) in which he welcomes the opportunity for self-defence which Hammilton's attack on his religious beliefs affords him: 'And suirlye in my awin persoun I have found this proverb trew, Virescit vulnere virtus.' Fowler may well have known of Queen Mary's use of the same motto at this date from its use on her 1557 *virescit* jetton.

32. The device had previously been described in Paolo Giovio's *Dialogo dell'imprese militari et amorose*, Rome 1555, and illustrated in the edition of Giovio published by Rouille in Lyon, 1560 under the title *Le sententiose imprese*.

33. Russell, *The Emblem and Device in France*, 1985, p. 175.

34. The other two medals have reverses with, in one case, the *Nunquam nisi rectam* device showing a ship in a storm which is recorded by all four descriptions of the Bed of State, and in the other with the *Aliamque moratur* device showing three crowns discussed in Chapter 2. See Cochran-Patrick's *Catalogue of the Medals of Scotland*, 1884, pp. 6–16, listing 22 different medals of Mary Queen of Scots, some of which are also illustrated in Burns, *The Coinage of Scotland*, vol. 2, 1887, pp. 346–8.

35. Strong, 'My weepinge Stagg I crowne: *The Persian Lady* reconsidered', in *The Art of the Emblem. Essays in Honor of K. J. Höltgen*, 1993, p. 103, repr. in Strong, *The Tudor and Stuart Monarchy*, vol. 2, 1995, p. 303.

36. *Ibid.*, vol. 2, 1995, pp. 303–24, figs 214–22. Strong notes the syntactical concision, 'Such a reading would suggest that the middle motto should be completed: *Mea sic mihi [regina]* [Thus to me my Queen].' This supports his interpretation that the speaker is Essex. I suggest the missing word needed to complete the sense is a verb, not a noun, and that the sentiment it expresses is precisely that on the Marian medal, which may well have been known to Lady Essex. I have not been able to identify a classical source for the motto, and it is just possible the syntax was originally complete – there is enough space for it on the tree trunk – but, if so, vestiges would have been likely to show up when the painting was cleaned recently; a tendency to abbreviate familiar (and not so familiar) quotations to make them more clipped and allusive was, however, conventional for *imprese* mottoes.

37. Franks, 'Notice of permissions given at Paris to John Acheson to make dies with the portrait of Mary Queen of Scots', *Proceedings of the Society of Antiquaries of Scotland*, 1872–73, pp. 506–7.

38. Southwell, *Collected Poems*, 2007, p. 41. The same Latin motto is used years later by Pierre le Moyne in his *De l'art des devises*, 1666, pp. 326–7, a Jesuit emblem book which perpetuates its Catholic usage. I am indebted to Anne Sweeney for first drawing my attention to Southwell's 'Decease, Release' and

to Peter Davidson for much inspiration and help with this research.
39. On Southwell and the Howards, see Devlin, *The Life of Robert Southwell, Poet and Martyr*, 1956, pp. 131–7; see also Howard, Duke of Norfolk, *Lives of Philip Howard…and of Anne Dacres*, 1857, p. 196, where Southwell is described as the countess's 'spiritual Director'.
40. Devlin, *Life of Robert Southwell*, 1956, p. 147, citing Lambeth Palace Library, Bacon Papers, MS 655.
41. W.J. Walter first made the connection with Mary Stuart when he printed the poem for the first time in 1817; at least one manuscript leaves the name blank in line 14, quoted above, but Anthony Bacon's note on the copy he apparently received within weeks of its composition leaves no room for further editorial doubt; one editor's perverse opinion that it might refer to Anne of Denmark since one copy of the poem has the name 'Anna' in line 14 and Queen Anna was certainly a crypto-Catholic may be dismissed as a piece of pure editorial silliness, if only because the alliteration of 'Mary' and 'Martyr' is required in this line, confirming the beautiful parallelisms on which not only the poem's two titles but also its whole structure rests. See Southwell, *Poems of Robert Southwell*, 1967, pp. lxxx and 143, for this editorial confusion.

Chapter 4: Birds and Beasts

1. The Chartley inventory confirms this in its list of 52 'diverses fleurs' in cross stitch, of which 32 are described as 'non-coupées' and the rest 'coupé chascune en son quarré'; to this it adds 24 different sorts of birds described as 'tirés au naturel' and 'non coupés', with 106 further examples which have begun to be cut, 16 quadrepeds, including a lion attacking a boar, and 52 fishes of various sorts. See Labanoff, *Lettres*, vol. 7, 1844, pp. 240–41.
2. Victoria and Albert Museum, T80-1924, see North, 'The Falkland Jacket: sources, provenance and interpretation of an emblematic artifact', *Emblematica*, vol. 14, 2005, pp. 127–53; the detached blackwork embroidered sleeve, Victoria and Albert Museum T.11-1950, is illustrated in Arnold, *Queen Elizabeth's Wardrobe Unlock'd*, 1988, fig. 274.
3. It is only the conventionalised Latin spelling which authorises the usual reduction of his name, since Latin avoids such triple consonants; I follow Braun, *Conrad Gessner*, 1990, in preferring the German form of his name; bibliographic records and library searches must still be pursued under the name Gesner however.
4. Hackenbroch, *English and Other Needlework: Tapestries and Textiles in the Irwin Untermeyer Collection*, 1960, p. xxii, fig. 44.
5. The surviving glass, which was restored and reassembled at the Victoria and Albert Museum following its discovery and prior to its return to Gorhambury in 1939, is described and illustrated by Michael Archer in two articles in *Country Life* (3 June and 10 June 1976); Archer makes a persuasive case for dating the stained glass to the period of Francis Bacon's ownership of the house built by his father Sir Nicholas Bacon in the 1560s; very similar stained glass was executed in the 1620s by the immigrant Dutch artist Abraham van Linge at Lydiard Park in Wiltshire, and the Gorhambury glass may well be his work (*Country Life*, 10 June 1976, p. 1454).
6. Bath, *Renaissance Decorative Painting in Scotland*, 2003, ch.7.
7. Bath, 'The sources of John Abbott's pattern book', *Architectural History*, vol. 4, 1998, pp. 49–66.
8. Wellisch, 'Conrad Gessner: a bio-bibliography', *Journal of the Society for the Bibliography of Natural History*, vol. 7, 1975, p. 151.
9. Wellisch, 'Conrad Gessner', 1975, p. 162.
10. The network also included Guillaume Rondelet, whose *L'histoire des poissons* (1558) has woodcuts illustrating quite a few of the marine creatures found in the embroideries, including the sea scorpion (p. 169), hammerhead shark (p. 304), seal (p. 343), she-dolphin (p. 344), scolopender (p. 358), sea lion (p. 360), monkfish (p. 361) and cockle crab (p. 298), sea urchins (p. 414). Rondelet's illustrations are so close to Gessner's however as to leave little doubt that they are copies, and there is no evidence that the embroiderers used Rondelet rather than Gessner as their source for any of these marine creatures.
11. Swain, *Needlework of Mary Queen of Scots*, 1973, figs 29 and 44.
12. Gessner, *Historia animalium*, vol. IV, 1560, p. 174.
13. Boece, *The History and Chronicles of Scotland*, vol. I, 1821, p. 179.
14. This copies what Gessner calls 'The fabulous horse of Neptune as shown in ancient pictures' (*Historia*, vol. IV, p. 182), though Gessner also has a perfectly accurate illustration of what we would call a seahorse, 'Hippocampus', *Icones*, 1560, p. 182, which is copied in the fragmentary 'LOCVSTE OF THE SEA' panel now forming part of Victoria and Albert embroidery T33: F-1955.
15. Boece, *Scotorum historia*, 1527, fols vii–viii. Bellenden translates: 'It wes said be Schir Duncane Campbell to us, that out of Garloll, an loch of Argyll, the year of God M.DX yeris, come ane terrible beist, as mekil as ane grew-hound, futit like ane ganar, and straik doun gret treis with the dint of hir tail: and wer not the remanant huntaris clam up in strang aikis, they had bene all slane in the samin maner. Eftir the slauchter of thir men, scho fled speidlie to the loch. Sindry prudent men belevit gret trubill to follow in Scotland, be appering of this beist; for scho was sene afore, and ay trubil following thairefter' (*History and Chronicles of Scotland*, vol. I, 1821, p. xxxi).
16. Boece, *History and Chronicles of Scotland*, vol. I, 1821, p. xxxi.
17. 'Anser Bassanus vel Scoticus, avis marina. Scotice vulgo a Solendguse. German. dici potest Solendganz oder Schottengans' (Gessner, *Historia animalium*, vol. III, 1555, p. 158).
18. Wellisch, 'Conrad Gessner', 1975, p. 161.
19. Boece, *History and Chronicles of Scotland*, I, 1821, p. xxxvii.
20. Swain, *Needlework of Mary Queen of Scots*, 1973, pls 69 and 85.
21. Thevet, *The Newe Founde Worlde, or Antarticke*, 1568, fol. 94a.
22. The feather cloak from the Musée de l'Homme is illustrated in Thevet, *Les singularitéz de la France antarctique*, 1982, p. 39.
23. *Collection of Inventories and other Records of the Royal Wardrobe and Jewelhouse 1488–1606*, 1815, p. 328.
24. Durkan, 'Giovanni Ferrerio, Gesner and French affairs', *Bibliothèque d'humanisme et renaissance: travaux et documents*, vol. 42, 1980, p. 350.

25. Gessner, *Historia animalium*, vol. II, 1554, p. 2
26. Boece, *History and Chronicles of Scotland*, vol. I, 1821, pp. xxxix–xl.
27. Durkan, 'Giovanni Ferrerio', 1980, p. 351.
28. Shelfmark Typ.SWZ.B51.FG.
29. Glasgow University Library holds another copy of the complete *Historia animalium* (including the *Icones* volumes), shelfmark Bh5-b.1-3, which carries the owner's signature 'Jo. bellenden' beside the printer's mark and, in the same hand, the date '4.Ma 1598', with the inscription 'Si deus pro nobis quis contra nos. Rom.8.31'. This is not the translator of Boece, who died in 1550, but undoubtedly a relative; on the Bellenden family and their extensive literary connections see Van Heijnsbergen, 'Literature and history in Queen Mary's Edinburgh', in MacDonald *et al.* (eds). *The Renaissance in Scotland: Studies Offered to John Durkan*, 1994, pp. 191–8.
30. Wellisch, 'Conrad Gessner', 1975, pp. 172–3.
31. *Tabula Monstrorum marinorum atque mirabilium ferarum, quae in partibus Septentrionalibus, tam in terra quam mari inveniuntur. Literae monstris additae, extra tabulam ostendunt, quid per singula monstra animalia tabulam intelligitur* [Table of sea monsters and wonderful wild animals, which are found both on land and sea. The letters added to the monsters show, outside the picture, what particular monsters the picture is to be understood as showing]: Munster, *Cosmographiae universalis*, 1550, p. 1002. This large woodcut is signed 'HRMD', which has been identified as Hans Rudolf Manuel Deutsch. Munster's book was certainly known in Scotland since the copy in St Andrews University Library, shelfmark Roy G96.M8B50, was presented to the library by Regent Murray.
32. Levey, *An Elizabethan Inheritance: The Hardwick Hall Textiles*, 1998, p. 36.
33. Zulueta, *Embroideries by Mary Stuart and Elizabeth Talbot at Oxburgh Hall*, 1923, p. 9.
34. Swain, *Needlework of Mary Queen of Scots*, 1973, pl. 77.
35. Gessner, *Historia animalium*, vol. III, 1555, p. 639.
36. On Gessner's use of Alciato see Bath, 'Some early English translations of Alciato: Edward Topsell's *Beastes* and *Serpentes*', *Emblematica*, vol. 11, 2001, pp. 393–402.
37. *OED* s.v.
38. Swain, *Needlework of Mary Queen of Scots*, 1973, p. 78; cf. Swain, *Figures on Fabric: Embroidery Design Sources and their Application*, 1980, p. 27
39. The arms of the dauphin are included with the other royal arms that define Mary's family connections painted at this time on the heraldic ceiling in the Palace of Holyroodhouse.
40. The stitches on the two Hardwick panels are identified by Santina Levey, *An Elizabethan Inheritance: The Hardwick Hall Textiles*, 1998, pp. 57–8.
41. Nevinson, 'English domestic embroidery patterns of the sixteenth and seventeenth centuries', *Walpole Society Journal*, vol. 28, 1939–40, p. 6.
42. Junius, *Emblemata*, 1565, no. 4.
43. Faerno's moral is: *Qui tenuem amicum laedit, huic, si humanitus/ Impune fuerit, imminet vindex Deus* [S/he who damages a weak friendship, even if s/he remains unpunished after the manner of men, calls down the vengeful God].
44. See Swain, *Needlework of Mary Queen of Scots*, 1973, p. 78.
45. Nevinson, 'An Elizabethan herbarium: embroideries by Bess of Hardwick after the woodcuts of Mattioli', *The National Trust Year Book*, 1975–76, p. 6.
46. Gessner, *Icones animalium*, 1560, p. 19; Swain, *Needlework of Mary Queen of Scots*, 1973, pl. 43.

Chapter 5: The Language of Flowers

1. Labanoff, *Lettres*, vol. 7, 1844, p. 239.
2. Swain, *Figures on Fabric: Embroidery Design Sources and their Application*, 1980, p. 32.
3. See Hearn, *Dynasties: Painting in Tudor and Jacobean England 1530–1630*, 1995, no. 29, pp. 63 and 73–4.
4. Nevinson 'An Elizabethan herbarium: embroideries by Bess of Hardwick after the woodcuts of Mattioli', *The National Trust Year Book*, 1975–76, p. 67.
5. See Grigson, *The Englishman's Flora*, 1975, p. 355.
6. *Ibid*, p. 430.
7. Grigson, *The Englishman's Flora*, 1958, p. 385.
8. Grigson, *The Englishman's Flora*, 1975, p. 194.
9. Labanoff, *Lettres*, vol. 7, 1844, p. 246.
10. The expression is Daniel Russell's, *Emblematic Structures in Renaissance French Culture*, 1995, p. 9.

References

Alciato, A., 1531. *Emblematum liber*. Augsburg: Steyner.

Alciato, A., 1551. *Emblemata*. Lyon: Bonhomme.

Alciato, A., 1997. *Emblemata*, P. Laurens and F. Vuilleumier (eds). Paris: Klinksieck [facs. repr.]

Amboise, A., 1621. *Devises royales*. Paris: R. Boutonne.

Arnold, J., 1988 *Queen Elizabeth's Wardrobe Unlock'd*, Leeds: W.S. Maney and Sons.

Arthur, L., 1995. *Embroidery 1600–1700 at the Burrell Collection*. London: John Murray.

Bath, M., 1994. *Speaking Pictures. English Emblem Books and Renaissance Culture*. London: Longman.

Bath, M., 1998. 'The sources of John Abbott's pattern book', *Architectural History*, vol. 4, 1998, pp. 49–66.

Bath, M., 2001. 'Some early English translations of Alciato: Edward Topsell's *Beastes* and *Serpentes*', *Emblematica*, vol. 11, pp. 393–402.

Bath, M., 2003. 'Alciato and the Earl of Arran', *Emblematica*, vol. 13, pp. 39–52

Bath, M., 2003. *Renaissance Decorative Painting in Scotland*. Edinburgh: National Museums of Scotland.

Bath, M., 2004. 'Mary Stuart's Bed of State', in J.F. van Dijkhuizen, P. Hoftijzer, J. Roding and P. Smith (eds), *Living in Posterity: Essays in Honour of Bart Westerweel*. Hilversum: Verloren, pp. 29–38.

Bath, M., 2005. 'Mary Stuart's "Byrd of America"', *History Scotland*, vol. 5, no. 3, pp. 16–23.

Bath, M., 2007. 'Ben Jonson, William Fowler and the Pinkie ceiling', *Architectural Heritage: Journal of the Architectural Heritage Society of Scotland*, vol. 18, pp. 73–86.

Bath, M., 2007. 'Emblems from Whitney on an embroidered valance in the Burrell Collection', *Society for Emblem Studies Newsletter*, no. 41 (July), pp. 7–8.

Bath, M., 2007. 'Embroidered emblems: Mary Stuart's Bed of State', *Emblematica*, vol. 15, pp. 5–32.

Bath, M., 2007. 'John Dunstall's emblems of Mary Queen of Scots', *Review of Scottish Culture*, vol. 9, pp. 1–9.

Bath, M., 2007. 'Was there a Guise Palace in Edinburgh?', in R. Gowing and R. Pender (eds), *All Manner of Murals*. London: Archetype Publications, pp. 11–21.

Bath, M., 2008. 'An emblematic embroidery in the Burrell Collection', *Emblematica*, vol. 16 (in press).

Belon, P., 1555. *L'histoire de la nature des oyseaux, avec leurs descriptions, et naïfs portraicts retirez du naturel*. Paris: B. Prevost.

Belon, P., 1555. *La nature et diversite des poissons, auec leurs pourtraicts, representez au plus pres du naturel*. Paris: C. Estienne.

Belon, P., 1555. *Les observations de plusieurs singularitez et choses memorables, trouvées en Grèce, Asie... et autres pays estranges*. Paris: G. Cavellat.

Bennet, H., 'Three Scottish embroideries', *Proceedings of the Society of Antiquaries of Scotland*, 107, pp. 330–32.

Berger, R.W., 1999. *Public Access to Art in Paris: A Documentary History from the Middle Ages to 1800*. University Park, PA: Penn State University Press.

Bie, J. de, 1636. *La France metallique*. Paris: Jean Camusat.

Boece, H., 1527 *Scotorum historia*. Edinburgh:

Boece, H., 1821. *The History and Chronicles of Scotland*, trans. J. Bellenden, 2 vols. Edinburgh: W. and C. Tait.

Bossy, J., 1991. *Giordano Bruno and the Embassy Affair*. New Haven, CT: Yale University Press.

Bossy, J., 2001. *Under the Molehill: An Elizabethan Spy Story*. New Haven, CT: Yale University Press.

Braun, L., 1990. *Conrad Gessner*. Geneva: Slatkine.

Bruno, G., 1584. *Lo spaccio della bestia trionfante*. London: J. Charlewood.

Bruno, G., 1964. *The Expulsion of the Triumphant Beast*, A.D. Imerti (trans. and ed.). Lincoln, NE: University of Nebraska.

Budiansky, S., 2005. *Her Majesty's Spymaster: Elizabeth I, Sir Francis Walsingham, and the Birth of Modern Espionage*. London: Viking Books.

Burns, E., 1887. *The Coinage of Scotland Illustrated from the Cabinet of Thomas Coats Esq*, vol. 2. Edinburgh: A & C Black.

Calendar of State Papers Relating to Scotland and Mary Queen of Scots, vol. 2: 1563–1569, ed. J. Bain, Edinburgh 1900.

Calendar of State Papers Relating to Scotland and Mary Queen of Scots, vol. 5: 1574–1581, ed. J. Bain, Edinburgh 1900.

Calendar of State Papers Relating to Scotland and Mary Queen of Scots, vol. 9: 1586–1588, ed. W.K. Boyd, Glasgow 1915.

Camden, W., 1614. *Remaines, Concerning Britaine*. London: [s.n.]. [1st edn 1605.]

Camden, W., 1615–17, *Annales rerum anglicarum et hibernicarum, regnante Elizabetha*. London: William Stainsby for Simon Waterson.

Camden, W., 1970. *Remaines, Concerning Britaine*. London: [repr.].

Camden, W., 1625. *Annales: The True and Royal History of the Famous Empresse Elizabeth*, trans. Abraham Darcie. London: Benjamin Fisher.

Camden, W., 1688. *The History of the Most Renowned and Victorious Princess*

Elizabeth, London: R. Bentley [repr. ed. W.T. MacCaffrey, Chicago, University of Chicago, 1970].
Camerarius, J. 1590. *Symbolorum et emblematum ex re herbaria*. Nuremberg: J. Hofmann and H. Camoxi.
Catalogue of the Tercentenary Exhibition of Mary Queen of Scots, Peterborough, 1887.
Cochran-Patrick, R.W., 1884. *Catalogue of the Medals of Scotland*. Edinburgh: David Douglas.
Collection of Inventories and other Records of the Royal Wardrobe and Jewelhouse 1488–1606, 1815. Edinburgh: H.M. General Register House.
Collinson, P., 1987. *The English Captivity of Mary Queen of Scots*, Sheffield: Sheffield History Pamphlets.
Cummings, R., 2007. 'Alciato's illustrated epigrams', *Emblematica*, 15, pp. 193–228.
Devlin, C., 1956. *The Life of Robert Southwell, Poet and Martyr*. London: Longman.
Drummond, W., 1711. *The Works of William Drummond of Hawthornden*. Edinburgh: James Watson.
Durant, D. N., 1977. *Bess of Hardwick: Portrait of an Elizabethan Dynast*. London: Weidenfeld and Nicolson.
Durkan, J., 1953. 'The beginnings of Humanism in Scotland', *Innes Review*, vol. 4, pp. 5–24.
Durkan, J., 1980. 'Giovanni Ferrerio, Gesner and French affairs', *Bibliothèque d'humanisme et renaissance: travaux et documents*, vol. 42, pp. 349–60.
Durkan, J., 1981. 'Giovanni Ferrerio, Humanist: his influence in sixteenth-century Scotland', in K. Robbins (ed.), *Religion and Humanism*. Oxford: Blackwell, pp. 181–94.
Erasmus, D., 1539. *Proverbes or Adagies*, trans. Richard Taverner. London: Richard Bankes.
Erasmus, D., 1703. *Opera omnia*. Leiden: P. van der Aa.
Faerno, G., 1563. *Fabulae centum*. Rome: Vincentius Luchinus.
Ferro, G., 1623. *Teatro d'imprese*. Venice: Giacomo Sarzina.
Fleming, D.H., 1897. *Mary Queen of Scots from her Birth to her Flight into England: A Brief Biography*. London: Hodder and Stoughton.
Fowler, W., 1914–40. *The Works of William Fowler*, H.W. Meikle, J. Craigie and J. Purves (eds), 3 vols. Edinburgh: William Blackwood and Son for the Scottish Text Society.
Franks, A.W., 1872–73, 'Notice of permissions given at Paris to John Acheson to make dies with the portrait of Mary Queen of Scots', *Proceedings of the Society of Antiquaries of Scotland*, 1872–73, pp. 506–7.
Fraser, A., 1969. *Mary Queen of Scots*. London: Weidenfeld and Nicolson.
Gatti, H. (ed.) 2002. *Giordano Bruno: Philosopher of the Renaissance*. Aldershot: Ashgate.
Gessner, C., 1551. *Historia animalium I: De quadrupedibus viviparis*. Zürich: Froschauer.
Gessner, C., 1554. *Historia animalium II: De quadrupedibus oviparis*. Zürich: Froschauer.
Gessner, C., 1555. *Historia animalium III: De avium natura*. Zürich: Froschauer.
Gessner, C., 1560. *Historia animalium IV: De piscium et aquatilium natura*. Zürich: Froschauer.
Gessner, C., 1553. *Icones animalium quadrupedum viviparorum et oviparorum*. Zurich: Froschauer.
Gessner, C., 1560. *Icones animalium quadrupedum viviparorum et oviparorum*, 2nd edn enlarged. Zurich: Froschauer.
Gessner, C., 1555. *Icones avium omnium*. Zürich: Froschauer.
Gessner, C., 1560. *Icones avium omnium*, 2nd edn enlarged. Zürich: Froschauer.
Gessner, C., 1560. *Icones animalium aquatilium*. Zürich: Froschauer.
Gibb, W., 1890. *The Royal House of Stuart*. London: Macmillan.
Giovio, P., 1555. *Dialogo dell'imprese militari et amorose*. Rome: Antonio Barre [repr. Lyon by Rouille 1559 for the first time with illustrations, and in 1560 under the title *Le sententiose imprese*].
Giovio, P., 1585. *The Worthy Tract of Paulus Iovius*, S. Daniel (trans.). London: Simon Waterson.
Goldsmith, O. 1774. *History of the Earth and Animated Nature*, 8 vols. London: J. Nourse.
Green, H., 1870. *Shakespeare and the Emblem Writers*. London: Trübner.
Grigson, G., 1975. *The Englishman's Flora*. London: Paladin.
Gristwood, S., 2003. *Arbella: England's Lost Queen*. London: Bantam.
Guy, J., 2004. *My Heart is my Own: The Life of Mary Queen of Scots*. London: Fourth Estate.
Hackenbroch, Y., 1960. *English and Other Needlework: Tapestries and Textiles in the Irwin Untermeyer Collection*. London: Thames & Hudson.
Hargrave, F., 1776–81. *A Complete Collection of State Trials*, 7 vols, 4th edn. London: T. Wright *et al*.
Haynes, A., 2004. *The Elizabethan Secret Services*. Stroud: Sutton Publishing.
Hearn, K. (ed.) 1995. *Dynasties: Painting in Tudor and Jacobean England 1530–1630*. London: Tate Publishing.
Henkel, A. and Schöne, A., 1967. *Handbuch zur Sinnbildkunst des CVI. und CVII. Jahrhunderts*. Stuttgart: J.B. Metzler.
Historic Manuscripts Commission Calendar of the Manuscripts in the Possession of the Most Hon. the Marquis of Salisbury, K.G., London 1883–1976, 24 vols.
Hollstein, F., 1954–. *German Etchings, Engravings and Woodcuts 1400–1700*, 57 vols. Amsterdam: Sound & Vision Publishers.
Höltgen, K.J., 2002. 'The ruler between two columns: imperial aspiration and political iconography from Emperor Charles V to William of Orange', in M. Bath, P.F. Campa and D. Russell (eds), *Emblem Studies in Honor of Peter M. Daly*. Baden-Baden: Koerner, pp. 143–68.
Horapollo Nilus, 1551. *De sacris notis* [= *Hieroglyphica*]. Paris: Kerver [1st edn 1543].
Horapollo Nilus, 1950. *The Hieroglyphics of Horapollo*, G. Boas (trans). New York: Pantheon Books.
Howard, Duke of Norfolk (ed.) 1857. *The Lives of Philip Howard, Earl of Arundel, and of Anne Dacres, his Wife*. London: Hurst and Blackett.
Isselburg, P. and Rem, G., 1617. *Emblemata politica*. Nuremberg: [s.n.]
Jonson, B., 1925–52. *Ben Jonson: The Works*, C.H. Herford and P. Simpson (eds), 11 vols. Oxford: Clarendon Press.
Junius, H., 1565. *Emblemata*. Antwerp: Christopher Plantin.
Kemp, C., 2002. 'Lumine carens: zur Sonnenfinsternis in der Emblematik', in W. Harms and D. Peil (eds), *Polyvalenz und Multifunktionalität der Emblematik*, vol. 1. Bern/Frankfurt-am-Main: Peter Lang, pp. 303–18.
Kirke, H., 1911. 'An aristocratic squabble', *Derbyshire Archaeological Journal*, vol. 32, pp. 19–38.
Labanoff, A., 1844. *Lettres, instructions et mémoires de Marie Stuart, reine d'Écosse*, 7 vols. London: C. Dolman.
Lefuse, M., 1911. *The Life and Times of Arabella Stuart*. London: Mills and Boon.
Leisher, J. F., 1987. *Geoffrey Whitney's* Choice of Emblems *and its Relation to the Emblematic Vogue in Tudor England*. New York: Garland.
Le Moyne, P., 1666. *De l'art des devises*. Paris: S. Cramoisy.
Levey, S., 1998. *An Elizabethan Inheritance: The Hardwick Hall Textiles*. London: National Trust.
Levey, S. and Thornton, P.K., 2001. *Of Household Stuff: The 1601 Inventories of Bess of Hardwick*. London: National Trust.
Lockie, D.M., 1853. 'The political career of the Bishop of Ross', *University of Birmingham Historical Journal*, pp. 98–137.
Lovel, M.S., 2005. *Bess of Hardwick, First Lady of Chatsworth 1527–1608*. London: W.W. Norton.
MacDonald A., Lynch, M. and Cowan, I.B. (eds) 1994. *The Renaissance in Scotland: Studies Offered to John Durkan*. Leiden: E.J. Brill.
Masson, D. (ed.) 1891. *Register of the Privy Council of Scotland*, vol.10: 1613–1616. Edinburgh: H.M. General Register House.
Mattioli, P.A., 1558. *Commentarii in Dioscorides*. Venice: Vincent Valgrisi [1st edn 1554].

Mattioli, P.A., 1598. *Commentarii in Dioscorides*. Frankfurt: Bassaeus.

Munster, S., 1550. *Cosmographiae universalis*. Basel: H. Petri.

Murdin, W. (ed.) 1759. *A Collection of State Papers Relating to Affairs in the Reign of Queen Elizabeth ... Transcribed from Original Papers ... Left by William Cecil Lord Burghley, and Deposited in the Library at Hatfield House*. London: W. Bowyer

Nevinson, J., 1976 'An Elizabethan herbarium: embroideries by Bess of Hardwick after the woodcuts of Mattioli', *The National Trust Year Book 1975–76*. London: National Trust, pp. 65–9.

Nevinson, J. L., 1939–40. 'English domestic embroidery patterns of the sixteenth and seventeenth centuries', *Walpole Society Journal*, vol. 28, pp. 1–13.

Nevinson, J.L., 1966–68. 'The embroidery patterns of Thomas Trevelyon', *Walpole Society Journal*, vol. 61, pp. 1–38.

North, S., 2005. 'The Falkland Jacket: sources, provenance and interpretation of an emblematic artifact', *Emblematica*, vol. 14, pp. 127–53.

Olaus Magnus, 1554. *Historia de gentibus septentrionalibus*. Rome: I.M. de Viottis.

Ordine, N., 1999. *Giordano Bruno, Ronsard et la religion*. Paris: Albin Michel.

Palliser, B., 1870. *Historic Devices, Badges and War-cries*. London: Sampson Low.

Palmer, T., 1988. *The Emblems of Thomas Palmer: Two Hundred Poosies Sloane MS 3794*, J. Manning (ed.). New York: AMS Press.

Paradin, C., 1557. *Devises heroïques*. Lyon: Jean de Tournes [1st edn, Lyon, 1551; repr. Antwerp, Plantin, 1561].

Pollard, J.G., 1990 'England and the Italian medal', in E. Chancy and P. Mack (eds), *England and the Continental Renaissance. Essays in Honour of J. B. Trapp*. Woodbridge: Boydell Press.

Praz, M., 1975. *Studies in Seventeenth-century Imagery*. Rome: Edizione di Storia e Letteratura.

Robertson, J. (ed.) 1863. *Inventaires de la Royne Descosse Douairiere de France: Catalogue of the Jewels, Dresses, Furniture, Books and Paintings of Mary Queen of Scots*. Edinburgh: H.M. General Register House.

Rondelet, G., 1558. *L'histoire des poissons*. Lyon: Bonhomme.

Rosenthal, E.E., 1973. 'The invention of the columnar device of Emperor Charles V at the court of Burgundy in Flanders in 1516', *Journal of the Warburg and Courtauld Institutes*, vol. 36, pp. 198–230.

Rossi, Bartolomeo de', 1612. *Hieroglyphica*. Verona: B. Marino.

Russell, D., 1985. *The Emblem and Device in France*. Lexington KY: French Forum.

Russell, D., 1995. *Emblematic Structures in Renaissance French Culture*. Toronto: University of Toronto Press.

Russell, D., 2002. 'The ornamental image: memory, decoration, and emblems', in M. Bath, P.F. Campa and D. Russell (eds), *Emblem Studies in Honor of Peter M. Daly*. Baden-Baden: Koerner, pp. 191–213.

Scher, S. (ed.) 1994. *The Currency of Fame: Portrait Medals of the Renaissance*. London: Thames and Hudson.

Simeoni, G., 1560. *Le imprese heroiche e morali*. Lyon: Rouille [repr. Antwerp, Plantin, 1561].

Southwell, R., 1967. *The Poems of Robert Southwell*, N. Pollard Brown and J. McDonald (eds). Oxford: Clarendon Press.

Southwell, R., 2007. *Collected Poems*, P. Davidson and A. Sweeney (eds). Manchester: Carcanet Press.

Stevenson, D., 1988. *The Origin of Freemasonry: Scotland's Century 1590–1710*. Cambridge: Cambridge University Press.

Stewart, I., 1988. 'Review of D. Bateson, *Scottish Coins* (1987)', *Numismatic Circular*, 96, no. 2 (March), p. 48.

Stewart, I., 1983. 'Coinage and propaganda: an interpretation of the coin-types of James VI', in A. O'Connor and D.V. Clarke (eds), *From the Stone Age to the Forty-five*. Edinburgh: John Donald Publishers, pp. 450–62.

Strickland, A., 1842–43. *Letters of Mary, Queen of Scots, and Documents Connected with her Personal History*, 3 vols. London: H. Colburn.

Strickland, A., 1850–59. *Lives of the Queens of Scotland*, 8 vols. Edinburgh: Blackwood.

Strong, R., 1963. *Portraits of Queen Elizabeth I*. Oxford: Clarendon Press.

Strong, R., 1993. ' "My weepinge Stagg I crowne": The Persian Lady reconsidered', in M. Bath, J. Manning and A.R. Young (eds), *The Art of the Emblem. Essays in Honor of K. J. Höltgen*. New York: AMS, pp. 103–41 [repr. in R. Strong, *The Tudor and Stuart Monarchy: Pageantry, Painting, Iconography*, vol. 2, Woodbridge, Boydell and Brewer, 1995, pp. 303–24].

Strong, R. and Trevelyan Oman, J. 1972. *Mary Queen of Scots*. London: Secker and Warburg.

Stuart, Mary Queen of Scots, 1992 *Bittersweet within my Heart: The Love Poems of Mary, Queen of Scots*, R. Bell (ed.) San Francisco: Chronicle Books.

Swain, M., 1970. *Historical Needlework: A Study of Influences in Scotland and Northern England*. London: Barrie and Jenkins.

Swain, M., 1973. *The Needlework of Mary Queen of Scots*. New York: Van Nostrand Reinhold.

Swain, M., 1980. *Figures on Fabric: Embroidery Design Sources and their Application*. London: A & C Black.

Swain, M., 1986. *Scottish Embroidery: Medieval to Modern*. London: Batsford.

Swain, M., 1994. 'The Lochleven and Linlithgow Hangings', *Proceedings of the Society of Antiquaries of Scotland*, vol. 124, pp. 455–66.

Thevet, A., 1558. *Les singularitéz de la France antarctique*. Paris: heirs of Maurice de la Porte.

Thevet, A., 1982. *Les singularitéz de la France antarctique*, J. Baudry (ed.). Paris: Le Temps [repr. of 1558 edn].

Thevet, A., 1568. *The Newe Founde Worlde, or Antarcticke*. London: H. Bynneman.

Topsell, E., 1607. *The Historie of Four-Footed Beastes*. London: William Jaggard.

Tytler, P.F., 1828–43. *History of Scotland*, 9 vols. Edinburgh: W. Tait.

Valeriano Bolzani, G.P., 1556. *Hieroglyphica sive de sacris aegyptiorum literis*. Basel: T. Guarini.

Van Heijnsbergen, T. 1994. 'Literature and history in Queen Mary's Edinburgh', in A. MacDonald, M. Lynch and I.B. Cowan (eds), *The Renaissance in Scotland: Studies Offered to John Durkan*. Leiden: E.J. Brill, pp. 191–8.

Wardle, P., 1981. 'The embroideries of Mary, Queen of Scots: notes on the French connection', *Bulletin of the Needle and Bobbin Club (New York)*, vol. 64, pp. 3–14.

Watkins, S. and Fiennes, M., 2001 *Mary Queen of Scots*. London: Thames & Hudson.

Way, A., 1858. 'The signet-ring and silver bell of Mary Queen of Scots', *Archaeological Journal*, vol. 15, pp. 253–66.

Wellisch, H., 1975. 'Conrad Gessner: a bio-bibliography', *Journal of the Society for the Bibliography of Natural History*, vol. 7, pp. 151–247.

Wells-Cole, A., 1997. *Art and Decoration in Elizabethan and Jacobean England*. New Haven, CT: Yale University Press.

Whitney, G., 1586. *A Choice of Emblemes and other Devises*. Leiden: Plantin.

Wingfield Digby, G., 1963. *Elizabethan Embroidery*. London: Faber & Faber.

Yates, F.A., 1966. *The Art of Memory*. Chicago: Chicago University Press.

Young, A., 1987. *Tudor and Jacobean Tournaments*. London: George Philip.

Zulueta, F. de, 1923. *Embroideries by Mary Stuart and Elizabeth Talbot at Oxburgh Hall, Norfolk*. Oxford: Oxford University Press.

Index

Page references in bold indicate illustrations

Ab omni parte equaliter pungo panel 121, **122**, 139
Abbott, John 71
Acheson, John 66
Aelianus 71
Alciato, Andrea 23, 27, **28**, 41, 148
Aliamque moratur emblem 19, **42**, 43, 46–7, 55, 151
Altera securitas emblem 157
Ambo utroque tenent emblem 154
Amboise, Adrien d' 43, 151
Amoris sorte pares emblem 56
Ape of Turky panel **69**, 144
Arbella Stuart **12**, 13
Arctiora sunt virtutis panel 38, 127
Ardorem extincta lacrimae emblem 32, **37**, 156
Ardua deturbans emblem 30, 142
Armadillo, *see* Tatou panel
Arran, Earl of 2
Artem quaevis alit terra panel 138
Arundel, *see* Howard, Philip
Asperitate secures emblem 155
Asse panel 130
Aubépine, Guillaume, Baron de Châteauneuf 19
Aubigny, Agrippa d' 33–4
Auchmowtie, John 20
Aulus Gellius 63
Aut hanc aut super hoc emblem 150

Babington plot 5
Bacon, Anthony 67
Bacon, Sir Francis 71
Balfour, Sir James 61
Basta ch'io vivi emblem 152–3
Beauregard, Renée de *see* Rallay, Renée de
Bed of State 6, 11, 16, 17–21, 23, 26, 32, 42–7, 147–57
Bedingfeld, Sir Richard 12
Bees panel 128
Belon, Pierre 70, 72–5, 82, 108, 124, 131
Bess of Hardwick 1, 2, 3, 4, 11, 13, 14, 16, 29, 32–7, 69, 88–90, 113, 131

Bie, Jacques de **44**, 45, **66**, 148
Boare panel 130
Boate Fishe panel 144
Boece, Hector 73–4, 77, 78, 85
Bon Brek panel 103, 130
Brantome 8
Brennus 155
Breton, Hector le 63
Bruno, Giordano 19, 44–7, 151
Buke panel 132
Bull Bayted panel 132
Burnett Alexander, arms of 63, 64, **64**
Burrell Collection, Glasgow 7
Butterflies panel 129
Byrd of America panel, Marian Hanging 78, **79**, 85, 128
Byrde of America panel, Cavendish Hanging **79**, 80, 85, 132
Byrde of Paradyse panel 130

Caeca fortuna est panel 138
Camden, William 49–55, 153, 155, 156
Camel panel 132
Camerarius, Joachim 41
Cancer panel 129
Castelnau, Michel, Sieur de Mauvissière 45
Catte panel 111, **111**, 145
Cavendish, Elizabeth 12
Cavendish, Grace 142
Cavendish, Henry 142
Cavendish, Mary 12–13
Cavendish, William 13, 35–6, 131
Cavendish Hanging
   Byrde of America panel **79**, 80, 85, 132
Cecil, Sir William (later Lord Burleigh) 4, 55
Cercerel panel 131
Chamel of Indye panel 130
Charles IX 28, 43, 142
Chartley inventory 5, 6, 15, 19, 60, 62, 113, 124
Civet Catte panel 131
Clouet, François ii, 33, 37

Cock of Maurtain panel 130
Cock of th'Alpes panel 143
Cockatrice panel 128
Cocke panel 130
Cockle Crab panel 145
Comite mercurio emblem 150
Contino intra tuum pel panel 143
Cordile panel 132
Coronam ne carpito emblem 120, 137
Crane panel 130
Crocodil panel 130
Cum larvis non luctandum emblem 28
Cum Minerva manum quoque panel 121, 138
Curle, Elizabeth 55
Cushion covers
   Europa and the Bull 90, **90**
   Hardwick 107, 108–11, 135–6

Dabit Deus his quoque finem emblem 54, **54**, 154
Dacre, Anne, Countess of Arundel 12–13, 55–7, 67
Daniel, Samuel 27
Darnley, Henry Stewart, Lord 3, 4, 5, 24, 39–42, 55, 58
Dat gloria vires emblem 38–42, 113, 127, 155
Dederitne viam emblem 151
Delphin panel 101, **101**, 129
Dickson, Alexander 47
Ditat servata fides emblem 31, **31**, 142
Divinae vindicta emblem 20, 156
Dog Fish panel 143
Donec emerserit undis panel 149
Donec totum impleat orbem emblem 45, 149
Donne, John 113
Dotrel panel 106, **106**, 133
Dowker panel 144
Dragon panel 128, 130
Drummond of Hawthornden, William 4, 6, 8, 16, 17–21, 23, 27, 43, 51–7, 147–57
Dunstall, John 53–7, 154, 155, 156
Durkan, John 85

169

Eape panel 143
Earlshall (Fife) 71
Elephant panel 11, 144
Elizabeth I 2, 19, 26, 45, 49, 54, 55, 56, 58, 66, 87, **89**, 111, 115
Eloquium tot lumina emblem 50, 52, **52**, 53, 156
Emblems
   Aliamque moratur 19, **42**, 43, 46–7, 55, 151
   Altera securitas 157
   Ambo utroque tenent 154
   Amoris sorte pares 56
   Ardorem extincta lacrimae 32, **37**, 156
   Ardua deturbans 30, 142
   Asperitate secures 155
   Aut hanc aut super hoc 150
   Basta ch'io vivi 152–3
   Comite mercurio 150
   Coronam ne carpito 120, 137
   Cum larvis non luctandum 28
   Dabit Deus his quoque finem 54, **54**, 154
   Dat gloria vires 38–42, 113, 127, 155
   Dederitne viam 151
   Ditat servata fides 31, **31**, 142
   Divinae vindicta 20, 156
   Donec totum impleat orbem 45, 149
   Eloquium tot lumina 50, 52, **52**, 53, 156
   En ma fin git mon commencement 157
   Et lepores 27, 148
   Eventus rei in manu dei 113–14, 116, 130
   Extinctam lachrimae 32–3, 36, 131
   Fortitudo eius 152
   Fortuna comites 17, 156
   Fructus calcata 51, 52, 153
   Idem intus et extra 151
   Il mal me preme 26, 154
   Illa peremptum 56
   Impunitas ferociae parens 110, 111, 135
   In fide societas 153
   Ingenii largitor 32–3, **33**–4, 129
   Invidia integritatis assecla 40, 41
   Ipsa sibi lumen 19, 53–4, **54**, 153
   Je suis ung mal 150
   Latet anguis in herba 37, **37**
   Llos llenos de dolor 24, 27, 149
   Magnatum vicinitas 150
   Malo oppressus 27
   Manet ultima caelo 42–7, **43**, 151
   Mea sic mihi prosunt 64–7, **65**, 147
   Medio occidit die 155
   Monstrant regibus astra 30, **30**, 141–2
   Moveor nec rapior 153
   Ne nimium crede colori 128
   Ne volutetur 24, 149
   Nodos virtute 30, **30**, 142
   Non inferiora secutus 7–8, **8**, 30, 113, 127, 142
   Non quae super terram 155
   Nunquam nisi rectam 31, **32**, 149
   Nutrisco et extinguo 7, 23, **24**, 153
   Per vincula crescit 26, 51, **51**, 155
   Pervigiles virtus 155
   Pietas revocabit 52, **52**, 154
   Pietate et justicia 29, 142
   Ploret picea 24, 150
   Ponderibus virtus innata resistit 26, 50–51, **51**, 155
   Premit et hæret 148
   Pulchriori detur 114, **115**, 127
   Quae cecidere resurgent 52, 152
   Quid nisi victis dolor 155
   Quis contra nos 30–31, **31**, 57, 142
   Sa vertu m'atire 8–9, 52, 60, 127, 153
   Securitas altera 25
   Sic dulcia in amarum 154
   Sub herba latet anguis 37, **37**, 127
   Tamen leo 57
   Tantus mihi fulgor 155
   Te stante virebo 25–6, **25–6**, 44, 149
   Terrena obcecant 154
   Trino non convenit orbis 152
   Undique 151
   Unum quidem sed leonem 58, 148
   Unus non sufficit 44, 45–6, **46**, 148
   Ut casus dederit 152
   Ut superis visum 52, **52**, 151
   Vias tuas domine 31, **31**, 142
   Virescit vulnere virtus 14, 26, 37–8, 58–65, **60–65**, 127, 150
Emery, Nicolas 66
En ma fin git mon commencement emblem 157
Erasmus 27, 113, 118–22, 124, 130, 137–9, 142, 143, 148
Estriche panel 131
Et lepores emblem 27, 148
Europa and the Bull cushion cover 90, **90**
Eventus rei in manu dei emblem 113–14, 116, 130
Eworth, Hans 114–15, **116**
Extinctam lachrimae emblem 32–3, 36, 131
Extra publicam viam ne deflectas panel 118, **119**, 138

Fables 7, 16–17, 31, 33, 57–8, 69, 100, 101, 108–11, 113, 129, 135–6, 148
Faerno, Gabriello 17, 108–11, 124, 135
Falcon panel 145
Falkland bodice 170
Fauconet panel 131
Fecem bibat panel 130
Felicitas vera panel 138
Feras non culpes panel 121, **122**, 138
Ferrerio, Iovanni 78, 82, 85, 124
Ferro, Giovanni 152
Fitzwilliam, George 55
Fortitudo eius emblem 152
Fortuna comites emblem 17, 156
Fotheringhay Castle 5–6, 20, 55
Fowler, William 14, 17–18, 19, 43, 46, 52, 53, 117, 147–57
François I 7, 9, 23, 24, 127, 153
François II 2, 3, 24, 29, 43, **44**, 45, 46, 60, 62, 143, 148, 153, 154
Fratrum inter se ire panel 137
Froschauer, Christoph 40, 42
Fructus calcata emblem 51, 52, 153
Fugacia sic speciosa panel 113, 130
Fyrete panel 130

Galen 72
Galloway, Earls of 63–4, **64**
Gene Skyn panel 71, **71**, 144
Gessner, Conrad 11, 40–42, 70–102, **70**, 111, 124, 125, 128–34, 143–5
Gheeraerts, Marcus 65, **65**
Giovio, Paolo 24, 27–8, **28**, 149
Gleade panel 131
Gor Glut panel 143
Gorhambury 71
Great Munkey panel 144
Greek Anthology 148

Habeas extra lutum pedes panel 143
Hand bell, Mary's silver 55, 60–62, **61**–2, 150
Hangings
   Cavendish Hanging, Byrde of America panel 79, **80**, 85, 132
   Marian Hanging, Byrd of America panel **78**, 79, 85, 128
Hardwick cushion covers 107–12, **107**–8, 135–6
Hardwick Hall 17, 108, 109, 117, 124, 137, 141, 145
Harte panel 128
Hearon panel 144
Henri II 24, 32, 77, 82, 84, 131, 149
Henri III 19, 24, 42–7, 151
Henry VIII 2, 157
Hillyard, Nicholas 89
Hobreau panel 144
Holbein, Hans 40
Holyroodhouse, Palace of 10, 111, 141, 143, 145
Homer 27
Horapollo 57–8, **58**, 148
Horse panel 129
Hostium munera panel 142
Howard, Anne, *see* Dacre, Anne, Countess of Arundel
Howard, Philip, Earl of Arundel 12, 13, 31, 50, 55–8, 67
Hullot panel 145

Idem intus et extra emblem 151
Il mal me preme emblem 26, 154
Illa peremptum emblem 56
Impunitas ferociae parens emblem 110, 111, 135
In fide societas emblem 153
Ingenii largitor emblem 32–3, **33**–4, 129
Integritas vi robora panel 114, 131
Intra tuum peliculum panel 143
Invidia integritatis assecla emblem 40, 41
Ipsa sibi lumen emblem 19, 53–4, **54**, 153
Isselberg, Peter 41

James II 7
James V 2
James VI/I 3, 6, 17, 19, 20, 47
Jay panel 128
Je suis ung mal emblem 150
Jonson, Ben 4, 6, 16, 17, 51, 147–57
Judgement of Paris 114–15, **116**, 127
Junius, Hadrianus 24, 26, 27, 40, 41–2, 109, **110**, 111, 124, 135, 154
Jupiter panel 143

INDEX

Kerver, Jacques   57–8
Knotted Serpentes panel   104, **104**, 132

Laing, David   19
Las pennas passan panel   12, 15, 28–9, **29**, 36, 57, 141–2
Latet anguis in herba emblem   37, **37**
Leicester, Robert Dudley, Earl of   25–6, 45
Lennox, Margaret Douglas, Countess of   5
Lennox, Matthew Stewart, 4th Earl of   **12**, 14, 55
Leonem ne stimules panel   138
Leparde panel   131
Leslie, John, Bishop of Ross   5, 85
Levey, Santina   2
Lewiston, Lady   4
Lindsay of the Mount, Sir David   63
Lion of the Sea panel   75–6, **75**
Llos llenos de dolor emblem   24, 27, 149
Lockey, Rowland   **12**
Locuste of the Sea panel   143
Lyone panel   128

Magnatum vicinitas emblem   150
Malo oppressus emblem, 27
Malum consilium panel   138
Manet ultima caelo emblem   42–7, **43**, 151
Marcus Aurelius   71
Marguerite de Navarre   8, **8**, 30, 127
Marian Hanging, Byrd of America panel   78, **79**, 85, 128
Martial   71
Mary of Guise   2
Mattioli, Pietro A.   103–7, **103–7**, 114, **114**, 117–23, **117–23**, 129, 130, 131, 137–9, 142, 143, 145
Mauvissière, *see* Castelnau
Mea sic mihi prosunt emblem   64–7, **65**, 147
Medici, Catherine de   2, 6–7, 11, 32–5, 37, 131, 156
Medio occidit die emblem   155
Melvin, Andrew   16, 20, 55
Minutula pluvia panel   137
Mole Worte panel   131
Monster of the Sea panel   144
Monstrant regibus astra emblem   30, **30**, 141–2
Montagu, Viscount   12, 13
Moveor nec rapior emblem   153
Mule panel   132
Munster, Sebastian   88, 141
Murer, Jos   87

Natura ea que nocent panel   138
Nautilus panel   144
Navarre, Marguerite de *see* Marguerite de Navarre
Ne nimium crede colori emblem   128
Ne volutetur emblem   24, 149
Nemo bene imperat panel   139
Nequicquam sapit panel   137
Nevinson, J.   109–11, 118, 135
Newte panel   144
Nodos virtute emblem   30, **30**, 142
Non hora somniamus panel   143

Non inferiora secutus emblem   7–8, **8**, 30, 113, 127, 142
Non quae super terram emblem   155
Norfolk, Thomas Howard, 4th Duke of   5, 50, 55, 58–60, 131
Nullum speciosum panel   138
Nunquam nisi rectam emblem   31, **32**, 149
Nutrisco et extinguo emblem   7, 23, **24**, 153

Oculis magis habenda fides panel   138
Olaus Magnus   88–9, **88**, 90, **92–3**, **95**, 141
Omnes sibi esse melius volunt panel   138
Omnia ex disponentis panel   139
Omnium rerum vicissitude est panel   138
Once panel   86–7, 128
Onocratalus panel   144
Ordine, Nuccio   45
Ospray panel   144
Oudry, Pierre   3
Ovid   38
Oxburgh Hall   12, 127

Panels
  Ab omni parte equaliter pungo   121, **122**, 139
  Ape of Turky   **69**, 144
  Arctiora sunt virtutis   38, 127
  Artem quaevis alit terra   138
  Asse   130
  Bees   128
  Boare   130
  Boate Fishe   144
  Bon Brek   103, 130
  Buke   132
  Bull Bayted   137
  Butterflies   129
  Byrd of America   78–9, **79**, 85, 128
  Byrde of America   **79**, 80, 85, 132
  Byrde of Paradyse   130
  Caeca fortuna est   138
  Camel   132
  Cancer   129
  Catte   111, **111**, 145
  Cercerel   131
  Chamel of Indye   130
  Civet Catte   131
  Cock of Maurtain   130
  Cock of th'Alpes   143
  Cockatrice   128
  Cocke   130
  Cockle Crab   45
  Contino intra tuum pel   143
  Cordile   132
  Crane   130
  Crocodil   130
  Cum Minerva manum quoque   121, 138
  Delphin   101, **101**, 129
  Dog Fish   143
  Donec emerserit undis   149
  Dotrel   106, **106**, 133
  Dowker   144
  Dragon   128, 130
  Eape   143
  Elephant   **11**, 144
  Estriche   131

  Extra publicam viam ne deflectas   118, **119**, 138
  Falcon   145
  Fauconet   131
  Fecem bibat   130
  Felicitas vera   138
  Feras non culpes   121, **122**, 138
  Fratrum inter se ire   137
  Fugacia sic speciosa   113, 130
  Fyrete   130
  Gene Skyn   71, **71**, 144
  Gleade   131
  Gor Glut   143
  Great Munkey   144
  Habeas extra lutum pedes   143
  Harte   128
  Hearon   144
  Hobreau   144
  Horse   129
  Hostium munera   142
  Hullot   145
  Integritas vi robora   114, 131
  Intra tuum peliculum   143
  Jay   128
  Jupiter   143
  Knotted Serpentes   104, **104**, 132
  Las pennas passan   12, 15, 28–9, **29**, 36, 57, 141–2
  Leonem ne stimules   138
  Leparde   131
  Lion of the Sea   **75**, 76
  Locuste of the Sea   143
  Lyone   128
  Malum consilium   138
  Minutula pluvia   137
  Mole Worte   131
  Monster of the Sea   144
  Mule   132
  Natura ea que nocent   138
  Nautilus   144
  Nemo bene imperat   139
  Nequicquam sapit   137
  Newte   144
  Non hora somniamus   143
  Nullum speciosum   138
  Oculis magis habenda fides   138
  Omnes sibi esse melius volunt   138
  Omnia ex disponentis   139
  Omnium rerum vicissitude est   138
  Once   86–7, 128
  Onocratalus   144
  Ospray   144
  Peacock   143
  Pecuniae obediunt omnia   138
  Pelican   **96**, 128
  Per publicam viam ne ambules   118, **119**, 121, 138
  Phenix   128
  Phesant   128
  Pie   143
  Poole Snyte   144
  Porphyry   98–9, **98**, 130
  Pye of Persia   81, **82**, 130
  Quail   131

171

Quayle 144
Quod caret alterna 138
Reindeer 95, 130
Rhinocerote of the Sea 76–7, 90, **94**, 129
Robin 99, **100**, 130
Sand Cockles 105, **105**
Satius est initiis mederi 138
Satyr 131
Scolopender 90, **91**, 129
Scorpions 107, **107**, 131, 134
Sea Hors 76–7, **76**, 144
Sea Moonke 72–3, **73**, 129
Seele 143
Sementem alii faciunt 138–9
She Dolphin 69, 129
Shofler 96, **97**, 144
Sneiles 129
Solen Goose 77, 78, 85, 128
Spider 106, **107**, **107**, 133
Steinbock 143
Sterlin 130
Stork of the Montaynes 86, 87, 130
Su 82, **83**, 133
Swalloe 131
Tatou 82, **84**, 131
Thorne Back 90, 129
Tiger 129
Troute 129
Turkie Cocke 131
Turtel Dove 128
Unicorn 128
Ut plures sapiendum 137
Ut sementem feceris 139
Vera felicitas semper illesa 115, **117**, 131
Vera virtus periculum affectat 131
Virtutis praemium 118, **118**, 138
Vitia occulta minus noxia 121, **123**, 138
Water Owle 144
Zyphwhale 90, **92**, 128, 143
Paradin, Claude 23–5, **24–5**, 30–1, **31–2**, 37,
  57, 109, 111, 124, 127, 129, 136, 141–2, 149,
  152, 153, 154, 157
Paulet, Sir Amyas 5, 6, 20, 51
Peacock panel 143
Pecuniae obediunt omnia panel 138
Pelican 63–4, 96, **96**, 144
Pelican panel **96**, 128
Per publicam viam ne ambules panel 118, **119**,
  121, 138
Per vincula crescit emblem 26, 51, **51**, 155
Pervigiles virtus emblem 155
Phenix panel 128
Phesant panel 128
Philip II, King of Spain 55
Pie panel 143
Pietas revocabit emblem 52, **52**, 154
Pietate et justicia emblem 29, 142
Pinkie House, Musselburgh **16**, 17, 20
Pliny 30
Ploret picea emblem 24, 150
Plutarch 41
Ponderibus virtus innata resistit emblem 26,
  50–51, **51**, 155
Poole Snyte panel 144

Porphyry panel 98–9, **98**, 130
Premit et hæret emblem 148
Prestongrange, Lothian 32, **35**, 129
Primavera, Jacopo 57, **57**
Pulchriori detur emblem 114, **115**, 127
Pye of Persia panel **81**, 82, 130

Quae cecidere resurgent emblem 52, 152
Quail panel 131
Quayle panel 144
Quid nisi victis dolor emblem 155
Quis contra nos emblem 30–31, **31**, 57, 142
Quod caret alterna panel 138

Raith, James 17
Rallay, Renée de (née Beauregard) 3, 5, 14, **15**
Randolf, Thomas 3
Reid, Robert 85
Reindeer panel 95, 130
Rhinocerote of the Sea panel 76–7, 90, **94**, 129
Ridolfi plot 5
Robin panel 99, **100**, 130
Ronsard 8
Russell, Daniel 64

Sa vertu m'atire emblem 8–9, 52, 60, 127, 153
Sadler, Sir Ralph 5
Saint-Germain-en-Laye 7
Salamander, *see Nutrisco et extinguo* emblem
Salomon, Bernard 90, **90**
Sand Cockles panel 105, **105**
Satius est initiis mederi panel 138
Satyr panel 131
Savoy, Duke of 152
Scolopender panel 90, **91**, 129
Scorpions panel 107, **107**, 131, 134
Sea Hors panel 76–7, **76**, 144
Sea Moonke panel 72–3, **73**, 129
Securitas altera emblem 25
Seele panel 143
Sementem alii faciunt panel 138–9
Senlis, Jacques de 55
Seton, Alexander, 1st Earl of Dunfermline 17
Seton, Mary 4
She Dolphin panel 69, 129
Shepherd Buss embroidery 23
Shofler panel 96, **97**, 144
Shrewsbury, Elizabeth Talbot, Countess of, *see*
  Bess of Hardwick
Shrewsbury, George Talbot, 6th Earl of 1, 4, 5,
  15, 82, 143
Sic dulcia in amarum emblem 154
Sidney, Sir Philip 44, 49
Simeoni, Gabriele 24, 29, 30, 31, **31**, 64, 65, 135,
  141–2
Sinclair, Henry 77, 85, 124
Sneiles panel 129
Solen Goose panel 77, 78, 85, 128
Solis, Virgil 90, **90**
Southwell, Robert 31, 57, 66–7
Spider panel 106, **107**, 133
Steinbock panel 143
Sterlin panel 130
Stork of the Montaynes panel 86, 87, 130

Strong, Roy 65
Stuart, Arbella *see* Arbella Stuart
Su panel 82, **83**, 133
Sub herba latet anguis emblem 37, **37**, 127
Suffolk, Henry Grey, Earl of 87
Sunflower 7, 8, 9
Swain, Margaret 12–13, 15, 72, 78, 111
Swalloe panel 131

Talbot, Alethea 12–13
Talbot, Mary 14
Tamen leo emblem 57
Tantus mihi fulgor emblem 155
Tatou panel 82, **84**, 131
Te stante virebo emblem 25–6, **25–6**, 44, 149
Terrena obcecant emblem 154
Thevet, André 77–84, 128
Thomann, Johannes 87
Thorne Back panel 90, 129
Tiger panel 129
Topsell, Edward 87, 124–5
Toucan, *see* Byrd of America
Trino non convenit orbis emblem 152
Troute panel 129
Turkie Cocke panel 131
Turtel Dove panel 128

Undique emblem 151
Unicorn panel 128
Unum quidem sed leonem emblem 58, 148
Unus non sufficit emblem 44, 45–6, **46**, 148
Ut casus dederit emblem 152
Ut plures sapiendum panel 137
Ut sementem feceris panel 139
Ut superis visum emblem 52, **52**, 151

Valeriano Pierio 58
Vase, Pierre 27
Vera felicitas semper illesa panel 115, **117**, 131
Vera virtus periculum affectat panel 131
Vias tuas domine emblem 31, **31**, 142
Villegagnon, Nicolas de 77–8, 84–5
Virescit vulnere virtus emblem 14, 26, 37–8,
  58–65, **60–65**, 127, 150
Virgil 8, 45, 128
Virtutis praemium panel 118, **118**, 138
Vitia occulta minus noxia panel 121, **123**, 138
Vredeman de Vries, Hans 32, **33–5**, 129

Walsingham, Sir Francis 17–18
Wardle, Patricia 6–7
Watch, silver pocket 9, 51–5, 152, 153, 154, 155
Water Owle panel 144
Way, Albert 61
Wellisch, Hans 77
Wells-Cole, A. 129
White, Nicholas 4
Whitney, Geffrey 23, 25–6, 41

York Conference 4, 58
Young, Alan 25, 49–50

Zulueta, Francis 9, 141, 145
Zyphwhale panel 90, **92**, 128, 144